Consulting

FOR

DUMMIES®

2ND EDITION

Consulting

FOR

DUMMIES®

2ND EDITION

by Bob Nelson and Peter Economy

WILEY

Wiley Publishing, Inc.

Consulting For Dummies®, 2nd Edition

Published by
Wiley Publishing, Inc.
111 River St.
Hoboken, NJ 07030-5774
www.wiley.com

Copyright © 2008 by Wiley Publishing, Inc., Indianapolis, Indiana

Published simultaneously in Canada

For general information on our other products and services, please contact our Customer Care Department within the U.S. at 877-762-2974, outside the U.S. at 317-572-3993, or fax 317-572-4002.

For technical support, please visit www.wiley.com/techsupport.

Wiley also publishes its books in a variety of electronic formats. Some content that appears in print may not be available in electronic books.

Library of Congress Control Number: 2008924957

ISBN: 978-0-470-17809-6

Manufactured in the United States of America

10 9 8 7 6 5 4 3

WILEY

About the Authors

Bob Nelson (San Diego, CA) is founder and president of Nelson Motivation, Inc., a management training and consulting firm based in San Diego, California. As a practicing manager and a best-selling author, he is an internationally recognized expert in the areas of employee recognition, rewards, motivation, morale, retention, productivity, and management. He is author of the best-selling book *1001 Ways to Reward Employees* (Workman) — which has sold over 1.5 million copies worldwide — and coauthor of the best-selling book *Managing For Dummies,* 2nd Edition, with Peter Economy (Wiley), as well as 18 other books on management and motivation.

Bob has been featured extensively in the media, including television appearances on CNN, CNBC, PBS, and MSNBC; radio appearances on NPR, USA Radio Network and the Business News Network; and print appearances in the *New York Times*, the *Wall Street Journal*, the *Washington Post*, and many more. He writes a weekly column for *American City Business Journals* and a monthly column for *Corporate Meetings & Incentives*, among others.

Dr. Nelson received his PhD in management from The Peter F. Drucker Graduate Management Center of Claremont Graduate University in suburban Los Angeles, and received his MBA in organizational behavior from The University of California at Berkeley. For more information on products and services offered by Nelson Motivation, Inc. — including speaking or consulting services — call 800-575-5521. Visit Bob at his Web site: www.nelson-motivation.com.

Peter Economy (La Jolla, CA) is a freelance business writer and publishing consultant who is associate editor of the Apex award-winning magazine *Leader to Leader*, and coauthor of the best-selling book *Managing For Dummies,* 2nd Edition, with Bob Nelson (Wiley), *Giving Back* with Bert Berkley (Wiley), *The SAIC Solution* with J. Robert Beyster (Wiley), as well as the author or coauthor of more than 30 other books on a wide variety of business and other topics. Visit Peter at his Web site: www.petereconomy.com and be sure to check out his Free Book Project at: www.booksforfree.org.

Dedication

To the many unsung consultants who quietly dedicate their working lives to helping others reach their goals.

Authors' Acknowledgments

We would like to give our sincere thanks to the talented consultants whose personal experiences helped bring this book to life, including Bill Eastman, Peter Psichogios, and Ray Wilson. Thanks also to Bill VanCanagan for his expert legal advice on the manuscript.

Bob and Peter are especially appreciative of all the talented folks at John Wiley & Sons, especially Joyce Pepple, Stacy Kennedy, and Alissa Schwipps for their infinite wisdom, guidance, and support on this project.

On the personal side, Bob would like to acknowledge the ongoing love and support of his father Edward, his wife Jennifer, and his children Daniel and Michelle. Peter thanks his wife Jan, and his children Peter J, Skylar, and Jackson, for love everlasting. *May the circle be unbroken.*

Publisher's Acknowledgments

We're proud of this book; please send us your comments through our Dummies online registration form located at www.dummies.com/register/.

Some of the people who helped bring this book to market include the following:

Acquisitions, Editorial, and Media Development

Senior Project Editor: Alissa Schwipps

(Previous Edition: Pamela Mourouzis)

Acquisitions Editor: Stacy Kennedy

Copy Editor: Christy Pingleton

(Previous Edition: Tina Sims, Michael Simsic)

Editorial Program Coordinator: Erin Calligan Mooney

Technical Editor: Ray Wilson

Senior Editorial Manager: Jennifer Ehrlich

Editorial Assistants: David Lutton, Joe Niesen

Cartoons: Rich Tennant (www.the5thwave.com)

Composition Services

Project Coordinator: Katherine Key

Layout and Graphics: Reuben W. Davis, Alissa D. Ellet, Melissa K. Jester, Christine Williams

Proofreaders: Cara Buitron, John Greenough

Indexer: Potomac Indexing, LLC

Publishing and Editorial for Consumer Dummies

> **Diane Graves Steele,** Vice President and Publisher, Consumer Dummies

> **Joyce Pepple,** Acquisitions Director, Consumer Dummies

> **Kristin A. Cocks,** Product Development Director, Consumer Dummies

> **Michael Spring,** Vice President and Publisher, Travel

> **Kelly Regan,** Editorial Director, Travel

Publishing for Technology Dummies

> **Andy Cummings,** Vice President and Publisher, Dummies Technology/General User

Composition Services

> **Gerry Fahey,** Vice President of Production Services

> **Debbie Stailey,** Director of Composition Services

Contents at a Glance

Table of Contents

Introduction

· ·

*A*nyone can become a consultant. Becoming a *successful* consultant, however, is a different story. Prospering as a consultant requires you to have expertise that others are willing to pay you to provide, and it requires having good business skills. Oh. And it requires some amount of motivation on your part to *want* to consult for others.

Writing this book was a labor of love for us. We are both consultants and have been for many years. If we don't do a good job, we don't get paid. And if we don't get paid, we don't eat. Our goal is to provide you with the skills you need to become a successful consultant, whether you're a beginner who is just getting his business off the ground, or an experienced consultant who wants to fine-tune her already successful practice.

As you may have already discovered or suspected, consulting can be an exciting and rewarding profession — and not just in a financial sense. Working with people to help solve problems can be an immensely satisfying thing to do. Of course, in the real world, consulting involves much more than tapping your client's head with a magic wand and watching all the problems go away.

Consulting For Dummies, 2nd Edition, is specifically written to address the unique needs of both new and experienced consultants as well as consultants-to-be. If you're new to the business, you can find everything you need to know to be successful and in demand. If you're an experienced consultant, we challenge you to shift your perspective and take a fresh look at your philosophies and techniques — what's working for you and what's not. We offer some new approaches and techniques to help you take your business to a higher level.

About This Book

Consulting For Dummies, 2nd Edition, is full of useful information, tips, and checklists that any consultant or consultant-to-be can use right away. Whether you're just thinking about becoming a consultant or you're already a seasoned pro, you can find everything you need to make consulting fun and profitable for you and your clients.

The good news is that the information you find within the covers of this book is firmly grounded in the real world. This book is not an abstract collection of theoretical mumbo-jumbo that sounds good but doesn't work when you put it to the test. We've culled the best information, the best strategies, and the best techniques for consulting from people who already do it for a living — including us. This book is a toolbox full of road-tested solutions to your every question and problem.

Consulting For Dummies, 2nd Edition, is *fun,* which reflects our strong belief and experience that consulting can be both profitable and fun. Nobody said that you can't get your work done while making sure that you and your clients enjoy yourselves in the process. We even help you to maintain a sense of humor in the face of upcoming deadlines and seemingly insurmountable challenges that all consultants have to deal with from time to time. Some days, you will be challenged to your limit or beyond. However, on many more days, the satisfaction of resolving a production bottleneck, recommending a new accounting system, or installing a new client-server computer network will bring you a sense of fulfillment that you never could have imagined possible.

The material in this book is easy to access. What good is all the information in the world if you can't get to it quickly and easily? Have no fear; we have designed this book with you, the reader, in mind. Here's how to find the precise information you seek:

- ✔ If you want to find out about a specific area, such as gathering data or setting up a home office, you can flip to that chapter and get your answers quickly — faster than you can say, "The check's in the mail." Let the table of contents and index be your guides.

- ✔ If you want a crash course in consulting, read this book from cover to cover. Forget squandering lots of money on high-priced seminars and videos or spending countless nights poring over some fly-by-night correspondence course. Forget learning by trial and error. Everything you need to know about consulting is right here.

We know from personal experience that consulting can be an intimidating job. Consultants — especially those who are just learning the ropes — are often at a loss as to what they need to do and when they need to do it. Don't worry. Help is at your fingertips.

Conventions Used in This Book

When writing this book, we included some general conventions that all *For Dummies* books use. We use the following:

- ✔ **Italics:** We *italicize* any words you may not be familiar with and provide definitions.
- ✔ **Boldface type:** We add **bold** to all keywords in bulleted lists and the actual steps in numbered lists.
- ✔ **Monofont:** All Web sites and e-mail addresses appear in `monofont`.

Also, we should note that, in this book, we use the term consultant quite loosely. We define a *consultant* simply as someone who sells his or her unique expertise to someone else, often on an hourly basis. There are many different kinds of consultants, from those who advise businesses on how to become more effective to those who advise lawyers on which members of a jury they should try to remove before a trial to those who can help you set up your home computer's wireless network.

What You're Not to Read

While we spent hours and hours — and many late nights — writing the words you'll read in this book, we know that you won't want to read it all. Truth be told, it's highly likely you won't need to. So, we make it easy for you to identify "skippable" material by sticking it into sidebars. This is the stuff in the gray boxes that's interesting and related to the topic at hand, but not absolutely essential for the success of your consulting business.

Foolish Assumptions

While we were writing this book, we made a few assumptions about you. For example, we assume that you have at least a passing interest in starting your own business that specializes in helping others solve their problems or capitalize on opportunities. Maybe you're already a consultant, or perhaps consulting is something that you might like to try. We also assume that you have a skill or expertise for which your friends, relatives, or clients will be willing to pay. This expertise may be providing your advice on anything from postage stamp collections to Internet consulting to aerospace engineering services. One more thing: We assume that you don't already know everything there is to know about consulting and that you're eager to acquire some new perspectives on the topic.

How This Book Is Organized

Consulting For Dummies, 2nd Edition, is organized into seven parts. Each part addresses a major area of the how, what, or why of becoming a consultant — and growing your business. Because of this organization, finding the topic that you're looking for is simple. Whatever the topic, you can bet that we cover it someplace! Here's a quick overview of what you can find in each part.

Part I: So You Want to Be a Consultant

Consultants are many things to many people. In this part, we provide an overview of the entire book, and then consider how to determine whether or not consulting is for you, before diving into the topic of starting your own consulting business.

Part II: Getting Your Consulting Business Off the Ground

Consulting is just like any other business — there are certain things you need to do to get it off the ground and running smoothly. This part focuses on starting up a successful consulting business as well as the financial, legal, and ethical considerations that you will encounter along the way. Finally, we take a look at how to set your fees.

Part III: The Short Course in Consulting

Consulting can be done one of two ways: the right way or the wrong way. In this part, we discuss the right way. We explain how to clearly diagnose the client's problem (and write a winning proposal), collect data effectively, and analyze it quickly and efficiently. Finally, we talk about how to give feedback to your clients and ensure that your advice gets implemented.

Part IV: Selling Your Consulting Services

To be a successful consultant, you have to learn how to sell your services (and yourself) effectively. This part considers the selling process and how to spread the word about your business. We consider how to build business through current clients, as well as how to build business with new ones.

Part V: Taking Care of Business

In this part, we dig a bit deeper into the business side of consulting, taking a close look at contracts and negotiating deals, keeping track of time and money, communicating with clients, and troubleshooting the kinds of issues and problems that every businessperson has to face from time to time.

Part VI: Taking Your Consulting Business to the Next Level

Once your consulting business is well established, you'll want to take it to the next level to make it even more successful than it already is. In this part, we consider different approaches to build on your success, including the use of advanced pricing strategies and enhancing your image and reputation.

Part VII: The Part of Tens

Here, in a concise and lively set of short chapters, you find tips that can really launch your consulting practice into orbit. In these chapters, we address using the Internet and other publicity tools to market your services, avoiding consulting mistakes, writing proposals, negotiating contracts, and building business with existing clients.

Icons Used in This Book

To guide you along the way and point out the information you really need to know about consulting, this book uses icons along its left margins. You see the following icons in this book:

This icon points you to tips and tricks to make consulting easier.

Watch out! If you don't heed the advice next to these icons, the entire situation may blow up in your face.

Remember these important points of information, and you'll be a much better consultant.

These real-life anecdotes from yours truly and other consultants show you the right — and occasionally wrong — way to be a consultant.

Where to Go from Here

If you are a new or aspiring consultant, you may want to start at the beginning of this book and work your way through to the end. A wealth of information and practical advice awaits you. Simply turn the page and you're on your way!

If you're already a consultant and you're short of time (and what consultant isn't?), you may want to turn to a particular topic to address a specific need or question. If that's the case, the Table of Contents gives a chapter-by-chapter description of all the topics in this book, and the thorough index can help you find exactly what you're looking for.

Regardless of how you find your way around *Consulting For Dummies*, 2nd Edition, we're sure that you'll enjoy getting there. If you have specific questions or comments, please feel free to visit our Web sites at www. nelson-motivation.com (Bob) or www.petereconomy.com (Peter). We would love to hear your personal anecdotes and suggestions for improving future revisions of this book, and we promise to take every one of them to heart.

Here's to your success!

Part I
So You Want to Be a Consultant

The 5th Wave

By Rich Tennant

"Try to keep your head above water! Swim parallel to the beach until you're out of the riptide! Keep your insweep at a 60 degree diagonal and your head pointed forward!"

In this part . . .

Although the term *consultant* can mean different things to different people, if you've decided to become one, then you need to decide exactly what it means to you. In this part, we take a 50,000-foot overview of the topic, and then dig in a bit deeper by exploring whether or not consulting is right for you. We show you how to assess your own skills and preferences, and how to prepare to make the move to consulting. Finally, we consider exactly what you need to do to take the plunge into starting your own consulting business — as painlessly (and profitably) as possible.

Chapter 1

Introducing the Wonderful World of Consulting

In This Chapter
▶ Understanding what a consultant is and why people become consultants
▶ Exploring the contents of this book
▶ Taking the consulting challenge quiz

Consulting has taken the world of business by storm, and it seems today that there is a consultant to do most anything you could ever want done. A consultant can be a partner in a large management consulting firm or a freelance writer. A consultant can be a self-employed Web site designer or a part-time cosmetics salesperson. A consultant can be an architect who works out of his or her home, an expert witness hired to testify at the latest Trial of the Century, or a virtual stock trader who provides investment advice to clients around the globe over the Internet.

In this book, we use the term consultant quite loosely. We define a *consultant* as someone who sells his or her unique expertise to someone else. This expertise can be anything from showing someone how to properly lay out, plant, and fertilize an organic vegetable garden, to analyzing and recommending changes to a complex aerospace manufacturing operation.

So, while many people think of consultants only in terms of the narrow field of professional management consulting — firms such as KPMG, Bain & Co., PricewaterhouseCoopers, and others that specialize in fixing "broken" organizations — the world of consulting is much bigger than that. Anytime someone pays you for your unique expertise or advice — whether it's creating a snazzy Web page for a friend's business, measuring the stress that a Category 4 hurricane might exert on a new home, or suggesting where to dig a new water well on a ranch in Wyoming — you are acting as a consultant.

In this chapter, we consider the many reasons why energized and talented people like you are becoming consultants, and then we briefly cover the topics of starting up your own consulting firm, understanding the consulting process, selling your services, and taking your business to the next level, all of which are covered in more detail later in the book. Finally, we invite you to take our nifty Consulting Challenge Quiz, which helps you determine whether you have what it takes to become a successful consultant.

The Reasons for Consulting: Money, Yes . . . But What Else?

Men and women from all walks of life with all manner of experience and expectations have reasons for becoming consultants. Some are leveraging their knowledge to help their clients, while others enjoy the variety of assignments that consulting can bring. Some prefer working for large, diversified consulting firms — with offices scattered all across the globe — while others are simply tired of working for someone else and ready to start their own consulting firms in a spare bedroom of their house. Still others are just looking for a way to make some extra money.

Whatever your reason for becoming a consultant, businesses of all sorts — and individuals and organizations — are using consultants more than ever. According to market research published in 2007 by consulting experts Kennedy Information, both consulting revenues and profits are up in the United States across the board, and are projected to continue to grow well into the future. One key reason for this is that skilled consultants can be brought into an organization on short notice, fix a problem, and then move on to another organization in need. No need to hire someone, pay them a salary, and provide them with benefits and a retirement plan.

And although some think that money is the main reason people choose to become consultants, that's not really what it's all about. Sure, a lot of people make good money as consultants — make no mistake about it. But to many people, the benefits of being a consultant go far beyond the size of their bank accounts. This section talks about some of the most compelling nonmonetary reasons people enter the consulting field.

Leveraging your talent

Everyone is especially knowledgeable about at least one thing. You may, for example, have worked for 20 years as a construction loan specialist for a large bank. When it comes to construction loans, saying that you are an expert is probably an understatement. And because of the huge network of contacts that you have developed over the years, many other organizations could benefit from your unique experience.

Or you may enjoy exploring the Internet in your spare time. You've built many Web pages for yourself and your friends, and you always keep up with the latest in authoring tools and other developments. Although you work at a grocery store as a cashier ten hours a day, five days a week, you always manage to find time to pursue your favorite hobby. Would it surprise you to find out that many businesses would hire you and pay you good money to build and maintain Web pages for them? It shouldn't — that's what consultants do.

Being tired of working for someone else

Most people have dreams of what they want to do with their lives. Some dream of buying their own home. Others dream of establishing a career or family. Still others dream of winning the lottery and moving to Bora Bora. However, in our experience, one of the most common dreams — the one that everyone who works in an organization dreams at least once or twice a day — is the dream of being your own boss.

It's not that all bosses are bad. Both of us have had many great bosses over the years, and we hope that we have been good bosses to those who have worked for us. Most people, however, are born with a strong desire to be independent and to make their own decisions rather than to have others make their decisions for them. And when, as time goes on, you begin to know more about what you do than your supervisors or managers, working for someone else can become especially difficult.

Getting laid off or fearing you will be

The days of having a job for life are long gone. Today's economy is one of rapid change and movement. As companies continue to search for ways to cut costs, they increasingly turn to hiring temporary workers or contracting work out to consultants. Having a job today is no guarantee of having one tomorrow. When you work for a company — no matter how large — you can be laid off at any time, for almost any reason, with little or no notice. If you're lucky, you get a severance package of some sort — maybe a few weeks' or a few months' pay. If you're not so lucky, your last day is just that, and you're on your own.

Becoming a consultant is a good way to ensure your financial future in the face of economic uncertainty. Why? One, because you control the number of jobs you take on and how much or how little extra work you want to keep in reserve. Two, because you can often make more money consulting for a firm than you can as an employee of that same firm. Many companies are more than willing to pay a premium to hire an expert consultant to do the same job that an employee could do for much less money.

Having a flexible second source of income

If you want a flexible second source of income, then consulting is just what the doctor ordered. When you're a self-employed consultant, you set your own schedule. If you want to work only on weekends, you can decide to work only on weekends. If you want to do your work late at night, that's fine, too. And because you decide exactly how much work you take on, you can work for one client at a time or many clients at once. Decisions about your schedule and your workload are all up to you.

And another thing: If you conduct your business from your home, this second source of income can mean a sizable write-off on your income taxes. The government allows owners of home-based businesses to take a variety of tax deductions that are not available to most other individuals. Even if you don't work out of your home, you can write off the majority of your business-related expenses. Check out Chapter 5 for some basic information about the tax benefits of becoming a self-employed consultant. More detailed information can be found in the most current edition of *Taxes For Dummies,* by Eric Tyson, Margaret A. Munro, and David J. Silverman (Wiley).

Finding a higher calling

Many organizations benefit greatly from the services of good consultants because they generally bring with them an independent and objective outside perspective. Unfortunately, many small businesses and noncommercial organizations cannot afford to pay for a consultant's expertise like most larger, well-established businesses can. Schools, churches, charities, and other community-based organizations rely on members of the community to provide expertise and assistance. Many consultants make a regular practice of providing their expertise to community organizations at no charge as a way of giving back. (We discuss this concept more in Chapter 20.) If you are one of these people, you may already be consulting without even realizing it!

Why would anyone want to do that?

✔ If you really believe in something — whether it's the goals of a particular political candidate or your kid's elementary school — then the psychological benefits are much greater than any financial benefits.

✔ The work you do for your favorite charity or community group may get you noticed, resulting in paying work. Most community organizations are supported by a variety of people from all walks of life. The network that you establish with these individuals can be invaluable to you in your working life as well as your social life. Although establishing a network of contacts may not be the main reason that you decide to offer your services to the group of your choice, it's not the worst thing that could happen to you, is it?

Preparing to take a step up

More than a few consultants have parlayed their consulting skills and experience into top executive jobs — often with the companies that had employed them as consultants. Before Robert Kidder became CEO of Duracell, Inc., and later chairman and CEO of Borden, Inc., he was a management consultant at McKinsey & Company. John Donahoe, named CEO of eBay in 2008, was a consultant at Bain & Company for more than 20 years (as was his predecessor, Meg Whitman, who consulted for Bain for eight years). And Hubert Joly, a former McKinsey & Company consultant, was recently tapped to serve as president and CEO of hospitality industry giant Carlson.

So, if your ultimate goal is to take a step up in your corporate career, then honing your skills — and building your business network — as a consultant might be just the ticket.

Taking the First Steps toward Becoming a Consultant

While many consultants work for someone else — in all sorts of companies, in all sorts of industries — for many others, a major attraction of becoming a consultant is starting their own consulting firm. The good news is that many millions of consultants have successfully made the transition to being their own bosses and are enjoying the financial, professional, and lifestyle benefits that result. The bad news is that starting up your own consulting firm — and keeping it on an even keel — is a lot of hard work.

Understanding the consulting process

If you hope to become an effective consultant, then you should be familiar with the most effective approaches to consulting. People have been consulting for hundreds — maybe thousands — of years. Over these many years, a five-step method to consulting has emerged that is the standard approach for many consultants today — whether self-employed or working for someone else. This five-step consulting process includes

1. **Defining the problem**

2. **Collecting data**

3. **Problem solving**

4. **Presenting recommendations**

5. **Implementing recommendations**

No matter what kind of consulting you do, you will find that your efforts will be focused on this approach, which will help you find the answers your clients seek.

Finding your forte

Before you can start your own successful consulting firm, you need to be certain of the kind of consulting you want to do. Some of you will find the answer obvious — "I want to help small engineering firms learn how to better use computer-aided design software to their benefit," or "I want to show young couples how to plan now for their financial futures." However, some of you won't be quite so sure. In this case, you need to assess your skills and personal preferences to help you decide. And whether or not you already know what kind of consulting firm you'd like to start, you need to be sure there's a market for what you want to do.

Taking the leap

Finally, once you've decided that you do indeed want to start your own consulting business and you know what kind of consulting you want to do, you need to decide when the time is right, and exactly how and when you'll make the transition from your current employer to the new world of self-employment. This requires assessing your professional, financial, and personal considerations, and creating a step-by-step plan for making the transition, a topic we cover in detail in Chapter 3. While some self-employed consultants simply walk into their boss's office one day and quit — starting their own business that very moment — others make the transition over a period of weeks, months, or even years.

Keys to making your business a success

According to the U.S. Small Business Administration (SBA), there are four key indicators of business success.

✔ **Sound management practices:** An ability to manage projects, handle finances, and communicate effectively with customers

✔ **Industry experience:** The number of years you have worked in the same kind of business you intend to start and familiarity with suppliers and potential customers

✔ **Technical support:** Your ability to seek out and find help in the technical aspects of your business

✔ **Planning ability:** An ability to set appropriate business goals and targets, and then create plans and strategies for achieving them

Beginning Your Own Consulting Firm

The first thing to keep in mind when starting up your own consulting firm is that you are starting your own *business*. If this business happens to be home-based, then there is good news for you: According to surveys conducted by IDC/LINK, an average of only about 5 percent of home-based businesses fail each year. So, after five years, only approximately one-quarter (25 percent) of home-based businesses fail — far less than the average failure rate of more than 50 percent for all businesses after five years.

The many issues that need to be addressed as you begin building your consulting business are the same as those faced by most other businesses, from setting up an office to securing support services and dealing with legalities, taxes, and insurance. You have to figure out how much your services are worth, and then find the means to track down and engage those who are willing to pay for them. Communicating and problem-solving naturally come into play along the way.

Getting started

You need to attend to a variety of matters when starting up your own consulting firm — from getting your business set up (including finding a space for it in your home or elsewhere, and getting office equipment and supplies) to securing the services of a good accountant, banker, and perhaps even a lawyer. We cover these topics in detail in Chapter 4. In addition, there are legal issues to consider, such as deciding what form of business to adopt, picking a name for your business, and dealing with zoning laws, licensing, and permits. And, of course, you need to set up a bookkeeping system and be prepared to pay your taxes, buy insurance, and perhaps secure health care and other benefits. These subjects are the focus of Chapter 5.

And there's one more thing you need to address when starting up your own consulting firm: the fees you'll charge your clients to consult for them. Many different approaches exist for setting your fees. Ultimately, you need to adopt fees that are appropriate for your industry, that create value for your clients, and that provide you with enough profit to make a good living. If your fees are too high, you may not get enough business to stay afloat. However, set your fees too low, and you may find yourself swamped with business, but not really making any money. Ideally, you'll find a win-win approach where both you and your clients are happy with the results. Chapter 6 is dedicated to helping you zero in on this magic number.

Selling your services

Like any other kind of business, consultants have to sell themselves — their expertise, their experience, their ability to get the job done — and convince someone to pay the kind of fee that makes consulting worth their while. In a way, every consultant — at least, every *successful* consultant — is also a salesperson. And the better salesperson you become, the better able you will be to land the clients and projects you need to become profitable and to grow your business.

Selling your services involves many different parts of an equation that add up to a client signing a contract with your firm. These parts include such things as identifying the real decision-maker in your client's company, making a sales pitch, promoting your business, building business and referrals through your current clients, and building business with new clients. We tackle all of these topics in Part IV. Remember: The success you find as a consultant is often directly proportional to the time and expertise you apply to the selling process.

Taking care of business

As we say many times in this book, consulting is a business, and you need to plan accordingly to attend to its unique needs. Every consultant relies on contracts to formalize agreements with clients: How long will an engagement take? What work will be accomplished? How much will your client pay you for your services — and when? Negotiating agreements with your clients is a vital skill for consultants. We cover the subject of contracting in detail in Chapter 16.

Also of great importance is the tracking of your time (the hours you put into a particular project) and your money (the fees that are attributable to a particular project). This involves setting up and maintaining client activity logs or time sheets, and creating budgets. Turn to Chapter 17 for more on these issues.

You'll also need to be sure that you become an expert communicator — in writing, over the telephone, and via e-mail and other technology-enabled modes of communication. Chapter 18 discusses the ins and outs of communication. Finally, your business *will* run into problems and challenges from time to time — every business does. Whether the challenge is poor cash flow, getting clients to pay, or finding the right client for your kind of business, recognizing that there is a problem — and then correctly diagnosing and solving it — is a critical skill that you'll need to master if you want to help ensure your long-term success as a consultant. We dedicate Chapter 19 to troubleshooting issues such as these.

Taking Your Business to the Next Level

Building and growing a consulting business that will be successful over a long period of time involves more than the basics of setting up your office, finding good clients, working through the consulting process, becoming an effective salesperson, negotiating contracts, and keeping track of your time and money. You also have to understand how to tune up your firm's growth engine (the subject of Chapter 20), how to integrate advanced pricing strategies into the way you do business (see Chapter 21), and how to create a top-rank image and reputation in your particular industry (turn to Chapter 22).

Many consultants are happy building a certain level of business and then simply maintaining it. If that's the situation you're in and you're happy with it, then that's perfectly fine. However, if you dream of building a consulting business that will expand to hire others and serve customers in a variety of markets — outside of your city or state, or even internationally — then you'll want to do what it takes to move your business to the next level. Who knows? Maybe you'll be so successful that you will have to hire a consultant or two along the way to help you with your own business.

The Consulting Challenge Quiz

Maybe you're thinking that this consulting thing may not be such a bad idea. Now the big question is: Do you have what it takes to become a consultant? Do you want to find out? Then simply take the Consulting Challenge Quiz. It's quick, it's easy, and it's guaranteed to help you sort fantasy from reality. Don't forget to total your score at the end of the test to see where you fit.

Quizzing yourself

Here are the questions. Read each one and circle the answer that comes closest to your personal feelings. If you're not sure how to answer a question on your first attempt, move on to the next question and come back to the tricky one later.

1. Do you like to solve problems?

   A. Yes, solving problems is my sole reason for being.

   B. Yes, I like solving certain kinds of problems.

   C. Can I trade one of my problems for one of yours?

   D. Is there someone else who can solve them?

   E. No. Yuck. Never.

2. Can you set your own goals and then follow them to completion?

   A. I don't know what I would do if I didn't always have goals to pursue.

   B. Yes, I set my own goals, but I don't always follow up on them.

   C. I haven't tried before, but if you show me how, I will.

   D. I don't set my own goals; they set themselves.

   E. Sorry, I don't have any goals.

3. Are you an independent self-starter?

   A. I don't need anyone to tell me what to do — let's get going!

   B. I'm independent, but I sometimes have a hard time getting motivated to do things on my own.

   C. No one has ever let me make my own decisions before. I kind of like the idea of doing things on my own, though.

   D. Hum a few bars, and maybe I can sing it.

   E. Do I have to be?

4. Are you confident about your ability to get the job done?

   A. Without a doubt.

   B. I'm fairly certain.

   C. I'm not sure.

   D. Can we discuss this some other time?

   E. Absolutely, unequivocally not.

5. Do you enjoy pursuing tasks to completion, despite the obstacles in your path?

    A. I am very persistent.

    B. Usually, although I sometimes avoid tackling problems directly.

    C. As long as we understand upfront that no one is perfect.

    D. Is any task ever truly complete?

    E. Some things were just never meant to be done.

6. Can you adapt to rapid changes?

    A. My middle name is change.

    B. It's easier for me to adapt to good changes than to adapt to bad changes.

    C. If you've seen one change, you've seen them all.

    D. As long as it's you who changes and not me.

    E. I am a rock.

7. Are you creative?

    A. Just give me a pencil and a piece of paper, and you'll have your solution in five minutes.

    B. Usually, but it depends on what mood I'm in.

    C. Let me think about that for a while.

    D. Why expend a lot of effort creating something that someone else has probably already figured out the answer to?

    E. I like things the way they are.

8. Do you like to work with people?

    A. Working with people is what makes work fun.

    B. Definitely — some people more than others, however.

    C. Yes — it definitely beats working with trained seals.

    D. I really prefer my computer.

    E. I want to be alone!

9. Are you trustworthy, loyal, honest, and brave?

    A. All of the above and more!

    B. Well, three out of four isn't bad, is it?

    C. How about two out of four?

    D. I'd like to believe that there are other, more important human qualities.

    E. Next question, please.

10. Are you interested in making a decent living?

A. My opportunities are unlimited.

B. Sure, as long as I don't have to work too hard at it.

C. I don't know; I'm pretty comfortable the way things are now.

D. Just how do you define decent?

E. I'm going to win that lottery one of these days!

Analyzing your answers

Get out a calculator right now and add up your results. Give yourself 5 points for every A answer, 3 points for every B, 0 points for every C, –3 points for every D, and –5 for every E. Don't worry. We'll wait right here until you're done. Finished? Okay.

We have divided the possible scores into six separate categories. By comparing your total points to the points contained in each category, you can find out whether consulting is in your future.

25 to 50 points: You are a born consultant. If you're not already working for yourself as a consultant, we strongly suggest that you consider quitting your job right now and start passing out your business card to all your friends, acquaintances, and prospective clients. Read this book for tips on how to sharpen your already well-developed skills.

1 to 24 points: You definitely have potential to be a great consultant. Consider starting your own consulting practice in the very near future, but make sure you keep your day job until you've got enough clients to keep you afloat. Read this book to understand the basics of consulting and find out how to grow your new business.

0 points: You could go either way. Why don't you try taking this test again in another month or two? Read this book to ensure that you pass next time.

–1 to –24 points: We're sorry to tell you, but consulting is not currently your cup of tea. We strongly recommend that you read this book and then take this test again. If you don't do better after all that, then maybe working for someone else isn't the worst thing that could happen to you.

–25 to –50 points: Forget it. Your DNA just doesn't have the consulting gene built into it. Sell this book to one of your co-workers right now. Maybe he or she will score higher on this test than you did.

More than 50 or less than –50 points: Take your calculator to the nearest repair shop and get it fixed!

Chapter 2

Determining Whether Consulting Is Right for You

*H*ow do you decide whether starting a consulting business is the right thing for you? You may have arrived at this decisive point in your life because you feel you're able to contribute more if you own and operate your own consulting firm. Or you may believe that starting a consulting business of your own can be a much more lucrative proposition than working for someone else (and, in many cases, it can be). Yet another possibility is that you simply like the idea of calling the shots in your life, and not having to answer to a boss.

Whatever your reason, becoming an independent consultant can be the key that unlocks the door to the rest of your future, if you just take a small step forward and give it a try. And you don't have to do it all at once. You can (and, indeed, our advice is that you *should*) keep your current day job while you try out consulting in your spare time.

In this chapter, we help you determine what you *really* want to do with your life and what skills you have that can get you where you want to go. We also help you determine whether what you want to do is marketable enough to allow you to make a living at it. (Making a living at whatever you decide to do is always a plus!) Finally, we tell you how to do some simple test-marketing of your business ideas to see which ones are likely to fly and which ones may be better suited to papering your parakeet's cage.

Note: If you're already a consultant, then this chapter is probably not for you. You've already stepped onto the consulting path, and you're likely looking for new ways to improve your practice — so skip ahead to the topics we cover later in this book that are important to you.

Pondering Your Preferences

Undoubtedly, you like to do certain kinds of work more than others. Take a moment right now to think about the things you most like to do on the job. Perhaps your great love in life is to create massive computer spreadsheets. Maybe you really like to read and analyze legal contracts. Or is your number-one favorite duty making travel reservations for your organization's salespeople?

One problem with a career in most organizations is that you may very well be promoted right out of the things that you enjoy doing the most, into new duties that you find much less enjoyable. If you're talented in a particular area of technical expertise — whether it's creating advertising campaigns, writing complex software programs, or building houses — you'll inevitably be recognized for your skill and eventually promoted into a supervisory or management position. When this happens, suddenly your job changes from one of, say, creating advertising campaigns to one of coaching a team of *employees* to create advertising campaigns. And although you may still do some creative work, suddenly your day is chock-full of management activities, such as budgeting department resources, controlling expenditures, counseling employees, building teamwork, attending endless meetings, and filling out forms for anything and everything you can imagine. Before you know it, you're doing tasks that have nothing to do with what you really enjoy doing — creating advertising campaigns, writing software programs, or building houses.

In this section, your job is to decide exactly what you enjoy doing the most — at work and otherwise. Your goal is to identify new work opportunities that allow you to do the things you enjoy. Think in terms of a new career where *you* — not someone else — decide which things you do. Don't worry now about whether you can make money at it. Making money is indeed an important consideration (that is, if you want to be able to afford to eat, or avoid living in a cardboard box on the street), and we look into that later in this chapter.

What do you really like to do?

Start this exercise by considering what you really like to do. Our belief is that if you like to do it — *really* like to do it — you can do it well. And doing the things that you like to do well generates success. For the moment, forget about the things you just sort of like to do or the things you feel wishy-washy about. Be honest with yourself — don't put on your list things that someone else thinks you should like to do. Instead, look deep within yourself to tap into your own feelings. Use the space that follows each question to write in your ideas. Or photocopy the pages so that you can go through the exercise again in a few months or a few years.

What would your ideal day look like ten years from now? Divide it into 30-minute increments, and describe what you'd be doing during each part of your day.

What would your perfect job be? Visualize it. Smell it. Taste it. (Okay — don't taste it.) What would you do every day? How would you spend your time? With whom would you work?

List your most positive and enjoyable work experiences. What about these experiences made them so enjoyable? Exactly what skills were you applying?

What are your five favorite things to do at work? Why do you like each of these five things?

1. _____
2. _____
3. _____
4. _____
5. _____

What are your five favorite things to do away from work? Why do you like each of these five things?

1. _____
2. _____
3. _____
4. _____
5. _____

What strengths would you bring to your dream job? What gaps in knowledge or experience would you need to fill to start working in your dream job?

A visualization exercise

As you work on getting in touch with the things that you like and the things that you dislike, you can amplify the effectiveness of the process by participating in a visualization exercise. First, find a nice, cozy chair where you can relax — away from the phones or the hustle-bustle of your home or office. Turn down the lights and let your mind wander. No, don't go to sleep — you need to be awake for this one. Visualize your ideal life. What's a typical day like in your ideal life? Start at the very beginning of your day when you wake up and work through it until you go to bed at night. Ask yourself the following questions:

Where are you living?

How do you wake up?

Who do you wake up with? (That is, do you have a spouse? Children? A dog?)

What time do you wake up?

What clothes do you put on?

What do you eat for breakfast?

Who do you eat breakfast with?

Where do you go to work?

How do you get there?

Who do you see at work?

What does your work environment look like?

What does it smell like?

What do you do at work?

Who do you talk to?

What do you talk about?

Continue to work through your typical day in your ideal life — the rest of the morning, lunch, afternoon, the commute home in the evening, dinner, after dinner, and bedtime. Ask detailed questions about what you're doing, where you're doing it, when, and with whom. Use the results of this exercise to help guide you in your answers to what you really want to do with your life.

What do you really dislike doing?

Just as you have things that you really like to do — both on and off the job — you invariably have things that you really can't stand to do. The next step in this exercise is to zero in on the things that you really don't like to do. Again, be honest with yourself — now's the time to get it all out on the table. (Don't worry; we're not going to show this to your boss.)

What would your worst job be? What would you be doing every day? With whom would you be working? How would you be spending your time?

List your most negative and least enjoyable work experiences. What about these experiences made them so unbearable? Exactly what skills were you applying?

What are your five least favorite things to do at work? Why are these your least favorite things?

1. _____
2. _____
3. _____
4. _____
5. _____

What are your five least favorite things to do away from work? Why are these your least favorite things?

1. _____
2. _____
3. _____
4. _____
5. _____

Assessing Your Skills

It's one thing to want to do something — to be in tune with your likes and dislikes — but it's another thing altogether to have the skills and expertise needed to carry out your selected endeavor successfully. To get a sense of whether a particular brand of consulting is really in your future (or in your *present,* for that matter), first you need to take the time to assess the skills that you bring to the task. In the sections that follow, we help you do just that.

What are you really good at?

Assuming you've had years of experience in the business world, you undoubtedly excel in certain tasks. Perhaps you are the world's greatest budget forecaster, or maybe you have an incredible eye for displaying products in department store windows to increase sales. Whichever skills you excel in, now's the time to get in touch with them.

What are your most outstanding job skills (for example, accounting or negotiating), and what makes you so skilled in those particular areas?

What things have other people told you that you do well?

What personal qualities (for example, analytical ability or persistence) do you possess that support your most outstanding job skills?

What are the top five essential duties of your current job?

1. _____
2. _____
3. _____
4. _____
5. _____

What special training or classes have you taken to improve your job skills?

What special certificates, licenses, or registrations do you possess for your current job (for example, CPA or general contractor's license)?

What aren't you so good at?

Figuring out what you're not good at is just as important as figuring out what you are good at — in fact, it can save you a lot of time and heartbreak. However, deciding what you're not good at is often easier said than done. Why? Because many people have an idealized vision of what they *think* they ought to be good at, whether they are or not. For example, you don't admit that you're lousy with figures and discard that option from your list of possibilities. Instead, you say, "One of these days I'm going to concentrate on getting better at working with numbers," leaving the possibility open. The implicit assumption is that you should hang on to every possible avenue to the future, regardless of the improbability that you'll ever go there. Truth be told, that's not the best approach. Although the motive behind thinking this way is noble, this kind of thinking only diffuses your focus and concentration, distracting you from the things that you do best.

What job skills (for example, accounting, negotiating, and so on) are you least comfortable with, and why are you uncomfortable with them?

What personality traits (for example, decisiveness or persistence) would you work to improve to enhance your job skills and why?

What tasks do you avoid and why?

Matching Your Skills with Your Preferences

After you assess your likes and dislikes, your skills, and the areas that you are less skilled in, you can put all this information together to create a coherent picture of who you are and what kind of consultant you're meant to be — if you're meant to be one at all. You may be surprised to find that the perfect job for you bears little resemblance to your current job. On the other hand, you may be surprised to find out that you're not cut out to be a consultant. Whatever the result, you need to know one way or the other.

To begin this exercise, review all the comments that you wrote under the section titled "What do you really like to do?" The point of this section is to allow you to unleash your imagination and consider what kind of work you really want to do. For a moment, forget that you have been a bank teller in Toronto your entire working life, or a waitress in a truck stop in

Little America, Wyoming, for the last ten years. As you read through your responses, take time to step back, close your eyes, and visualize your answer to each question.

Think about what kinds of consulting businesses you could start that would allow you to apply your personal preferences. Don't be shy — now's the time to let your imagination go wild. Try to list *at least* five possible consulting businesses. Jot them down here:

1. _____

2. _____

3. _____

4. _____

5. _____

Next, review your responses under the section titled "What are you really good at?" Your responses to the questions in this section don't necessarily indicate that you want to do something, only that you're good at it. And if you need some additional training to get the credentials you need, weigh the amount of time and money that you need to get them. Step back and visualize the kinds of consulting businesses that you could start based on your answers. Again, think of at least five business possibilities and list them here:

1. _____

2. _____

3. _____

4. _____

5. _____

Now compare your lists. Do you have any possibilities in common? Yes? Great! Circle them right now with a big red marker. You don't have *any* in common? Go through the exercise again and *really* let yourself go — dive deep within yourself and tap into your true self. When you start your new consulting business, the idea is to pick something that lets you do what you want to do with your life, but also to choose something that you're good at or that you can get good at in a reasonable amount of time.

If you've tried to find the right consulting business, but keep coming up dry, then perhaps prompting a consulting business idea would be helpful. For example, you can intentionally peruse the local magazine racks for ideas of how others spend their time to see if anything is triggered.

Finally, review your responses to "What do you really dislike doing?" and "What aren't you so good at?" Do any of your responses to the questions in these sections cause you to delete any of the consulting possibilities that you circled with that big red marker? Yes? Then take that big red marker and put a big *X* through them. No? Good. Enter the surviving items of this exercise in the space below.

Now complete the following sentences for each item:

I am in the _____ consulting business.

I help my clients _____ .

Congratulations! You have identified the consulting businesses that best match your desires *and* your talents. Because of this synergy, you have the best chance for success if you pursue one or more of these opportunities. Of course, success takes more than a great idea. You have to have clients who are willing to pay you for your services in order for your idea to be profitable. However, before we dive into that issue, let's do one more thing first: some research.

Simple research can help make sure that your idea of what a consultant does is similar to real life. With the Internet it's a pretty simple task. Some basic questions to answer as you do your research are

- ✔ What does this type of consultant do for his or her clients (write reports, develop and deliver training, create designs, and so on)?
- ✔ Does the work include a lot of travel?
- ✔ Does the work include long, slowly paced projects or short, quick-turnaround projects?
- ✔ Does the work require working closely with others in the company or is it pretty much a solitary effort?
- ✔ What types of clients does the consultant typically work with (for example, big or small companies)?
- ✔ What industries do the clients typically work in?
- ✔ Who in the company does the consultant work with (the CEO, the engineering staff, the human resources department)?

A side benefit of this research is that you will start to identify potential competition or potential collaborators down the road.

Is Your Idea Marketable?

Should you or shouldn't you? Only you can decide whether to become an independent consultant.

Unfortunately, trying to predict whether your consulting business will be successful or go down in flames is a difficult task. Many new businesses succeed each year, but many fail. How will yours fare? Only time will tell. Many factors add up to potential success or disaster in running your own business: your drive to succeed; the availability of clients who are willing to pay for your services; and your ability to satisfy your current clients, attract new clients, and make a profit.

Truth be told, there are very few really new ideas out there. Chances are that someone else is already doing the type of consulting you are considering. Do some online research and talk with other consultants doing this work. In this section, we address some of the most important issues surrounding your decision about whether to take the plunge. Before you quit your day job, give serious consideration to these issues.

Who are your clients and what are their needs?

You may have a great idea, but unless you also have clients who need your services and are willing to pay for them, all you have is an idea. Ideas don't pay your bills; *clients* do. Identifying your clients and their needs — defining and describing them — is an important step in determining whether you have a viable idea.

So who are your clients, and what do they need? You need to be able to list real names and phone numbers, not just stuff like "anyone who needs an online presence for their business," or "a vast quantity of investors who aren't being served adequately by big brokers."

As you consider exactly who your clients are and what they need, ask yourself the following questions:

  ✔ **Who are your most likely clients?** Make a list. Name names and list phone numbers and addresses. You can find clients by looking in the Yellow Pages or in industry trade magazines, by networking, or by researching possible firms of interest on the Internet. In many cases, these first clients will come from current or recent work engagements. Or they may come from referrals by co-workers, customers, or suppliers and vendors. You have to be careful about letting people know what you're doing if your day job employer has a problem with you working as a consultant — even in your spare time.

✔ **Exactly what do your clients need?** As you develop your list of likely clients, note what each client needs. For example, your targeted clients may need someone to offer training in skills for new managers. The best way to find out what your clients need is by talking to them one-to-one. Will you provide *exactly* what they need, or are you going to try to sell them on something they don't need? (We highly recommend that you always only do the former!)

✔ **What advantages do you offer over your competitors?** Although you may have a great idea, other consultants can probably offer much the same services to your potential clients (yes — it's true!). Determine why your clients would pick you over your competitors, and then concentrate on those advantages. Also consider what advantages your competitors offer over your consulting business. If you're not sure, ask your clients. They'll probably be happy to point out the pluses and minuses of you *and* your competition. A simple tool is to draw up a table with the list of competitors down the left column and a list of their offerings across the top. Include your business in the table and you'll see where you are different from your competition.

Can your business become profitable?

Doing what you want to do with your life instead of working as just another cog in the wheels of some humongous bureaucratic maze of an organization is a great goal. Consulting is, above all, about freedom — the freedom to decide what *you* want to do and then to pursue it. However, don't forget one minor detail. Unless you recently won the lottery, found the largest undiscovered diamond mine on the continent in your backyard, or inherited the McLaren F1 race team, you have to make a profit if your consulting business is to live long and prosper.

To determine whether your business can be profitable, do the math and take the following items into account:

✔ **What are your anticipated revenues?** Consider potential clients and decide the level of revenues that you can reasonably anticipate bringing in for several different periods — a month, a quarter, and a year. Be conservative; this is not the time to go manic. Do some outside research to discover what your competitors charge and the amount of business *they* bring in each year.

✔ **What are your anticipated expenses?** List all your potential expenses for several different periods — a month, a quarter, a year. Think hard. You don't want to forget anything. Do a reality check by examining your canceled checks and credit card statements. Typical expenses for a consulting firm include

- Rent

- Salary/compensation (if you absolutely must have a minimum take-home pay amount)

- Utilities (electricity, gas, water)

- Professional services (accountant, lawyer, etc.)

- Computer equipment

- Advertising

- Phone

- Cable/Internet connections

- Web site

- Furniture

- Office supplies (paper, staples, pens)

- Travel (airfare, rental cars, hotel)

- Postage, overnight delivery fees

- Insurance

- Subcontracting (work outsourced to other firms)

It's always best to underestimate revenues and overestimate expenses.

✔ **Do your anticipated revenues exceed expenses or vice versa?** This is the $64,000 question. When your revenues exceed your expenses, the leftovers are called *profit*. Profit is good. When your expenses exceed your revenues — especially for a prolonged period of time — this is called a "going-out-of-business plan." This kind of plan is definitely *not* good. Although you should expect your consulting business to need several months to a year or more to become profitable, the sooner you can make more money than you spend, the better! Remember — Fido needs to be fed!

Is the timing right?

In business, as in life, timing can be everything. Although hard work and persistence can overcome almost any obstacle, having the right product for the right client at the right time is also important. For example, if you had started an Internet consulting firm in 1990, you would have starved — and quickly. In 1990, few people or companies had heard of the Internet, much less established a presence on it. However, if you had started the same business yesterday, you'd have more than enough to do for a long time to come.

Consider the following when you try to determine whether your timing is right:

✔ **Does what you want to do provide a needed service?** You may have the greatest idea since sliced bread, but you may find that no one wants or needs your product. This is why all the big Fortune 500 companies spend tons of money on marketing studies, focus groups, and product opinion surveys. You don't want to spend a great deal of time and money chasing a market that just isn't there. Before you start your consulting practice, survey the market you want to enter and determine whether real clients will spend real money for what you have to sell. You can find out if people need your service by making phone calls to potential clients, conducting focus groups, or using a variety of other market research methods.

✔ **Are you too far ahead of your time?** You may have an idea that is so great, and so far ahead of its time, that your clients aren't even aware that they need it. When you're *too* far ahead of your clients, convincing them that they need your services can take a great deal of time and effort. If you're on the cutting edge of the kinds of services you offer, don't get so far out on the edge that your clients can't catch up to you!

✔ **Are you too far behind the times?** On the other hand, jumping into a presumably hot field only to find that your potential clients' attention has already moved on to the next big thing is even easier. For example, total quality management (TQM) was a pretty hot field for several years and attracted loads of attention from a wide array of clients and consultants. Now, however, firms that once embraced TQM have left it far behind as they've moved to the next business-fad-of-the-month. If you were to start a firm specializing in TQM today, you'd be hard-pressed to line up enough business to keep your lights on, much less make a profit. As you decide on a consulting specialty, look toward the future — where your customers are heading — instead of to the past, where they've already been.

Do You Have What It Takes?

This question goes way beyond the nuts and bolts of starting and running a successful business. It goes to your personality, your motivation, your personal support systems, and more. If you prefer the security of working for a large corporation and the thought of being out on your own makes you break into a sweat, maybe *full-time* consulting isn't for you. Take it slow and work your way into it.

Don't forget that you can consult on a part-time basis while you continue to hold down a conventional full-time job. In fact, this is exactly what we recommend. You don't need to abandon your regular job to start your own consulting business. A much better idea is to work into it gradually, building your business as you go, until you're ready to make the jump to a full-time consulting business of your own. You *always* have the option of increasing the amount of time you devote to your consulting business and decreasing the amount of time you devote to your other job. If you become a victim of a downsizing, rightsizing, or reengineering, you'll be ready for it.

Consider these things when you're trying to decide whether you are cut out to be a consultant:

- ✔ **Do you dream of being your own boss?** Perhaps that's not quite the right question. Maybe it should be, "*How often* do you dream of being your own boss?" Being in control of one's life can be a very strong motivator for a consultant — a motivator strong enough to bring your enterprise great success through the sheer force of your desire to succeed.

- ✔ **Are you independent and a self-starter?** When you're an independent consultant, you don't have anyone to hold your hand. No one is there to make sure that you get out of bed in the morning, to tell you that you're not working hard enough, or to praise you for doing a great job. You probably won't run into anyone at the water cooler to socialize with, except maybe your cat or your 7-year-old daughter. It's all up to you. Are you up to the challenge? If you need to be jump-started on Mondays, then maybe consulting just isn't for you.

- ✔ **Can you support yourself as you establish your practice?** Although supporting yourself financially is important (for some reason, the people who supply you with the things you need to run your business expect you to pay them for their trouble), supporting yourself emotionally is just as important — perhaps even more so. Are you mentally ready to make the move to consulting? Do you have the support of your friends, relatives, and significant others? (A great indication of your significant others' support is whether they're willing to read this book too. If they are and do, they'll be aware of what you're doing and more likely to give you that nudge when needed!) Are you ready to answer the inevitable question: "Why would you leave that great job you have?" When you are comfortable with your answer to that question, you are truly ready to become an independent consultant.

Believe us: No one said that starting your own consulting business was going to be an easy proposition. Or, if they did, then they were stretching the truth more than just a bit. Starting any business is a risky proposition — U.S. Small Business Administration statistics reveal that the majority of new businesses are doomed to failure within five years after they start up. That's one of the potential downsides to starting your own consulting business, but the upsides can be very rewarding — not just financially, but also in terms of the personal satisfaction that comes from being in control of your own work and your own destiny. Take it from us. We both jumped off the 9-to-5 career merry-go-round to start our own companies — each more than 10 years ago. We would never go back, and we venture that you won't want to either once you've left that world behind. Instead you'll ask yourself why you didn't make the move sooner.

Chapter 3

Taking the Plunge into Consulting (Or at Least Getting Your Feet Wet)

. . . .

In This Chapter

▶ Understanding when the time is right

▶ Easing into consulting

▶ Starting out: First things first

. . . .

*T*aking the plunge into consulting is a big step for most people — *especially* those who have worked for traditional, established organiza- tions for most or all of their careers. For many, letting go of a traditional 9-to-5 job can be a time for deep soul-searching, introspection, and worry. *Am I disciplined enough to be my own boss? Will people be willing to pay for my knowledge and services, and how much will they pay? What will my family think if I decide to leave my regular job to start my own business? Am I ready to quit my job? Can I survive without getting a steady paycheck? How will I obtain benefits such as health insurance and a dental plan?* All of these questions — and many others like them — must be answered and dealt with before you can take the plunge. Listen carefully to the answers you give — they will ultimately determine whether you are ready to make the transition to independent consulting and whether you will succeed in your new endeavor.

So how do you make the transition to starting your own consulting business? And, perhaps more important, how do you know whether you're *ready* to make the transition? Is there a way to find out the answer to this question *before* you put your career (and potentially the welfare of both you and your significant others) on the line? Can you make the transition a little at a time, or does it have to happen all at once? And exactly how do you make your first moves towards becoming a consultant? Funny you should ask. Those just happen to be the very questions that we address in this chapter.

Deciding When the Time Is Right

Congratulations! If you've found your way to this particular section of this particular chapter, we can guess that you have decided to join the growing ranks of men and women who are taking control of their lives and their financial futures by becoming consultants or you're seriously thinking about it. Consider some of the factors that determine exactly when the timing is best for you. Don't be surprised if your answers differ from those of your family, friends, or co-workers — everyone has a unique schedule.

In this section, we examine some of the key issues that help you determine exactly when to make your move into consulting. This list is by no means exhaustive, so feel free to add any considerations that affect you individually.

Professional considerations

Before you can become a successful independent consultant, you have to attain a certain level of professional expertise. For example, if you expect someone to hire you to set up a new manufacturing quality system, you should have a strong base of experience in the area of manufacturing quality systems. If you spent your 20 years of experience behind the cash register at Starbucks developing a callus on your forefinger, you may have a tough time selling yourself as an expert in manufacturing (although you may have a great future in coffee-shop consulting).

If you're thinking about making a living as an independent consultant, be sure to keep the following professional considerations in mind:

- **Subject matter expertise:** Most people hire a consultant because they want the benefit of a consultant's extensive expertise. They know that hiring a competent consultant isn't an inexpensive proposition, but they also know that the overall price is less than specifically hiring or training an employee to do the same task. Before you become a full-time consultant, become an expert (or pretty darn close) in your field. When you ease into consulting by working on a part-time basis, you gain the benefit of learning while being supported by your full-time job.

- **Certifications and licenses:** In some cases, you may need to obtain special credentials before you can pursue your chosen vocation. For example, if you plan to become an independent financial adviser, you should give serious consideration to earning your Certified Financial Planner certification before you jump into the fray. Many other professions require extensive certifications or licensing before you can practice them. If you work for an organization that pays for your required training and testing, by all means take advantage of these resources. Getting a regular paycheck while earning your certification is better than trying to earn a living on your own while you pursue the necessary paperwork.

✔ **References:** The ability to point to a long list of satisfied clients is a critical selling point for any consultant. Try to do as many jobs as you can with as many customers as possible before you go out on your own. Not only can you take your current clients with you when you make the move to independent consulting, but you also can create a valuable network of associates that you can tap to locate new clients.

✔ **Organizational ability:** Making a business work takes more than printing up a set of business cards. You have to be organized, you have to have a plan, and you have to know (or find out) how to run a business. Running a consulting business is no different than any other business in that you have deadlines to meet, bills to pay, office facilities to secure, and associates and clients with whom you need to coordinate. Before you launch your new consulting business, take the time necessary to plan ahead and get organized. The time you invest before you get started pays for itself many times over after you are underway.

Financial considerations

Certainly, financial considerations weigh heavily in deciding when to become a consultant. Becoming complacent is easy when you're earning a decent wage and you're getting an attractive benefits package. However, what's here today can easily be gone tomorrow — none of us owns a working crystal ball, and you just don't know for sure what's going to happen in the future. We have far too many acquaintances who have been pushed out of organizations that are desperate to cut costs in any way possible. Businesses often don't care how many years you've worked there or how talented you are. When the budget ax falls, the results can be devastating if you're not ready with your own plan. So when you hear "Breaking Up Is Hard to Do" on the music system, grab a box and get ready to pack your personal things.

Before you go out on your own, however, you must be able to support yourself and any significant others who depend on you. Consider the following financial issues before you launch a consulting practice:

✔ **Weigh your income versus your expenses:** It's a simple rule of business and of life in general. To survive, your income has to be more than your expenses. If it's not, you go into debt. And if you go far enough into debt, eventually you're forced out of business when you file for bankruptcy. As you plan your consulting business, review all your projected sources of income and expenses. If your income exceeds your expenses, no problem — you can go forward confidently. However, if your expenses exceed your projected income as a consultant, figure out how to put yourself in a more favorable position before launching into full-time consulting. How? Consider the following approaches first, and then turn to Chapter 6 for detailed information on how to set your fees to optimize the amount of money you can make as an independent consultant.

- Increase the amount of work that you do.

- Increase the rates that you charge your clients.

- Decrease your expenses.

- Upgrade the type of clients you pursue to those who focus on the value you bring to the table, not on your rates.

✔ **Assess how much you have in savings:** It's been said that most people are only a few paychecks away from bankruptcy. That's just one reason why having money squirreled away in a savings account or other highly liquid asset, such as a money market account, is important. You should have some money saved, whether you're working for an established organization or working for yourself. Do you have enough money saved to get you through times when your business is down and your clients aren't paying their bills as quickly as you might like? You need at least three months' worth of living expenses — preferably more — to survive on your own. Assess your savings account and, if you find it lacking, direct as much money to it as you possibly can before you go out on your own. Believe us — when you need the funds to get through a particularly rough spot, you'll be glad you did.

✔ **Plan for the inevitable surprises:** Life is full of surprises, which can be both good and bad. A good surprise in business is an early payment from a client or a large, unexpected contract from a client you were about to write off. A bad surprise is finding out that a client has decided to file bankruptcy before paying your bill or receiving a notice that the Internal Revenue Service wants a much larger piece of your income than you planned to contribute this year. Again, you have to be financially prepared for surprises — especially bad ones. Make sure that your income is sufficient and that you have adequate savings to get you safely past bad surprises.

Personal considerations

You have other considerations besides professional and financial ones when you decide to become an independent consultant. Think about these personal considerations:

✔ **Friends and family:** What will your friends and family think about your choice to become a consultant? In some cases, everyone may be incredibly supportive of your move. In other cases — especially when you already have a good-paying career and will be giving up a steady paycheck and benefits — your friends and family may question your sanity in deciding to become an independent consultant. *Have you lost your mind? Why would you want to do that?* You may have to counsel your family about your reasons for consulting and about your new role so that you don't become the "soccer spouse" if you have kids. Before you make the move to consulting, make sure you're clear about why you want to make the change. Explaining your decision to others is easier when you can first explain it to yourself!

✔ **Personal style:** Being your own boss means *being your own boss!* For example, when you work for an organization, you're almost always directed to complete a long list of tasks and assignments. However, when you're working for yourself, suddenly you have to direct and motivate yourself to get things done. Self-motivation can be a liberating, but frightening, prospect for someone who has been told what to do and when to do it for years. Self-employment requires lots of self-discipline. You still have to get up each morning and go to work, even when your office is only a few steps down the hall — or at a coffeehouse down the street — rather than 20 miles on the other side of town.

✔ **Lifestyle:** Becoming a self-employed consultant can mean quite a change in your lifestyle. Everything from the hours you work to where you work to how you work will likely change. Suddenly you may find yourself working at your computer before the rest of the family wakes up or long after they're tucked into their cozy beds. You may find that your clients don't live and work in your town and they need you to get on a plane to meet with them. And working solo means working solo — you may not be able to afford that associate or assistant your 9-to-5 job provided you.

✔ **Personal goals:** How does becoming a consultant fit into your personal goals? Do you have personal goals? Becoming a self-employed consultant isn't something that you should do on the spur of the moment. It requires serious advance planning and preparation. Whatever your personal goals, be they financial, professional, or whatever, make sure that consulting fits into them.

Only you can decide when the time is right to leave your day job and step into a new world of unlimited opportunity — a world where you control the reins of your destiny. If the prospect of consulting seems too overwhelming right now, don't forget that you can make the transition from your current job to a career in consulting at your own pace — one small step at a time or one great leap forward. The choice is yours.

Preparing for Stops along the Way

Becoming a self-employed consultant isn't something that just happens to you one day. The decision to become a consultant deserves and requires significant planning to make it a successful reality in your life. Yes, some people do walk into their offices one day and quit to start their own businesses *before* they have developed an adequate client base, and others are fired or laid off before they have the chance to prepare. Most independent consultants, however, build successful businesses by making a stop or two along the way.

Working for an established consulting firm

Many self-employed consultants have found a very natural transition from a full-time regular job to independent consulting by making a stop along the way as an employee for a consulting firm. For example, Peter has a friend who worked for a company for 15 years — all the while gaining valuable experience and company-paid training. He was lured away by a large international consulting firm and was put to work doing consulting jobs for firms in the industry that he had left. Eventually, after he sharpened his consulting skills and established a huge network of industry contacts, he started his own successful independent consulting business.

Moving from a big organization to an established consulting firm to your own independent consulting business offers numerous advantages:

- ✔ If you stay with your big-organization position long enough, you can collect retirement or a pension after you leave.

- ✔ While working for an established consulting firm, you develop and hone strong consulting and client skills while you learn the ins and outs of the consulting industry. Plus, working for a recognized consulting firm represents a seal of approval of your expertise.

- ✔ You may work with consultants who are providing services to your big organization; observe what they do right and discover what you can do better.

- ✔ You have the opportunity to develop a valuable network of contacts that may become the client base of your own consulting business.

- ✔ Your former employer may retain you as a consultant. Because you already know the company, its customers, and its competitors, you can contribute immediately with no additional training or orientation.

Working part time

Easing into your consulting business on a part-time basis is one of the safest *and* least painful ways to make the transition. For most consultants-to-be, this is the best approach. On the plus side, you can keep your regular job as long as you like while you maintain your consulting business on a part-time basis. On the minus side, doing both jobs can create occasional scheduling headaches. For example, imagine what you would do if an emergency at your regular job required you to fly to Rio de Janeiro on the same day that you were supposed to present your final recommendations to an important consulting client.

Both jobs can peacefully coexist, however, with careful planning and extra work on your part. For example, you can keep one master calendar to ensure that you don't have unanticipated scheduling conflicts. And, if you need to take a leave from your regular job to do some work for a consulting client, you can request permission for the leave far enough in advance to minimize the negative impact of your absence on your current organization. You can also set up regular "office hours" — time when you're not at your regular job — so your consulting clients can contact you. Here are some of the positive outcomes of doing your consulting on a part-time basis:

✔ You can try various consulting alternatives and build a strong client base while maintaining the security of your regular full-time job.

✔ You retain your health insurance and other important job benefits (a steady paycheck, for one!) as long as you remain in your regular job.

✔ If your foray into the wonderful world of consulting doesn't work out, you can easily return to your regular job and try consulting again some other time.

Who knows? You may build up such a successful business that you have no choice but to quit your regular job and go into independent consulting on a full-time basis.

Working full time

Pursuing a regular full-time job while running a full-time consulting business can be very demanding on your schedule and on your sense of reality (*Where am I? Who am I working for today?*). As such, it may be one of the least pre-ferred options. Yet, holding two full-time jobs *is* an option for many people as they make the transition from their regular jobs to careers as independent consultants. On the plus side, not only can you fully immerse yourself in the wonderful world of consulting, but you can also start developing a solid client base and generating significant consulting revenues — greatly acceler-ating your transition — all within the safety and security of your regular job. On the minus side, you could possibly — quite literally — work yourself to death. (This is probably not what you had in mind when you decided to become an independent consultant.)

We can't, with a clear conscience, recommend taking on full-time consulting business on top of a full-time job. However, if you decide to go that way, moving from a regular job to independent consulting by pursuing your new business on a full-time basis can work to your benefit in the following ways:

✔ You get the best of both worlds — a steady salary and benefits from your current job *and* full immersion in your new consulting endeavor.

✔ By building a base of consulting clients and income more quickly than you can by consulting on a part-time basis, you can greatly accelerate your transition to full-time independent consultant.

✔ You can get some excellent tax write-offs as a consultant that you can apply against your regular job.

✔ You'll sleep great at night because you'll be so tired from working two full-time jobs.

In the event that you decide to consult on the side, we recommend that you notify your current employer to be sure that you're not in either direct or indirect competition.

Landing a big contract

For some people, starting an independent consulting business is an all-or-nothing kind of thing. Bob has a business acquaintance who submitted proposals to a variety of potential clients while working in a full-time position as an employee of an organization. When Bob's acquaintance was selected as the successful bidder on a million-dollar contract, she had all the motivation and reason she needed to quit her job and dive into independent consulting on a full-time basis. If you consider this route, have an adequate base of consulting business lined up before you make the move to full-time consulting, and don't, we repeat, *don't,* submit your resignation before you have a signed contract in your hands! We discuss the ins and outs of writing winning proposals in Chapter 7.

Starting up your independent consulting practice by landing a big contract offers these advantages and more:

✔ You don't have to leave the security of your full-time job until you win a big contract.

✔ Producing and submitting contract proposals to potential clients in your after-work hours is easy. You must limit such work to after-hours to prevent conflicts of interest and future legal hassles with your current employer.

✔ If you don't land a big contract, all you have lost is some of your time and the cost of copying your proposals and mailing them out.

Immersing yourself completely

Finally, you have another way of shifting to independent consulting: total immersion. You may go to work one day and, because of a reorganization, be notified that you have been selected to be laid off: *Here's your check, please clean out your desk, thank you very much for all your fine work, don't call us, we'll call you.* Or you may reach the end of a long career of service to your organization and decide to retire. Or maybe you just can't stand the idea of spending one more day in your office doing the job you do or answering to a boss you no longer respect, and you quit.

Although total immersion isn't always the *best* way to start an independent consulting business — you may not be able to keep your personal financial boat afloat very long without a steady paycheck, for example — it *does* offer the following benefits:

- ✔ You can focus *all* your work energy on establishing a successful consulting business.

- ✔ Being out of work has a special way of focusing your attention on the real necessities in life: paying your rent or mortgage, buying food, and making your car payments. Who was it — Louis Something-or-other — who during the French Revolution stated, "Standing on the gallows really focuses the mind"?

- ✔ If your former employer established a pension or retirement plan for you, you may be able to tap into those funds to help get your business off the ground and buy yourself time as you establish a client base.

Taking the First Steps

Assume for the moment that you have decided that you're ready to take the consulting plunge. Whether you decide just to stick your toe in first or to give it all you've got, testing the water before you jump in is always a good idea. Testing the water is simple when you're at home in your bathtub, but when you're starting a new business — *your* new business — you have to do more than just check the temperature to make sure that you don't get burned! Following are a few tips that can help you take those first steps as you get your consulting business off the ground.

Talking to people who do what you want to do

You don't need to reinvent the wheel. Many people before you made the transition to independent consulting — including some, no doubt, who are doing exactly what *you* want to do. Some have succeeded beyond their wildest dreams, and others haven't. You can learn more from someone who is already doing what you want to do than you can from going to any school or sticking a book under your pillow at night.

Peter Economy consults!

Beginning in 1990, Peter Economy (www.peter economy.com) worked toward his goal to leave his 9-to-5 career as an administrative manager and build a successful, full-time, home-based consulting business. In 1996, this dream came true when he finally cut loose the anchor that he called his job and began consulting full-time. Actually, the job cut him loose when he was notified that funds had run out for his position and he was laid off. However, when additional funds were secured a few days later and his office called him back into work, Peter thought about it for a minute — and then declined the offer. Since that very day more than 10 years ago, he hasn't looked back. In addition to coauthoring books, Peter provides writing services to a variety of clients, gives editorial advice to other authors, writes magazine articles, and corresponds with *For Dummies* readers worldwide via e-mail. Bob interviewed Peter to get an idea of why someone would leave a "secure" 15-year career to work for himself as a consultant.

Consulting For Dummies: Good morning, Peter. Long time no see.

Peter Economy: Yeah right, Bob.

CFD: Okay, here's the million-dollar question: Why did you decide to become a consultant?

Economy: Geez — you're getting right to the point, aren't you? I guess there are three main reasons why I wanted to become a consultant. Number one, I always wanted to be my own boss. I had been a manager for years, but during the entire time that I was working in the world of business, I always had to respond to someone else's needs and priorities — not my own. It seemed that I was so busy fighting other people's fires that I didn't have enough time left to prevent my own.

CFD: Even when you were a vice president for that computer operations company?

Economy: Especially when I was a vice president at that computer operations company. The higher up I got in the organization, the more I was subject to the personal whims and foibles of those in upper management. If they sneezed, I jumped! Anyway, now *I* decide my priorities. I decide the projects I want to work on, how much I'm going to charge my clients, and when and where I will do the work. I don't have to show up early at the office or stay late just to impress my boss. The color of my tie and the size of my pinstripes are no longer issues. My work speaks for itself.

CFD: So your clients are more concerned with the final product, not what you were wearing when you created it or whether you called in sick on Friday or whether you attended the mandatory off-site management meeting?

Economy: Right. They don't care how I create products; they care only about the quality of the results and that I deliver them when I promise to.

CFD: So what was your second reason for becoming a consultant?

Economy: The second reason was economic security. Back when I started getting serious about building a consulting practice, I saw that the company I worked for depended on government business to remain prosperous, and that business was quickly drying up. Many of my friends and co-workers were laid off by their employers, and I was afraid that I might very well be next. This suspicion was borne out when I was laid off from my last career job twice due to lack of funding.

CFD: Yeah, there's nothing like getting laid off to light a fire under you!

Economy: That's for sure. Now the amount of money I make is directly proportional to the amount of effort I put into my work. If I work, I get paid. If I don't work, I don't get paid. However, I know that if I work hard and do the best possible job for my clients, I will have plenty of business to do, and I will be much more successful than I could ever be working for someone else.

CFD: But how were you able to build a consulting business while you were working in a full-time job?

Economy: Well, that leads to the third reason for my wanting to be a consultant: flexibility. By nature, consulting is a very flexible way to make a living. Because of this fact, I was able to squeeze occasional jobs into my schedule — usually at night and on the weekends. I might review a book for a publisher or ghostwrite a few chapters for a textbook or help fix another writer's manuscript — all in my spare time. Eventually, I was able to increase the level of consulting I did so that I could replace my full-time career job with a variety of different consulting jobs.

CFD: Wasn't leaving a steady paycheck and benefits scary? When you work for an organization, you can rely on a steady paycheck — regardless of your level of productivity. When you work for yourself, you never know where your next paycheck is coming from.

Economy: That's all true, but to me that's part of the price of freedom. Freedom is a two-edged sword. Not only do you have the freedom to

succeed beyond your wildest dreams, but you also have the freedom to fail beyond your wildest nightmares. However, I honestly believe that each one of us has a skill or talent that, if developed, can be the basis of a successful consulting business. The hard part is taking the first step and putting your dreams into action. It's not easy; but if you're willing to put your heart and soul into it, the rewards — both psychological and financial — soon outweigh the costs. And besides, then you too can sing, "I did it my way. . . ."

CFD: How did you overcome the financial and emotional adjustments that you obviously had to make?

Economy: To address the financial issues, my wife Jan and I sat down together and drew up a budget for our family — the first we'd ever done in our eight years of marriage. Once you work through the numbers and see that everything is going to be all right, a lot of the fear goes away. The emotional adjustments can't be made quite so easily. It takes a little time to get used to the idea of being completely responsible for yourself rather than being dependent on an employer. But it helped that, when I left my full-time job, I was emotionally ready to make the move. I wanted to be my own boss.

CFD: One last question. Is Economy really your last name?

Economy: Put it in your ear, Nelson!

Before you start your new business, seek out people who do what you want to do and talk to them — as often and for as long as you can. Schedule an appointment to meet them at work, or invite them to an informal get-together after work. Find out what things worked for them and what things didn't. Ask them about the good times and the bad times, and what you can do to bring about more of the former. You may find the flames of your desire to start your own independent consulting firm fanned to new heights by your acquaintances' enthusiasm. Who knows, they may even offer you a small project — a subcontract job — to get you started. Or the embers may die when you discover that what you *thought* you wanted to do really *isn't* what you want to do. Either way, you learn important lessons that can make you and your business much stronger. Besides, you're building an informed network of consultants who can help you expand your business.

Starting small

Given a choice, you are better off to start small and work your way up to larger projects as you hone your consulting skills. Why? One reason is that you can devote more of your time and attention to a small project than you can to a large one. If you are still working full-time in a traditional job, you have to fit the project into your schedule whenever you can — most likely at nights or on the weekends. We can guarantee from our personal experience that finding extra time to work on a small project is easier than finding time to work on a large project. Not only that, but you can learn the ropes of your chosen field at a pace that is comfortable to you, *and* you have a lot more time available to refine and polish your work.

Evaluating the results

How do you know whether your tentative first steps at consulting are taking you in the right direction? The way to find out is to evaluate your results:

- ✔ **Is consulting what you expected?** Many people have a glorified view of how wonderful consulting must be. Consulting is wonderful, but for many, the reality of consulting doesn't quite match up with the fantasy. Is consulting what you expected, or is it something less or more? If it's something less, then reconsider the type of consulting that you're doing or your approach to doing it. Don't worry — you may need several tries before you get it right!

- ✔ **Do you like what you're doing?** Don't forget: You're supposed to be having fun doing what you're doing. If you enjoy the consulting work that you're doing, great! If not, why not? Is your view likely to change as you get more involved in consulting and devote more of your life to doing it? Don't forget that the first few months (perhaps even the first few years) of transitioning to your own consulting business may be an emotional roller coaster for you and your loved ones. These highs and lows are a natural part of making a major life change. If you hang in there and keep trying, things will probably get better soon. If, however, you've been trying for some time and things *aren't* getting better, then maybe becoming a self-employed consultant isn't your cup of tea.

- ✔ **Do your clients like what you're doing?** Liking what you do is a great feeling. But knowing that your *clients* like what you do is equally important (at least if you want to pay the bills). If you plan to consult on a part-time basis only to supplement your current income, you don't need a lot of clients to keep your enterprise afloat. However, if you plan to pursue consulting on a full-time basis, you'll need lots of *very* satisfied clients to keep you fully employed. How do you find out whether they're satisfied? Ask them. You can do so in the form of a direct interview, a casual conversation, a feedback form, or a questionnaire. If you do good work at a fair price and are dependable, don't worry — they will come.

So are you ready to take the plunge? If your current job still has the advantage, don't feel that you need to make your move right away — consulting will always be there waiting for you. And in the meantime, you can make plans for the big move. However, if consulting has the edge, now may be the time to make the switch. If you do, we wish you the very best and offer this advice: Don't look back.

Part II
Getting Your Consulting Business Off the Ground

The 5th Wave   By Rich Tennant

"First Harry sold bowling balls, so he took me bowling. Then he sold golf clubs, so we took up golf. Now he's selling surgical instruments, and frankly, I haven't had a full night's sleep since."

In this part . . .

*E*very self-employed consultant started somewhere — at the beginning. In this part, we take a close look at exactly what it takes to start a successful consulting business, including the legal and financial ins and outs, taxes, and a topic of particular importance to consultants: ethics. We also delve deeply into the critical topic of determining what you're worth to your clients, and setting fees that reflect that value while helping you develop a profitable consulting business that's built to last.

Chapter 4

Setting Up Your Consulting Firm

● ●

In This Chapter

▶ Getting your home office off the ground

▶ Reviewing your home office checklist

▶ Securing support services

● ●

*A*s you can imagine, when you become a self-employed consultant, you need to find a new place to work. This most likely means creating an office in your home, or perhaps finding a small office outside the home. Regardless of where you decide to plant yourself and your new business, you need to set it up, and you need to find the kind of support services — accounting, banking, legal — that most people take for granted when working for an established company.

As you get set up, remember: *You're* the boss. You get to decide when and where you do business. If you want to rent an office downtown or in a suburban strip mall, you can do so. Many consultants (especially those who have employees) do rent office space, and they're very happy with that arrangement. However, you now have a chance to take a different path — one that offers an array of opportunities and benefits that you just don't get by working in a traditional office.

In this chapter, we focus on establishing a home office. We look into the space and furnishings you need to get started, and we review some of the financial incentives to establishing a home office and explain how you can take advantage of them. Finally, we talk about finding and using support services to your advantage.

Getting Your Home Office Up and Running

Setting up your office is probably the most fun part of running a business from your home. Remember all the lousy offices that you were crammed into in your past jobs? Remember the too-small desks, the uncomfortable chairs, the barely adequate computers, the stuffy air, and the generic music piped over the loudspeakers? This is your big chance to make up for all your previous employers' transgressions against your sensibilities and to design an office that meets your needs.

One more thing: This is also your chance to take advantage of the financial benefits that setting up a home-based consulting business can offer you. If you live in the United States and you play your cards right, the government can help you pay for your home office by making all your business expenses — as well as the portion of your housing expenses that is attributable to your home office — tax deductible.

This tax deduction can be a real financial benefit to you and your business; however, the government is *very* particular about exactly who is eligible to take the home-office deduction and under what circumstances. Writing off a part of your home as a business raises a red flag for government tax auditors, so be sure you know what you're doing. Consult with your tax adviser for more details on the home-office deduction, and while you're at it, pick up a copy of *Home-Based Business For Dummies,* 2nd Edition, by Paul and Sarah Edwards and Peter Economy, to find out more about the ins and outs of writing off your home-based consulting business.

In the event that setting up an office in your home isn't feasible or you prefer to work outside of your home, you may want to consider alternative arrangements that allow you to share office space and support services with others in situations similar to yours. For more on these options, see the section "Moving out of your home-based office" later in this chapter.

In this section, we explore the essentials of setting up your own home office — from the space to the equipment in it. You'll be spending a great deal of time in your office, so make it as nice a place to work as possible.

Your space

The total amount of space that you're going to need to set up a functioning home office depends on the nature of your consulting business. For most consultants, the ideal situation is to take over an existing bedroom or den and convert it into an office. Not only do you get plenty of space for all your furniture, equipment, and supplies, but a bedroom or den with a door also offers privacy — an important ingredient in *any* home office. In addition, a room that is 100 percent dedicated to your business is easier for you to use (and to deduct on your taxes).

Here are some key ingredients to setting up an inviting and productive workspace in your home:

- ✔ **Find an out-of-the-way place.** You don't want your home office to be in the center of your family's traffic pattern during the morning get-the-kids-ready-for-school rush, nor do you want it to be in a garage that fills with smelly fumes every time someone starts up the car. Ideally, your office should be a private sanctuary where you can focus on your work, not on everything *but* your work. On the flip side, if you find yourself working late into the night, your activities shouldn't bother your significant others. That can be a little difficult if you select your bedroom as your home office.

- ✔ **Make the space inviting.** You're going to be spending a *lot* of time in your home office, so you want it to be comfortable and inviting. It should have adequate heating and cooling in all kinds of weather. The walls should be freshly painted in a neutral color, and the windows should have blinds that enable you to control the amount of outside light that enters your office. What goes on the walls is up to you.

- ✔ **Provide for easy access.** Make sure your office is easy to access without disturbing the other members of your household. You don't, for example, want the only entrance to your office to be through the baby's nursery.

- ✔ **Have good lighting and plenty of it.** Good lighting is critical to your productivity. Ideally, your office will have both plenty of natural lighting from windows (most bedrooms are already well equipped in this department) and lighting from artificial sources, such as overhead lighting and desk lamps.

- ✔ **Ventilate the space early and often.** Make sure that your home office has access to plenty of fresh air. This is especially necessary if you have computers, printers, copiers, and other office equipment that generate gobs of ozone, dust, and heat.

- ✔ **Get wired.** Your home office needs plenty of grounded (three-prong) electric receptacles to plug in all your office equipment. Not only do you need outlets for your computer, but you also need outlets for your printers, a fax machine, an adding machine, a battery charger for your cellphone, desk lamps, a radio, and anything else that you may need to plug in. In addition to electricity, you need at least one phone line — maybe more — as well as a coaxial television cable if you're hooked up to a cable modem for Internet access.

✔ **Security is the best policy.** What would happen if someone stole your computer, along with all your disks and backup media? For some consultants, this incident would be an unqualified, magnitude seven, please-shoot-me-now-to-put-me-out-of-my-misery disaster. If you don't have a home security system tied to an alarm and a monitoring service, consider getting one. While you're at it, buy a small fireproof safe to store your backup disks — and make sure that you use it!

Your furniture

Your home office can be nothing more than a desk and a chair, or it can be a fully equipped suite with everything found in any commercial office, including fax machines, computers, copiers, and more. When you decide to furnish your home office, get good-quality furnishings that are both comfortable and built to last. You're going to be spending a lot of time in your office, so you should make it a joy — not an ordeal — to work there.

If you're watching your budget (and who isn't?), consider buying your furniture *used* instead of new. If you were laid off at your 9-to-5 job because of serious budget cutbacks and you liked your furniture or equipment, consider making them an offer of pennies on the dollar to take it home with you. Your former employer might just take you up on it. Keep an eye on Craigslist.org for great deals in your area. You may also want to consider renting or leasing your office furniture, although doing so may not be a great idea in the long run because you'll probably pay far more than if you just bought it to start with. Check your Yellow Pages or Internet listings for a rental company near you.

With that advice in mind, here are some key things to consider when you go shopping for office furniture:

✔ **Your chair:** If you're looking for a place to invest a little extra money in your office setup, the chair is the place. Spend the extra money to get a high-quality, ergonomically correct task chair. If you've used an ergonomic chair at work, you already know the importance of being in the correct working position — especially when you spend most of your time at your desk. Using a quality chair reduces fatigue and helps to prevent back pain and other ills that can occur when your posture is out of whack for long periods of time.

If you expect clients to visit, make sure that you have comfortable chairs available for them, too.

✔ **Your desk:** When shopping for your desk, think *big!* No matter how large your desk, by the time you load it up with a computer, a printer, a phone, a calculator, and a personal planner or two, you have precious little space left over to do your work. Get a sturdy desk — you don't want it to be rocking to and fro as you type up proposals. Also be sure that your desk has more than enough room to accommodate whatever you intend to put on it and still leaves you enough room to spread out your work. A large traditional office desk or even a sturdy worktable does just fine.

While you're shopping, make sure that you look for a desk that is at the proper height so that working on your computer is an ergonomic dream rather than an ergonomic nightmare. According to experts, a computer workstation should be at a height of about 28 inches off the floor. Ideally, your keyboard will be on an adjustable tray so you can find the most comfortable setting (which will probably be closer to a height of 25 or 26 inches).

✔ **Worktables:** A couple of worktables can give you the extra room you need to get your work done more efficiently and to stay organized. You don't need anything fancy here — a simple table with folding legs or a sturdy dining-room table works fine.

✔ **File cabinets:** You may be able to make do with a file drawer in your desk. If you deal with volumes of paperwork as a part of your consulting practice, however, you need additional filing space. An organized filing system is critical to your efficiency, so spend some serious time designing and implementing a filing system before you jump into your consulting business. Plenty of choices are available, and your ultimate decision depends on the amount of paperwork that you need to keep at hand. At a minimum, you should get a freestanding, four-drawer file cabinet. You can easily add more cabinets as the need arises. For long-term storage, pull the documents from your file cabinets and place them in the cardboard storage boxes commonly known as banker's boxes. You can then stick the storage boxes in a closet or in the garage. Reserve the space in your file cabinets for documents that you actively use and need to access regularly.

✔ **Bookshelves:** What would an office be without bookshelves? In addition to holding books, bookshelves are handy for a variety of other purposes. Peter's bookshelves — which are actually heavy-duty plastic storage shelves that he purchased at a large membership-warehouse club — are filled with books, boxes of business-oriented computer software, his laptop computer and related accessories, stacks and stacks of magazines for research, laser printer paper, inkjet printer paper, mailing envelopes, FedEx supplies, and his cherished compact disc player and stereo. No matter how many bookshelves you get, we can guarantee that you'll fill them up.

✔ **Supply storage:** Make sure to set aside a drawer or shelf to hold your office supplies. Pens, pencils, paper clips, staples, markers, printer ink cartridges, and all the other fruits of your office-supply shopping spree need a place safe from your dog, cat, or kids.

Your equipment

As with any office, your home office requires certain pieces of equipment and supplies for you to conduct business. For example, doing an in-depth automated spreadsheet analysis without a computer is pretty hard. And contacting your clients is hard as heck if you don't have a phone. You need the following basic equipment to get your business up and running:

- ✔ **Telephones:** You definitely need at least one telephone — maybe more. If you have only one phone, get a basic telephone with a hold button and speakerphone. Consider getting two telephone lines: one for voice and one for fax and Internet (if you're still using dial-up). Allow at least 24 to 48 hours for your local phone provider to get your service hooked up — more if the provider has to run new wiring from the street into your home.

  If you're like 99.9 percent of the rest of us, you'll also need a reliable wireless phone. Be sure to get one that will work wherever you may be traveling for your consulting services. And don't forget to get an answering machine or voice-mail service so that your callers can leave a message if you're not around.

- ✔ **Computer:** Your computer is the nerve center of your home office and an essential element in your consulting business. Get the best you can afford, and make sure it has the kinds of software that you need to get your work done. If you'll do most of your work at your home office, get a standard desktop computer. If you'll be on the road frequently or plan to spend much time with clients, consider getting a laptop computer. Bob's laptop is powerful enough to be used as his desktop computer simply by plugging in a monitor and keyboard. For software, a complete office suite, such as Microsoft Office, is a smart way to go. Microsoft Office contains word processing, spreadsheet, presentation graphics, and e-mail programs, all in one package. Also consider some of the latest Internet-based offerings such as the Google Office suite (`http://docs.google.com`), which can be accessed anywhere you can get an Internet connection.

- ✔ **Internet access:** Having access to the Internet is absolutely essential nowadays, and you've got lots of options for getting it. You can access the Internet with a telephone modem using a dial-up service, such as America Online, or you can piggyback onto your cable television service using a cable modem, such as that provided by Time Warner Road Runner. DSL service (which uses your existing phone line) and even satellite service are also possibilities. Depending on where you live, you may have access to a municipal Wi-Fi Internet service.

- ✔ **Fax machine:** If your computer has a data/fax modem, you can use it as your fax machine. However, if you don't want to leave your computer turned on all day long, you should buy a dedicated fax machine. Be sure to get one that uses plain paper — not the old-tech rolls of thermal paper. New fax machines have an added bonus: You can use most of them as copiers, printers, and scanners.

✓ **Network:** If you've got more than one computer in your home office — or if you want to hook your computer up with other computer-based devices (such as a digital video recorder, a video game system, and so forth), then you'll probably want to set up a computer network. You can choose to go with either a wired (generally using a router and Ethernet cables) or a wireless setup (using a wireless router). If you go with a wireless system, be sure to turn on password protection so your neighbors aren't tempted to borrow your service!

✓ **Copier/scanner:** If you need to make only a few copies of documents on an irregular basis, you can use your fax machine or scanner as a copier or rely on a local copying service, such as Kinko's. However, if you make lots of copies on a regular basis, buy or lease a decent office copier. To save yourself grief and headaches down the road, get one that, at a minimum, has an automatic document feeder and can handle legal-size as well as letter-size paper. Also get a service contract that guarantees service within one business day after you make your service call.

Whether you have a printer/copier/fax machine or just a plain printer, always, always, always have a stock of backup printer ink cartridges readily available to you. Nothing can raise your blood pressure faster than working against a fast-approaching project deadline and having your printer ink cartridges run out.

Other business essentials

The big stuff is out of the way. Now it's time to get down to the little things that really make an office an office. Remember those lousy pens that corporate standardized on to save money? Or those tacky desk calendars? Or how about those cheap yellow legal pads that fell apart more often than they held together? You never have to use any of those again. Now you decide what kinds of pens, pencils, paper, calendars, and other office supplies your office stocks.

When you set up your home office, stock up on plenty of office supplies. Visit your local office supply store or a large warehouse office-supply store and shop until you drop. Most of the large warehouse stores offer their own charge cards that include discounts and other benefits for using them — get one! Here are a few essentials for any well-equipped home office:

✓ **Writing utensils:** Get plenty of your favorite pens and pencils — now's your chance to really let go. In addition, buy an assortment of colored markers in sizes ranging from fine to broad. If you have a whiteboard in your office, you need special markers for that. And don't forget to stock up on those handy yellow highlighters, too.

✔ **Paper:** If you use your computer printer frequently or have an office copier, consider buying standard 20-pound paper by the case. Be sure to buy paper that is designed for the machine you intend to use it with, for example, a laser printer or a plain-paper fax machine. Also get some fancy 24-pound paper for sending letters to your favorite clients. Depending on your personal preferences, you may also want to buy some ruled pads of letter- or legal-sized paper, some note paper, and index cards.

✔ **Fastening devices:** An office without a stapler is not truly an office. Pick up a stapler and some matching staples to go with it. Buy plenty of paper clips (we like the jumbo size best), binder clips (get an assortment of sizes), and rubber bands. A roll of adhesive tape is a must, and a large roll of packing tape can be a real lifesaver from time to time.

✔ **Envelopes:** Stock up on #10 envelopes — these are the standard business size. If you plan to run them through your printer, make sure the box says that they are made for that purpose. Also get some 9-x-12-inch or 10-x-13-inch mailing envelopes so that you can mail documents without folding them.

✔ **Folders:** If you have a file cabinet, you need file folders to fill it up. You can choose from a wide variety of sizes, colors, and types, including hanging and non-hanging folders. Try out several different kinds of folders until you find the ones that work best for you.

Leveraging Support Services

Whether your business is small or large, there are certain things that only you can and should do — the things that bring you and your practice the greatest financial return. Similarly, you should always delegate certain things to others because doing them yourself takes you away from doing the things that bring you the greatest return. As an independent, self-employed consultant, you may find yourself constantly balancing the temptation to do everything yourself against the very real need to free up as much of your time as possible so that you can focus on the things you do best.

Your job is to use your time and resources in the most cost-effective way while maximizing their return. Our humble belief — borne over years of experience in business and consulting — is that the best way to accomplish this goal is to make effective use of support services. Support services are the full range of business services available to you — from clerical support to photocopying to legal and financial advice to a fully-equipped rented office — that enable you to spend less time doing the things that have a low return to your business and more time doing the things that have a high return.

Home office checklist

Here's a quick and easy checklist to use for setting up your home office that summarizes all the items listed in the section "Getting Your Home Office Up and Running." Now you don't have an excuse for not setting up an office right away!

✔ **Space:** Pick out a space in your home that is out of the way, quiet, and inviting. Make sure that it has adequate lighting and that it is sufficiently wired for electricity, phones, and data communications. If you don't have a home alarm and a fireproof data safe, consider getting them.

✔ **Furniture:** Get a comfortable, ergonomic task chair, as well as some comfortable chairs for your clients if you'll be meeting with them in your home office. Invest in a desk that is sturdy and large enough to accommodate your computer, peripherals, and your work.

Buy worktables, file cabinets, and bookshelves, too.

✔ **Equipment:** Buy a telephone for your office (and one for the road!) and invest in one or more phone lines, depending on your needs. Get the best computer you can afford and consider buying a plain-paper fax machine, unless you plan to use your computer to receive and send faxes. You'll definitely need Internet access for your e-mail and Web surfing, and you may need a network — wired or wireless — and an office copier as well.

✔ **Office supplies:** Go to your nearest office supply warehouse, grab a shopping cart, and go wild! Pens, pencils, staplers, tape, and more are all awaiting the opportunity to serve you.

In this section, we address the importance of leveraging your experience and focusing your efforts in making your business a success, and we consider the variety of different staffing options available to you. We also take a look at establishing workplaces outside a home office and how doing so can help make you a more efficient and effective consultant.

Getting a good assistant

Hiring an assistant is one of the quickest and most cost-effective ways to free up your time to focus on the things that you need to do and that bring your practice the greatest financial benefit. You don't have to make a major commitment to start out. Your assistant may be a spouse or significant other working on a part-time basis. Or perhaps a college student or a temporary employee may work for you a couple hours a day or a few days a week. As your workload increases, you can gradually extend your assistant's work schedule to meet your needs and the needs of your clients, or hire a full-time person or additional people as required.

Carefully chosen, a good assistant can deliver benefits far beyond taking care of clerical duties. Here are some of the benefits of hiring an assistant:

- ✔ **You save time.** An assistant can take over your rote tasks — answering the phone; responding to client inquiries; and sorting and prioritizing mail, voice-mail, and e-mail messages — freeing you to focus on client projects and securing new business.

- ✔ **You save money.** The financial value of your time probably far exceeds whatever you would pay an assistant. For example, you may make $100 an hour as a consultant, but your assistant may make a fraction of that — say, $8 to $10 an hour.

- ✔ **You make a more positive impression on your clients.** When clients are helped by an assistant, they are likely to be impressed and feel that they are receiving better service — and they probably are!

- ✔ **You create opportunities to get away from your office.** As a one-person business, you may feel that you have to be in your office all the time to make sure that you don't miss important client calls. Hiring an assistant enables you to get out of your office to visit clients and network with prospective clients.

- ✔ **You get another point of view.** No one has a monopoly on the truth. An assistant often can give you a second point of view or a second opinion. For a one-person operation, this can be a breath of fresh air.

As soon as you can afford to hire an assistant (can you afford not to?), do it! You'll be amazed at what you can do with all the time that suddenly becomes available — and so will your clients.

Finding a good lawyer, an accountant, and a banker

Every business needs occasional support from outside professionals such as lawyers, accountants, bankers, and others. Indeed, finding good professionals is one of the most important things you can do — besides finding lots of good clients — to ensure the success of your consulting business. In addition to the services they provide, you may find that these professionals become your trusted advisers. They often have broad business experiences from working with a variety of different clients, and they can offer good general business advice to you, too. They may even become a source of new clients for your business by referring others in their business community to you.

Before you sign on the dotted line, be sure to check your chosen professionals out thoroughly. The idea is to find someone who is not only talented and affordable, but who also can grow with you and your company and become a long-term partner and trusted associate. Consider the following when making your selections:

✔ **Qualifications:** Hire professionals who are as qualified and experienced as possible. Do not hire someone who merely dabbles in an area of professional expertise, or who does it as a hobby. You need someone who is a pro and is fully committed to your success.

✔ **Accessibility:** Make sure that the professionals you hire are available when you need them and aren't overcommitted with other clients.

✔ **Price:** While you should generally plan to pay more for more experience and skill, you shouldn't pay more than you need to. Don't be afraid to shop around for the best combination of skill, experience, and price.

✔ **Ethics:** The lawyers, accountants, bankers, and other professionals you work with should have ethical standards that are just as high as your own. Choosing someone with flexible ethics is asking for trouble.

✔ **Compatibility:** Ideally, you'll find someone who meets all of the above criteria and is also compatible with you and any business partners and associates you may have. Nothing is much worse than trying to work with someone you don't get along with.

Interview your prospective candidates (either in person or over the phone), asking questions that provide you with the following kinds of information:

✔ Does your candidate have specific experience working with home-based businesses?

✔ Does your candidate show an active interest in the future growth of your business?

✔ Does he or she keep abreast of the latest changes in the field as they pertain to your industry?

✔ What do the candidate's references say about his or her performance and reliability?

✔ What is the candidate's fee structure?

✔ Does your candidate have a network of other potentially beneficial contacts within your community (for example, loan officers at local banks)?

✔ Are you comfortable with the candidate, and are your personal philosophies compatible?

When asking for references, ask for clients who have businesses similar to your own. Talking with a reference who has recently started his own consulting business will give you a better idea of what to expect than one who has been a manufacturer, for example, for 20 years.

In the sections that follow, we consider the key professionals that self-employed consultants most often turn to for help and support.

Lawyers

An attorney's services are an important part of any business's — including an independent consultant's — support team. What can attorneys do for you? Here are some of the most common tasks attorneys take on for their small business clients:

- ✔ Choosing a form (legal structure) for your business
- ✔ Writing, reviewing, and negotiating business contracts
- ✔ Dealing with employee issues
- ✔ Helping with credit problems and bankruptcy
- ✔ Addressing consumer issues and complaints
- ✔ Working with rental or leasing agreements
- ✔ Outlining workers' compensation and social security benefits
- ✔ Advising you on your legal rights and obligations
- ✔ Representing you in court

Be sure to seek out an attorney who specializes in working with small businesses and startups. To find a good one, ask around. Check with your friends and business associates — particularly those who own small businesses. One more thing: Make a point of asking your attorney how much a particular task is going to cost *before* you engage his services, not after. A lawyer's bill for services is one place you do not want surprises.

Accountants

If you're not an expert in accounting (few independent consultants are), getting a good accountant is a must. As the owner of your own business, you need to know exactly how much money is going in and out of your bank accounts, and for what purposes it is being used. This knowledge allows you to assess the financial health of your company, and it provides the basis for determining how much you owe the government in taxes and other fees.

Inadequate record keeping is a key contributor to the failure of small businesses — including consulting firms. A good accountant can be worth his or her weight in gold, and usually becomes a long-term partner in the growth of your firm.

Here are some common tasks that accountants perform for their small-business customers:

- ✔ Small business startup, business sale, or business purchase
- ✔ Accounting system design and implementation
- ✔ Preparation, review, and audit of financial statements

✔ Tax planning

✔ Preparation of income tax returns

✔ Tax appeals

Find and select an accountant in much the same way that you select any other professional adviser. Check with friends and business associates for recommendations and references. Interview several candidates to be sure that your personalities are compatible.

A *certified public accountant (CPA)* is an accountant who has met his or her state's minimum educational requirements and passed a rigorous examination covering accounting, business law, auditing, and taxes. CPAs are required to have a college degree (this can be offset by extensive work experience, in some cases) and must meet an annual continuing education requirement. However, any skilled accountant — whether or not she has CPA after her name — may be just right for you and your business. It all depends on the experience and expertise that she brings to the table, as well as her willingness to be available to help you when you really need it.

Bankers

As the old saying goes, money makes the world go 'round. Your bank will inevitably play a central role in your consulting business — from maintaining checking and savings accounts, to providing tax depository services, to lending you money when you need it. These kinds of ongoing financial needs — and more — make finding and establishing a relationship with a good local banker a must.

Peter was shocked to learn, soon after he established a business account for his new corporation at a large local bank, that any checks over $500 would be put on hold for a week or more while the bank waited for them to clear. Yikes! In Peter's case, a combination of lots of begging, sweet talking, and threats to move his funds to another bank helped keep his cash flowing until his account aged enough for his bank to remove the automatic hold from his account.

Okay, so what kind of financial institution is right for self-employed consultants? A number of different financial institutions are available to you, and each has its own unique spin on the world of money and banking.

✔ **Banks** — including savings banks, savings and loans, and commercial banks — are the financial institutions of first choice for many businesses. Banks traditionally make a wide variety of loans, both commercial and consumer, and they're the place to go for special small-business loans offered in conjunction with the Small Business Administration (SBA). Most also offer special accounts designed specifically for businesses, along with a wide array of business-oriented products and services.

- ✔ **Credit unions** are similar to banks, but differ in that their members own them. This results in lower costs of operation, which are passed on to members in the form of lower interest rates on loans and higher savings interest rates. Credit unions are less likely than regular banks to offer special accounts and products and services for businesses and, in some cases, they may not even be able to accept your business as a customer.

- ✔ **Credit card companies** offer interest rates that are often significantly higher than the rates you would get on the same amount of money from a bank or credit union, yet countless entrepreneurs have financed their business startup and growth using credit card loans. Keep in mind that even if the credit card has your company name on it, you're likely to be personally responsible for the charges.

- ✔ **Commercial finance companies** specialize in working with businesses, usually in financing equipment leasing or purchases or the acquisition of inventory. The deals that commercial finance companies offer — particularly leasing — may offer attractive tax advantages and are worth checking out.

- ✔ **Consumer finance companies** are businesses that specialize in making loans to borrowers who have a hard time obtaining loans from their banks or credit unions, perhaps because they have defaulted on loans in the past or because their credit is already overextended. Consumer finance companies generally charge much higher rates than banks, credit unions, and credit card companies, so they should be considered a funding source of last resort for most businesses.

Be sure to establish a relationship with your banker (which most often means the branch manager) *before* you apply for a loan and *before* depositing a $10,000 check that will trigger an automatic hold. Consider moving your personal banking to the same bank. Depending on the extent of your personal financial assets, it may give your business instant importance. The relationship you build with your banker today will pay large dividends well into the future.

Outsourcing — You can do it, too!

After you establish your consulting business, you may find that you have far more clients who need your services than you have the time to accommodate. Unfortunately, one person can do only so much. When your workload exceeds the amount of time that you can devote to completing it, you have three choices:

- ✔ You can tell the client to find someone else to do the work.

- ✔ You can subcontract the work out to another firm.

- ✔ You can hire new employees to help you complete your assignments.

The first choice — rejecting the work — is clearly not the best option. Not only do you lose the opportunity to grow your business, but you also may be turning down a vital piece of business that you'll need if your other business goes away for some reason. And, believe us — you never know what business disaster may be waiting for you just around the corner.

Although you should turn away business that's not in your area of expertise or that's not profitable enough for you, few consultants have the luxury of turning away good, profitable work. If you repeatedly turn clients away, then after a while, they won't bother coming to you with their work.

The second choice — subcontracting the work out to another firm or independent consultant — can be a good idea, especially if the other firm occasionally sends work your way, too. This approach can work very well, so long as the quality is up to your own high standards and delivery times don't suffer. In most cases, your client doesn't even have to know that you're subcontracting out the work (be sure, however, to check your contract to see if you are legally required to notify your client in the event you subcontract work to another firm, or if you're personally required to do the work). However, no matter how accomplished and reliable your subcontractor may be, when you send work to another firm, you lose some amount of control over the process. You're still on the hook with your clients to assure the quality of the work done by your subcontractors, regardless of how good or bad it is.

This brings us to a third choice, one that gives you even more control over the work process: hiring employees to help you complete your assignments. If your increased workload is long-term in nature, then you may want to hire a "permanent" employee, that is, one with no defined term of employment. But what if the assignment is relatively small or short-term in nature? You don't want to hire an employee or two for a couple weeks and then have to lay them off. Through the modern miracle of temporary workers, you can expand and contract your staff as often as you like, without going through the trauma of hiring employees only to lay them off a short time afterward.

And "temps" — the common term for temporary workers — aren't limited to just secretaries and receptionists anymore. Computer programmers, technical writers, drafters, communications engineers, accountants, word processors, assemblers, customer service specialists, managers, and more are available through temporary employment firms. According to the people who keep track of such things, approximately 90 percent of all businesses use temporary workers from time to time. Why not you? To get an idea of what's available in your town, check out the Yellow Pages under "Employment — Temporary," or do an Internet search for temp agencies in your area.

Here are some of the advantages of using temporary workers to help you get through the inevitable surges in your workload:

- ✔ **Temporary workers are as temporary as you want them to be.** You can use temporary workers for a day, a week, a month, or a year — the time frame is up to you. And when you finish your assignment, you don't have to lay off your workers or give them two weeks' notice — the temporary employment agency merely reassigns your temps to another organization. No muss, no fuss.

- ✔ **There's no tedious hiring process.** You don't have to run an advertisement in the newspaper, read a mountain of resumes, and spend days interviewing job candidates. All you need to do is pick up the phone, call a temporary employment firm, and help is on the way — quickly and easily.

- ✔ **Temps are there when you need them.** You often can have a temporary worker at your office ready to work within a few hours of your call — certainly by the next business day. When you need someone quickly and you can't afford to mess around, calling a temp agency is one of the best and most reliable ways to meet your needs.

- ✔ **The temp agency pays all employee-related expenses.** You don't have to worry about trying to understand the tangled maze of payments that you have to make to the government whenever you hire an employee. In addition to an hourly wage, the temporary employment firm pays your worker's payroll taxes, social security, workers' compensation, and insurance, and, in some cases, provides health insurance, vacation pay, retirement savings plans, and other benefits.

- ✔ **Temporary employees can save you money.** You pay only for the time that your temporary worker works for you. You don't have to worry about paying for sick leave, vacations, or other downtime.

Moving out of your home-based office

The time may come in your independent consulting career when either you make enough money to hire some staff and build a fast-growing consulting firm that needs more space in a conventional office, or working at home is just not working for you — requiring you to either move your office out of your home, or go insane. Whatever the reason for moving out of your home-based office, the prospect of doing so can be exciting and scary all at the same time.

In this section, we explore of variety of options for moving your consulting firm out of your home-based office.

Renting or leasing office space

All kinds of businesses — small and large, young and old — rent or lease office space. (*Note:* The term *rent* usually applies to gaining use of a property in exchange for a monthly cash payment for a period of less than a year, while the term *lease* usually applies to a period of a year or more.) Before you decide to rent or lease office space, there are a variety of things to consider, including:

✔ How much space will you need? All sizes and shapes of offices are available in most areas of the country. Carefully consider the current needs of your business before making a long-term commitment to any space.

✔ Where is the best location for your office? Remember that for some kinds of businesses, being in the right location is *everything*. While many consultants can work most anywhere, some find that the cache that an address brings them — for example, the public relations consulting firm located on New York City's Park Avenue — is worth its weight in gold.

✔ Will this space accommodate your future growth plans? While you don't want to carry a bunch of empty offices on your overhead, you do want to have offices available to accommodate your future growth plans. Finding the right balance is a real challenge. Keep in mind that you can temporarily sublease space to another business while you're waiting for your own growth plans to kick in (so long as your lease allows you to sublease).

✔ How long will you need the space? The longer period of time you're willing to commit to, the longer the lease, and often the more flexible your prospective landlord will be in negotiating a favorable financial deal for you. However, you'll be in trouble if you've signed a long-term lease (say five years) and need to bail out sooner. You may be forced to pay the rent due for the balance of your lease, or at least until your landlord is able to find another tenant to take your space.

✔ Is the space configured to your exact needs? If not, you may have to undertake a short-term construction project (usually called *tenant improvements*) to bring the space in line with your needs. Many tenants negotiate an allowance for tenant improvements in their lease.

✔ Does your lease allow you to add more space easily if you need it? Some leases — and landlords — make it easy to add more space when you need it. Some don't.

✔ What expenses will you be responsible for, and which expenses will your landlord be responsible for? For example, if your air conditioning system breaks, will your landlord pay for repairs, or are you responsible for them? Leases for commercial properties come in three basic flavors:

   • *Gross lease*. The landlord pays for almost all the operating expenses of the property.

   • *Modified gross lease*. Some of the expenses of owning and operating the building are passed through to the tenants. For example, leases where the landlord pays all operating expenses except for certain items such as utilities, parking, or janitorial expenses are considered to be modified gross leases.

> • *Net lease*. The tenant pays the majority of the costs of operating the building, including property taxes, insurance, and maintenance costs. Leases in which the tenant pays almost all costs associated with operating the building are called *triple net leases.*

✔ Do you have all the furniture and equipment you'll need to outfit your new space? If not, then you'll need to buy or lease more.

✔ What utilities and communications equipment will need to be acquired and/or installed? Depending on the terms of your lease, you may need to contact electric, gas, telephone, Internet, and other utilities to arrange for service to your business. You may also need to acquire and install telephone and Internet networking equipment. Unless you're an expert at installing and setting up telephone and Internet equipment and networks, you may find hiring a communications consultant to be a very smart move.

✔ What kind of security systems will you need? While some consultants may find that a front door lock and key provide sufficient security, others may decide that only a complete, floor-to-ceiling system with window and door sensors, video cameras, infrared motion detectors, and smoke and entry alarms monitored 24/7 will do.

✔ What's the best way to find the space you need? If you're not a commercial real estate agent or broker, consider hiring one to find the right space for you and help negotiate your lease.

Of course, you can always buy an office space or building instead of renting or leasing one. To do so requires a lot more money upfront, and you may find that the tax advantages aren't as favorable as for renting or leasing. However, if you have the cash or purchase financing available to you, buying your own office can offer the kind of long-term appreciation and business stability that renting or leasing cannot.

Renting or leasing an executive suite

How would you like to have all the benefits of a fully staffed and equipped office without hiring any employees or buying any equipment? And not just any old office or one in the corner of your garage, nestled between the hedge trimmer and the geranium sprouts, but a real office with a desk, a door, and more. Don't get us wrong; we both have our own offices at home — and Bob has a traditional office as well — and we're very happy with them. Usually. But a home office (or a cold, empty, and lonely office in an office building downtown) may not be right for you.

Enter the executive suite. What's an executive suite, you ask?

An executive suite is a business that rents offices — by the hour, day, week, or month — to busy consultants and businesspeople like you. Everyone shares a common receptionist, conference rooms, kitchen, and more. Not only do you get access to an office in exchange for your money, but you also have a wide variety of business tools and services at your disposal — for a price, of course.

Why would anyone want to rent an executive suite? Many good reasons exist.

- ✔ **Flexibility:** You can rent an executive suite for an hour, a few hours a week, a couple weeks a month, or on a full-time basis for as long as you like. You can work out almost any arrangement.

- ✔ **Minimal capital outlay:** You have the choice of bringing your own furniture and office equipment or renting these items from your land-lord. According to executive suite industry estimates, the cost of using an executive suite is approximately 40 percent to 50 percent of the cost of setting up and staffing a comparable conventional office.

- ✔ **Turnkey operation:** When you rent an executive suite, you don't have to waste your time designing an office, installing electric and phone lines, hiring staff, and taking care of all those other details. With an executive suite, you can make one call today and have a fully functional office tomorrow.

- ✔ **Convenience:** In most cities, a wide selection of executive suites is available. You can therefore decide to locate your office near your home or close to your clients. And because you aren't tied to the long-term leases (typically three to five years) that are common in the commercial real estate market, you can quickly and easily pull up your roots and move to another executive suite or office if things don't work out.

- ✔ **Camaraderie:** One of the biggest complaints of consultants who work at home is that they miss the stimulation and company of being in a traditional office setting with other associates. Executive suites solve this problem by placing you in the midst of a group of other motivated businesspeople who share many of your goals and interests.

Of course, there are potential downsides to renting an executive suite as well, the main ones being that you may not need all the extras that an executive suite provides, or you might find these extras to be far more expensive than if you procured them yourself. If that's the case, then you should consider simply renting a vacant office space, and buying the equipment and services you need when you need them.

HQ (www.hq.com) — with more than 950 locations in more than 400 cities worldwide — is typical of this burgeoning industry. With clients ranging from individual consultants, salespeople, and entrepreneurs to huge companies such as Coca-Cola, Microsoft, and Sprint, HQ clearly provides a much-needed service to businesses of all sizes and persuasions. Check HQ's Web site for a complete listing of available services.

Many executive suites also provide travel booking, business meeting planning and coordination, and other business services on a pay-as-you-go basis. If you travel much as a part of your work, HQ offers unlimited access to any of its business lounges anywhere in the world through its membership program, Network Access (currently priced at a flat $300 a year). So the next time you're on a business trip to San Francisco, Toronto, or Paris — or most anywhere else you can imagine — you can set up shop in the nearest HQ business lounge.

Subleasing space from another business

Another way to achieve the same goal as using an executive suite, and save some money at the same time, is to sublease an office or offices from a business that has vacant space to fill, such as a legal, CPA, or real estate office. The setup is much the same as for an executive suite: You use a common receptionist and telephone service, and you share kitchen, mailroom, and other facilities — probably even the organization's copying equipment and computer network. However, you usually have to provide your own furniture, computer, and other equipment.

Meeting on the fly: Airport offices

For those of you who spend more than a little time on the road (or in the air), one of the best deals going for short-term office space is available in almost every major airport around the world. The big airlines — American, United, and others — have established clubs in these airports that offer a variety of facilities and services for the busy traveler. For example, at American Airlines Admiral's Club (www.aa.com/admiralsclub), not only can you check in for your next flight and partake of complimentary coffee, newspapers, and magazines, but you also have full use of telephones, offices, conference rooms, computers, fax machines, and other services, all for a fairly reasonable annual membership fee. These offices are also great for meeting associates and clients from multiple locations for up to three or four hours. You simply fly in, meet, and fly out.

Chapter 5

Getting a Grip on Legalities, Finances, and Ethics

*W*hether your consulting firm is a one-man or -woman operation or a vast global consultancy employing thousands, your firm is first and foremost a business. As the owner of the business, you have many things to consider beyond simply providing consulting services to your clients. You need to make a profit. You need to ensure that you're following the law — not just those national laws that get so much press, but also local laws and regulations that you may not even be aware of. You need to be able to track the financials of your business quickly and accurately, and you need to pay the appropriate taxes when they're due. And, of course, you need to be an ethical businessperson who sets an example for your employees.

In the pages that follow, we turn the spotlight on three key areas of building and maintaining your consulting business: legal, financial, and ethical. Get this consulting trifecta right, and you'll not only be able to sleep easier at night, but you'll also find you've got more time to focus on doing what you do best: consulting.

Taking Care of Legal Considerations

As anyone who has started a business knows, there are many dos and don'ts when it comes to the law. While you might be able to hobble along for some time ignoring the legalities of your consulting business, eventually they will catch up with you. So if you're getting ready to start your own consulting business, our advice is to take care of the legal considerations in the course of establishing your business and getting it off the ground. If you already have an established consulting firm but have neglected the legalities of your business, our advice is to take care of the legal considerations *now*.

Selecting a form (legal structure) for your business

You have no doubt noticed that some businesses have little taglines after their names — things such as LLC or Inc. These taglines are there because of the form of business that these companies selected at some point in their founding or development.

While this alphabet soup of letters seems simple enough, the reality is much more complex. When you pick a legal form for your business, you make an entire set of decisions that impact how your business can operate, how it is taxed, whether you'll be personally liable in the event of some catastrophic business occurrence, and much more.

In this section, we give you enough basic information on the topic to help you consider which legal structure may be right for your business. These are just the basics — you should contact an attorney or accountant to discern the specific advantages and disadvantages of each and to help you decide which is best for you. Many independent consulting firms start out as either a sole proprietorship or a partnership. It's simple, and it's inexpensive. As time goes on, however, many consulting firms consider the advantages and disadvantages of other available forms of business, especially in terms of liability and taxes. Be sure you put a lot of thought into deciding what form of business is right for you.

Note: This discussion is applicable to businesses based in the United States — consulting firms in other countries are subject to different rules.

Sole proprietorship

Most small businesses — including consulting firms — are *sole proprietorships,* whereby you are the one and only owner of the business. In a sole proprietorship, you report to the IRS the income you derive from your business on your Form 1040, along with any other personal income that you make during the course of the year. Any debts you incur as a sole proprietor are treated the same as your personal debts. Table 5-1 lists the good news — and the bad — about sole proprietorships.

Table 5-1	Sole Proprietorship
On the Plus Side	*On the Negative Side*
Owner has complete control over the business.	Sole proprietorships are generally seen as less prestigious than other forms of business.
Inexpensive to set up and operate.	Obtaining outside financing can be difficult.
Easy to start and to end.	The business dies with the owner.
Owner keeps all profits.	Owner is personally liable in the event of a lawsuit.

Partnership

In a *general partnership* form of consulting business, each partner agrees to provide specific skills, expertise, effort, and sometimes capital — while sharing the partnership's expenses — in return for an agreed-upon portion of the company's profits. The legal agreement spelling out these terms and conditions is called a *general partnership agreement*.

As with a sole proprietorship, profits in a partnership are taxed as personal income. However, the bad news is that partners are personally liable for debts and taxes. And if the partnership can't satisfy creditors' claims, then the personal assets (read house, car, dog) of the partners can be confiscated. Table 5-2 shows advantages and disadvantages in detail.

If you would like to avoid personal liability, you can set up a *limited partnership*. A limited partnership is a partnership in which some of the partners have a limited financial liability in the firm, generally the amount of money that they have invested. Limited partnerships must be registered and pay a *franchise fee* charged by the state to file a certificate of limited partnership.

Regardless of the type of partnership you enter into, be sure to have a lawyer draft your partnership agreement — the price you pay will be well worth the extra hours of sleep you'll enjoy every night.

Table 5-2	General Partnership
On the Plus Side	*On the Negative Side*
Two heads can be better than one.	Partners may not always agree on business decisions.
Business risks are shared by the partners.	Each partner is legally liable for actions of the other partners.
Partners may provide moral support to one another.	Partners often have disagreements and quarrels.
Government avoids interfering with partnerships.	When partnerships break up, things can get very messy.
Expenses are shared by all partners.	Profits are distributed to all partners.

Limited liability company

The *limited liability company* (LLC) offers flexibility in management the way a general partnership does, while offering the limited liability of a corporation. Limited liability companies are now legally recognized in all 50 states, the District of Columbia, and in many foreign countries.

Owners of LLCs are known as *members* — comparable to stockholders in a corporation or limited partners in a limited partnership. To form an LLC, you need to file articles of organization with your state's secretary of state. Each LLC member must also execute an operating agreement that defines the relationship between the company and its members. Check your state's procedures to find out what requirements apply to you.

The positive and negative aspects of LLCs are similar to partnerships, with the exception of the limitation of liability that corporations enjoy. Table 5-3 gives you some other pluses and minuses.

Table 5-3	Limited Liability Company
On the Plus Side	*On the Negative Side*
Limited liability for company's members (owners).	Many states require that LLCs include more than one person.
IRS rules allow LLCs to choose between being taxed as a partnership or a corporation.	Dissolve on the death of an owner.
Profit and loss can be allocated differently than ownership interests.	State laws for creating LLCs may not reflect the latest federal tax changes.

On the Plus Side	On the Negative Side
Simpler and cost less to set up and maintain than corporations.	More difficult and cost more to set up and maintain than sole proprietorships or partnerships.

Corporation

Corporations are legal entities that exist separately from their owners. Because of this legal separation, owners are generally not personally liable for actions on the part of the corporation. Corporations are identified by the familiar *Incorporated (Inc.)* or *Corporation (Corp.)* in or after their names.

If you're looking to raise significant amounts of money to get your consulting business off the ground, corporations can facilitate this process through the sale of corporate stocks or bonds. However, corporations are relatively expensive to start and maintain compared to other business forms, and the paperwork can be difficult to keep up with. Costs and procedures for incorporating vary from state to state. Contact your state's secretary of state for more information or contact a knowledgeable attorney or accountant. Table 5-4 describes some of the good news — and the bad — about corporations.

You've probably heard about a special type of corporation — an *S corporation* — that enables owners to overcome the problem of double taxation that regular corporations (called *C corporations*) often experience. Again, discuss this with an attorney or your accountant.

Table 5-4	Corporation
On the Plus Side	**On the Negative Side**
Higher overall business image than other forms.	Can be relatively expensive to start and operate.
May have tax advantages depending on the handling of benefits, dividends, and the owners' other sources of income.	Income must be allocated to owners according to their ownership interests.
Limited personal liability of owners and stockholders.	Lots of paperwork.
Can survive their owners. other forms of business.	Tax benefits may not compare well to
Relatively easy to sell.	The majority of shareholders must agree to sell the company.
Can raise money by selling stock and bonds.	Corporations are double taxed in some states.

Choosing and registering your business name

While the decision of what to name a business is easy for many consultants — Jane Smith and Associates, for example — for others, the decision requires no small amount of thought. Choosing the name of your company is one of the most critical decisions you make as you set up your business. While the right name can help pave the way to your success, the wrong name can have the completely opposite effect.

The best business names

- ✔ Describe the service or product that the business offers.
- ✔ Are protectable by trademark or service mark.
- ✔ Are novel and memorable.

Here are a few places to check whether your proposed business name is already in use:

- ✔ Local phone books
- ✔ Local courthouse, county recorder, and the office in your state responsible for registering business names
- ✔ Internet Yellow Pages, such as www.switchboard.com and www.info space.com, and search engines, such as www.google.com and www.yahoo.com
- ✔ Databases that facilitate trademark searches, such as the U.S. Patent and Trademark Office (www.uspto.gov) or NameProtect (www.name protect.com), or, better yet, an attorney specializing in trademarks and patents

If the name you have chosen for your business is your actual name, then generally no further action is necessary. However, if the name you've chosen for your business is *not* your name, in most states you'll be required to file a fictitious business name statement (also called a *doing business as . . ., DBA,* or *d/b/a*). This is also necessary if the business name implies greater ownership with such words as *And Company*, or *Associates*, or *& Son/Daughter.* There are some exceptions. If the legal entity is a corporation or LLC, for example, you probably won't have to file a fictitious business name statement unless you decide to do business using a name different than the one filed with the secretary of state.

Although regulations vary from state to state (check with your local authorities to be sure to get the exact information for where you plan to do business), fictitious business name statements are generally filed with the county clerk and may also have to be published in a newspaper of general circulation once a week for four successive weeks in the county where the principal place of business is located. Because the cost of publishing legal notices, such as fictitious business name statements, varies widely from newspaper to newspaper, it pays to shop around.

After your legal notice has been published for the required period of time, an affidavit of publication must be filed with the county clerk or requisite local or state agency within 30 days after publication. Again, check the requirements in your locale to be sure that you have a complete understanding of the filing requirements — before, not after, you start the process.

Dealing with zoning, licensing, and permit issues

Every business — including a consulting business — is subject to local zoning and licensing regulations. Unfortunately, working your way through the maze of government regulations can put you on the fast track to a big headache. However, you ignore these rules at your own peril. Some government bureaucrats would like nothing more than to find a reason to issue you a citation or a fine — or even shut you down.

Zoning regulations are in effect for a very simple reason — to maintain a reasonable quality of life for residential areas of a community. Many business uses of residential properties are specifically prohibited for this reason, unless a variance or exception is granted by the appropriate authorities.

Depending on the rules in your community, here are some of the things that zoning may impact:

- Advertising signage
- Parking and vehicle traffic
- The percentage of your home devoted to business
- The number of people you employ and the jobs you employ them to perform
- The use of hazardous materials and chemicals
- Noise, smoke, and odor

Keep in mind that your neighborhood may have additional covenants or other deeded restrictions on your business activities. Check your real estate purchase documents closely or check with your homeowner's association to see if such covenants or restrictions apply to you.

In addition to zoning issues, you may also be required to obtain certain licenses or permits to do business. For example, if your consulting services sometimes involve providing legal services, you may need a license to practice law in your state. Which ones will you need for your consulting business? Check with the city, county, and state authorities where your business is located or with your local chamber of commerce. Many government offices have departments specifically set up to help business owners through the maze of red tape. Be sure to take them up on their offer to help.

Finessing the Financial Stuff

If you (and your employees, if you have any) are the brains of your consulting business, then your financial systems are the blood vessels that bring the oxygen to keep that brain healthy. Money really does make the world go 'round, and consulting businesses are no exception to the rule. Indeed, if you've got your own consulting business, you know the joy that money coming into your business can inspire, and the worry that a lack thereof can also bring. In this section, we consider some of the financial issues of greatest importance to consultants and their firms.

Taxing matters

If there's one thing you can be certain of, it's that your consulting firm is going to owe taxes to somebody, somewhere. This is especially the case if you make a profit. The exact amount you owe and to whom it is owed depends on a variety of factors, including where you're located, the kind of business you conduct, and the form of business you select.

Surveying types of taxes

Here are some of the most common kinds of taxes that consultants and consulting firms can expect to pay:

- Income tax
- Self-employment tax
- Estimated tax
- Social security tax
- Unemployment tax
- Sales tax
- Excise tax

 ✔ Use tax

 ✔ Business tax

If you have a real, live consulting firm going with more than one or two employees, then some of these taxes — for example, social security and unemployment taxes — will become an everyday part of the way you do business. It's your job to get familiar with them and determine which ones you need to pay — and when you need to pay them. If you decide to ignore them — perhaps hoping they'll go away — you'll likely find yourself in very hot water at some point in the not-too-distant future. For more information about taxes, consult with a competent accountant. A certified public accountant (CPA) is your best bet.

Understanding the home-office deduction

If you live in the United States and you've decided to run your consulting business in your home, you may be eligible for something known as the *home-office deduction,* which reduces the taxes you pay to Uncle Sam. The home-office deduction allows you to claim expenses for the business use of your home.

However, like any other deduction, you must be sure you qualify before you take it. To qualify, you must meet the following requirements:

 ✔ **Your use of the business part of your home must be:**

 • **Exclusive:** A specific area of your home must be used only for your business. (***Note:*** There are special rules for qualified daycare providers and for people storing business inventory or product samples. See IRS Tax Tip 2007-53.)

 • **Regular:** The business part of your home must be used for business on a continuing, not just an occasional or incidental, basis.

 • **For your trade or business:** That is, for *your* business — not for someone else's business.

 ✔ **The business part of your home must be one of the following:**

 • Your principal place of business.

 • A place where you meet or deal with patients, clients, or customers in the normal course of your trade or business.

 • A separate structure (not attached to your home) that you use in connection with your trade or business.

The home-office deduction offers very real benefits to your consulting business. In addition to deducting your normal business expenses (paper, pencils, phone calls, and so on), you can also deduct a portion of the indirect expenses related to your entire home! Here are some of the most common indirect expenses that may be at least partially deductible under the IRS's home-office rules:

- Rent
- Mortgage
- Security system
- Housekeeping
- Household supplies
- Condominium association fees
- Trash collection
- Utilities (gas, electric, and so on)

Some tax experts believe that taking the home-office deduction raises a red flag with the IRS. This may or may not be true. Consult with an accountant, tax planner, or other tax professional before you take the home-office deduction for the first time. For more information, check out *IRS Publication 587: Business Use of Your Home,* which you'll find on the Web at www.irs. gov/pub/irs-pdf/p587.pdf.

Setting up a bookkeeping system — or not

Every business owner needs to know the exact status of the money going in and out of his or her consulting firm. A simple accounting system, such as one of the many excellent accounting software programs available on the market today, such as Quicken, QuickBooks, Microsoft Money, and Peachtree Accounting, can take care of your consulting firm's financial needs well into the future.

QuickBooks offers programs used by many small-business owners. Their key features include the ability to do the following:

- Print checks, pay bills, and track expenses
- Invoice customers and track payments and sales taxes
- Generate reports, including profit and loss, statement of cash flows, balance sheet, sales reports, and more
- Manage payroll and payroll taxes
- Track information for taxes and share information with an accountant
- Provide extensive tutorials and help functions

While these programs pride themselves on their relative simplicity, if you're not already pretty familiar with bookkeeping or accounting, we advise you to talk with an accountant for help in setting up and maintaining your system.

For more information on accounting and bookkeeping practices for small-business owners, check out *Small Business Financial Management Kit For Dummies* by Tage C. Tracy and John Tracy, or *Accounting For Dummies, 3rd Edition,* by John Tracy (both from Wiley).

If you're not the do-it-yourself type when it comes to financial matters, you have an alternative. You can turn the matter of your business bookkeeping over to a professional bookkeeper or accountant, who can take care of the heavy lifting for you.

Providing your own benefits

Most people who start their own consulting businesses already work for companies that provide a wide selection of benefits — everything from time off to healthcare to life insurance to retirement plans, and even to college tuition reimbursement. However, when you start your own business, it's up to you to decide what benefits are most important to you. You have to distinguish between benefits that are essential and those you can do without.

This means doing your homework and weighing the costs and benefits of each particular benefit. As you engage in this process, we believe you'll find that the best solution for you likely involves two key factors:

✔ Be sure to price your products and services high enough to cover the cost of health insurance. Studies show that the self-employed are more frequently uninsured than other parts of the workforce.

✔ Do your due diligence and guard against getting taken in by what appears to be inexpensive and adequate coverage, but turns out to be inadequate. Compare the coverage of several different insurance programs, along with the premiums you'll pay during the course of a year and the deductibles. Check with other consultants to see who they bought their insurance from, and what programs they signed up for. Check with your state insurance commissioner or other authorities to be sure non-name-brand insurance providers are on the up and up.

For most independent consultants, health insurance and retirement benefits are most important. Coincidentally, they can also be among the most difficult to deal with. Here are some options for getting past the difficulties:

✔ **Health insurance:** Affordable health insurance is almost an oxymoron — especially for the self-employed — and it can be difficult to obtain. Consider obtaining your health insurance through a professional association, which may be able to negotiate coverage for its members. In addition, some states, such as California, have a mandatory small-business insurance provision meaning that insurance companies must offer health insurance to companies with two or more employees. For more information, contact a local insurance agent.

✔ **Retirement:** Many different options are available with regard to retirement plans, including IRAs, 401(k)s, and more. Our suggestion is to take 10 percent (or as high a percentage as you can) off the top of every dollar that comes into your business and put it into a SEP-IRA or other retirement account. That said, be sure to check with your accountant for your specific situation.

Managing risk with insurance

Do consultants really need insurance? Even independent consultants working out of their homes? You bet they do. In today's let's-sue-'em-for-all-they've-got world of business, insurance is a must. Insurance is the kind of thing that you don't need until you need it. Remember: The many years of hard work that you've invested in your business can be lost in mere minutes due to a catastrophic loss. Take some time to set up proper coverage now — before you need it.

Talk with an insurance agent to determine exactly what kinds of insurance are needed for your business. Here's a list of some of the most common types of business insurance to help guide your discussions:

✔ **Basic fire insurance:** Covers property losses due to fire. Sometimes covers loss of business as well.

✔ **Extended coverage:** Protects against conditions not covered by fire insurance, including storms, explosions, smoke damage, and various other disasters.

✔ **Liability insurance:** Covers claims against the business for bodily injury incurred on the business's premises.

✔ **Product liability coverage:** Insurance against liability for products manufactured or sold.

✔ **Professional liability and/or errors-and-omissions insurance:** Protects the business against claims for damages incurred by customers as a result of providing them with professional advice or recommendations.

✔ **Vandalism and malicious mischief coverage:** Covers against property losses resulting from vandalism and related activities.

✔ **Theft coverage:** Protection from burglary and robbery.

✔ **Vehicle insurance:** Covers collision, liability, and property damage for vehicles used for business.

✔ **Business interruption insurance:** Payment of business earnings if the business is closed for an insurable cause such as fire, flood, or other natural disaster.

- ✔ **Workers' compensation:** Disability and death benefits to employees and others who work for you and are injured on the job. These are defined by state law.

- ✔ **Health insurance:** We've saved the best (and, for many home-based business owners, the most important) for last. Health insurance includes medical, dental, vision, and other coverage designed to maintain and promote employee health and wellness and to protect employees against catastrophic loss in case of injury or illness.

A homeowner's policy is usually not enough insurance to cover your consulting business in the event that you encounter a serious business problem. Most homeowners' policies provide only $2,500 of coverage for business equipment, and they do not insure you against risks of liability or lost income.

Doing the Right Thing: Ethics and You

What would you do if your best and most profitable client asked you to divulge some new product information from another client? What would you do if a client asked you to take your payments "under the table" and not report them to the Internal Revenue Service or other tax authorities? What would you do if a potential client offered to pay you a large amount of money to do a project that you know you're not qualified to perform?

Consultants face these kinds of ethical dilemmas every day of the week. Like a double yellow line painted down the center of an interstate highway, when it comes to ethical behavior, a clear line separates good behavior from bad behavior. The decisions you make in response to all the dilemmas you face determine which side of the line you walk on — the right side or the wrong side. Unfortunately, just as a thick fog can roll in and obscure the lines painted on a highway, so, too, can the line separating right from wrong become fuzzy and hard to see.

In this section, we consider some of the key elements of ethical behavior and ways to develop and implement a personal code of ethics.

Facing ethical land mines

Temptations to stray from the right side of the ethics line to the wrong side are all around you. You have a choice: You can do business the ethical way or the unethical way. It's that simple.

Our advice is to do business the ethical way. Not only will you sleep better at night, but your reputation will be enhanced and your clients will be glad that they have one less thing to worry about.

You never know who will plant an ethical land mine in your path or when it'll make its presence known. Be on the alert for the following kinds of ethical land mines:

- **Conflicts of interest:** A conflict of interest occurs when your personal interests or the interests of your business conflict with those of your client. An example is a government consultant who recommends that a client buy an expensive new fire-suppression system from one particular company without seeking competitive bids; unbeknownst to the client, however, the consultant is getting a kickback from the fire-suppression system manufacturer for each unit that clients buy.

- **Personal relationships:** When professional relationships between consultants and clients cross the line into the realm of personal relationships — particularly intimate personal relationships — ethical quicksand can't be very far away.

- **Ability to do the job (or lack thereof):** Are you really qualified to do the work that your client is hiring you to do? Do you already have far too many jobs lined up to be able to adequately handle new ones? Are you going to have to subcontract the work to another consultant or firm because you're too busy to do the work yourself? Your clients hire you because they assume — either through you telling them so or through your silence — that you are able to do the work. If, in reality, you can't, you'll soon find yourself in a major ethical quandary. You and your clients should agree to any subcontracting of work before you commence work.

- **Insider information:** As a consultant, you discover a lot of interesting and confidential things about your clients' operations, business plans, and strategies. Misusing this information is a serious breach of ethics. If, for example, you provide information gained from working with Company A to Company A's arch rival, Company B, as a part of the work that you do for Company B, you're committing a serious ethical infraction against Company A.

- **Fees and timekeeping:** Are your fees reasonable? Do you keep meticulous track of the time that you work for your clients? Do you have controls to ensure that one client isn't charged for another client's work and that clients aren't billed for work that is never done (such as while you're out of town meeting with other clients or working on another client's project when you should have been working on a project for the client you just billed)? Ethical land mines abound in this dangerous area of your practice. To make sure you stay on the straight and narrow path, check out our discussion on timekeeping in Chapter 17.

Developing your personal code of ethics

Ethics are important for anyone in business. They're particularly important to consultants because of the high level of trust that organizations grant them and because of the access that many consultants have to the confidential and proprietary inner workings of the firms that employ them. No single code of ethics is appropriate for everyone. So many different kinds of consultants exist that a set of rules that would be appropriate for one group — say, real estate brokers — would have little in common with a set of rules intended for another group — say, consulting engineers. However, some very basic ethical beliefs can and should form the basis for your personal code of ethics.

Here are some items that can form the basis for any consultant's code of ethics. Review them and consider using them as the basis for your own code of ethics.

- ✔ **Account for your time accurately and honestly.** If you're working on an hourly or other time-based system of billing, keeping track of your hours and reporting them to your clients accurately and honestly is up to you. Your client expects and trusts you to be truthful in your billing practices. To do any less is not only unethical but also a violation of your client's trust. And if your client can't trust you, he or she won't hire you again or refer you to friends or other associates.

- ✔ **Don't make promises you can't keep.** Although you may really want to impress a potential client with your amazing abilities, avoid making promises you can't keep in hopes of landing your client's account. Not only is this unethical — your client may be better off hiring someone who has more capabilities or better qualifications in a particular area — but you end up setting up yourself and your business for failure. Though there's nothing wrong with a little good old-fashioned optimism, don't blatantly make a promise that you know you cannot keep. If you're hoping that your client will forget you made the promise or that you can change the promised action to something you can achieve after you're selected to do the work, then you're not only fooling yourself but also doing your client a great disservice.

- ✔ **Follow through on your promises.** Part of becoming a successful consultant is doing what you say you're going to do. If you say that you will complete the project on March 31, then you should deliver the results on (or before, if you can) March 31 — not a day later. Suppose that you promise to come up with a complete landscaping design for $1,000. Unless your client does something that causes your incurred costs to skyrocket, such as adding more work to your project but not adding more money to your project budget, you should deliver your design for $1,000 and not a penny more. If, for some reason, you can't keep your promise no matter how hard you try, then inform your client as far in advance as possible and present a plan for curing the problem.

✔ **Don't recommend products or services that your clients don't need.** You may speak with clients who are absolutely, beyond-a-shadow-of-a-doubt certain that they know what is wrong with their organization. You need only propose to do what they say that you should do to land what could be a very lucrative contract. This is the consulting equivalent to shooting fish in a barrel. However, if you know that the course of action the client is suggesting is not the proper remedy, you should tell your client so and decline the offered work. In most cases, your client will appreciate your honesty, and your reputation will be elevated a few notches in your client's mind (and in the mind of anyone else your client tells this story to).

✔ **Be candid and give your honest opinion.** Your clients pay you good money for the benefit of your skills and many years of experience. When your clients ask for your opinion, be frank and honest, and don't try to sugarcoat the truth to make it more palatable.

✔ **Protect your clients' confidentiality.** When you are a consultant, you may often be placed in situations in which you have access to information that is proprietary to your clients, the release of which could cause them serious financial or other damage. Your clients have placed you in a position of trust. Don't violate that trust. If, for some reason, you want to publicize the fact that you're doing work for a particular firm — perhaps in a press kit or a proposal to another organization — ask your client for permission first.

✔ **Disclose conflicts of interest.** If you're a popular consultant in your field, preventing conflicts of interest from occurring can often be difficult. As organizations vie for your expertise, you may find yourself working on the same problem for two different companies that compete with one another in the marketplace. However, as soon as you discover a conflict — whether it's a potential conflict or an actual one — you should always disclose it to the affected client or clients and then take action to resolve it. This may mean assuring your clients that you won't transfer their confidential data from one company to the other, or it may mean signing information nondisclosure agreements. If the conflict can't be resolved through these means, then you may have to drop one of the two firms as a client.

✔ **Don't use inside information to your advantage.** While you're working for an organization, you may come across information that is closely held within the company and unknown to others outside the organization. For example, you may find out that the organization is about to patent a process that will certainly lead to a huge surge in the price of the company's stock. Not only is it unethical to use insider information to your advantage — in this case, to buy a large amount of the company's stock before the patent becomes public — but it is illegal as well.

✔ **Don't break the law.** At times, a client may ask you to do something that is not only against your personal sense of ethics but also obviously and blatantly illegal. Do not pass go and do not collect $200. Just go. And don't come back. Ever.

These guidelines look great on paper, but in the real world, you're going to face many situations that aren't quite so black-and-white. Everyone has a personal set of values and ethics, and what's right for one person may be wrong for another. The challenge is to find ways to keep to your values while also finding ways to work with a client whose values may not be exactly the same as yours. If your values are too far out of sync with your client's values, then don't hesitate to pull yourself off the job and find other clients whose values more closely match your own.

If you ever find yourself in an uncomfortable ethical situation, first talk to your client about it in an effort to determine an alternate course of action that is in accordance with your own values. Most clients will respect your perspective, even if they don't share it. If you can't find a way out of your ethical dilemma by working with the client on alternative actions, then walk away from the job, but in a way that doesn't offend your client. Whatever you do, don't burn bridges with your clients or poison the well for referrals to other clients.

Take some time to develop your own code of ethics. Type it up, hang it prominently in your office, and put it on your Web site. Above all, live the code of ethics that you have developed. A good operational rule is, if you have any doubts, don't do it!

The ICCA Code of Ethics

This is the Code of Ethics of the Independent Computer Consultants Association (ICCA), a national, not-for-profit organization based in St. Louis, Missouri, that provides professional development opportunities and business support programs for independent computer consultants. (Visit the ICCA's Web page at www.icca.org for further information.) The ICCA publishes the following Code of Ethics, copyrighted by ICCA, to serve as a model for its members and for the entire computer consulting industry.

✓ Consultants will be honest and not knowingly misrepresent facts.

✓ Consultants will install and use only properly licensed software on their systems as well as the clients' systems.

✓ Consultants will divulge any potential conflicts of interest prior to accepting the contract or as soon as possible after the conflict is discovered.

✓ Consultants will only represent opinions as independent if they are free from subordinated judgment and there is no undisclosed interest in the outcome of the client's decision.

✓ Consultants will ensure that to the best of their knowledge they can complete the project in a professional manner both in terms of skill and time.

✓ Consultants will keep the client informed of any matters relating to the contract even if the information is unfavorable, or may jeopardize the contract.

✓ Consultants will safeguard any confidential information or documents entrusted to them and not divulge any confidential information without the consent of the client.

✓ Consultants will not take advantage of proprietary information obtained from the client.

✓ Consultants will not engage in contracts that are in violation of the law or that might reasonably be used by the client to violate the law.

✓ ICCA member firms, their principals, and employees will uphold the principles of the ICCA and not commit acts discreditable to the ICCA.

Chapter 6

Setting Your Fees

• •

• •

*T*he topic of setting fees probably makes an independent consultant more uncomfortable than any other topic. Consultants are comfortable when they are recommending the placement of columns for proper support of a massive steel I-beam, the implementation of a new employee performance review system, or the installation of new software to run a company's Web server. After all, they're experts in those fields. But setting fees is often another matter altogether. Ask some consultants their price and watch the reaction. They suddenly get flustered and tentative. And if a client balks at a consultant's quoted price, explaining that other consultants do double the work for half the price, some of these same consultants will quickly discount their prices in a desperate effort to gain — or retain — the client's business, doing whatever it takes.

When you're a consultant, pricing your services is a constant balancing act. Set your fees too low, and you may not only be flooded with more business than you can handle, but you won't make enough money on the flood of business to recover your expenses and make a profit. Set your fees too high, however, and you may get a few high-fee jobs but not enough to keep your business afloat. The end result is that many consultants are in a constant state of uncertainty when pricing their services.

Understanding your value to your clients and then pricing your services appropriately is essential to your ability to make a living as an independent consultant. If you're going to thrive as a consultant, therefore, you need to do three things soon after you set up shop:

✔ Develop a fee structure that allows you to achieve your goals for financial and personal independence.

✔ Become a master at understanding and selling the value that you offer your clients and at getting your client to focus on *results* — not rates, activity, or time.

✔ Overcome any hang-ups that you have about putting a price on your time and selling your skills and services to others.

This chapter discusses putting a value on the expertise that you bring to your clients, determining how much you need to make for your business to thrive, structuring your fees, and deciding when to modify your fees and when to stand firm on them.

Determining What You're Worth to Your Clients

How much do *you* think you're worth to your clients? $1? $10,000? $1 million? More? If we really pressed you for an answer, we probably could get you to come up with a number. However, regardless of the number you select, it's meaningless unless it is based on what your *clients* think you are worth.

One of the first lessons to learn about pricing your services is that you should always focus on the value that you bring to your clients and not only on your *own* opinion of worth. In some cases, your clients' perception of your value may far exceed your own perception of your value. In other cases, your clients' perception of your value may be disappointingly less than your own perception of your value. The fact is that you really can't know how much you're worth to your clients until you talk to them and get a sense of the problems they face and the ultimate cost to them of a variety of alternate solutions.

In this section, we consider some factors that determine your value as a consultant to your clients.

Knowing why you're being hired

When exploring the philosophical question of how much you are worth to your clients, you may find it useful to explore why organizations hire consultants in the first place.

When faced with a problem, your clients have many different alternatives at their disposal for resolving it. The primary options include assigning a current employee to the task or hiring a new employee to take on the assignment. However, these approaches can often bring their own problems, and they may not be the most cost-effective ways to arrive at the best solution. In addition, when faced with hiring their own employees, your clients may not be able to find any candidates with a consultant's unique credentials and high level of expertise.

So why do organizations hire consultants? The following reasons are some of the most compelling:

- ✔ **Consultants are experts.** Expertise and knowledge are two of the main reasons that organizations hire consultants. Many people in an organization may be able to take on a necessary assignment, but it's often the case that none can do the job as quickly and efficiently as an expert consultant who every day lives and breathes the issue to be addressed. The end result of hiring an expert consultant is often an overall savings in time and money — many times with better results than if the assignment was performed in-house by the organization's employees.

- ✔ **Consultants are independent.** When an organization hires a consultant, it is hiring an independent contractor, not an employee. This simple fact has all sorts of implications. Consultants work closely with their clients, but consultants do not require the kind of direct supervision that employees performing comparable tasks do. And the client controls payment — if a consultant doesn't perform in accordance with the terms of the consulting contract, a client can by all rights withhold payment, or even terminate the contract and the relationship with that particular consultant.

- ✔ **Consultants are objective, outside third parties.** Consultants often bring a fresh point of view to an organization that may have lost its perspective. In many organizations — especially those where employees are afraid to speak against the status quo for fear of losing their jobs — only an outsider is willing to tell it like it is. Sometimes only an outside consultant can clearly see the broken organizational systems and dysfunctional management behaviors that disable the firm. Outsiders also can make recommendations that break through to the decision-makers who most need to hear them.

- ✔ **Consultants have dedicated time.** Time may be a precious element among an organization's existing staff and in short supply. A person or group may be assigned to a project and then later taken off the project because of conflicting priorities. An outside consultant, on the other hand, can focus on the task or project full time until the work is completed.

✔ **Consultants are flexible resources.** Most consultants make themselves available to their clients — especially their best clients — on a moment's notice. Indeed, more than a few consultants give their very best clients their home phone numbers and "secret" e-mail addresses. If an organization had to hire someone new to take on an assignment, *months* could be spent placing ads, performing interviews and reference checks, making a final selection, and bringing a new employee on board. On the other hand, if the organization wants to hire a consultant, one needs only to pick up the phone and a consultant can be at the organization's immediate disposal.

✔ **There's no long-term commitment.** When an employee completes a special project, an organization may find itself scrambling to place the person in another position within the organization — or be faced with laying-off the employee. When a consultant completes a special project, he or she simply goes away until the next time the organization needs the firm's services. There is no two-week notice, no termination, no layoff, no severance pay, no nothing. Consultants can and *do* develop long-term relationships with organizations, but only when these *organizations* desire long-term relationships with particular consultants or consulting firms.

✔ **Consultants are cost effective.** When you tally up the long-term costs of hiring an employee to take on a task versus bringing in a consultant to perform the same task for a defined period of time, going with a consultant may be more cost advantageous. An organization does not have to pay the consultant for health insurance, vacation time, 401(k) plans, or other benefits that it typically pays its employees. Using a consultant is a cost-effective alternative for organizations that need to solve a problem quickly and efficiently. We explore *why* this is true in the next section.

Seeing how much you can save your clients

Although all the considerations named in the section "Knowing why you're being hired" are important for determining your value to your clients, the ultimate question is: *How much more profit will your client earn by hiring you and your consulting firm?* Often this is measured by reducing costs, but sometimes it's best measured by increasing revenues. Regardless of how you get there, the higher the profit, the more value you provide to your clients. This justifies a hiring decision in your favor — regardless of the amount of money you charge.

The point is — and we're going to keep repeating this until you believe it — that you should focus on the *value* you provide to your client, not on the hourly rate or on the number of hours that you need to complete a job. Keep this distinction uppermost in your client's mind, too. You may believe that asking for a fee of $100 an hour is very optimistic at best and insulting to your client at worst. However, suppose that a client has to invest almost $100,000 a year to hire a full-time employee to have the same effect that you can have in 40 hours each month — for $48,000 a year. In that case, you provide incredible value to your client, especially if you happen to also provide a better work product than any employee can.

Here's an example of what we mean: Say that your client wants to create a high-profile media presence for her large mail-order clothing business. She has a choice: She can hire a part- or full-time employee, or she can hire you — the public relations expert to beat *all* public relations experts — for a fee that, at least on the surface, appears to be pretty steep. The first thing to consider is the cost of each alternative to your client. In Case A, your client decides to hire a full-time employee for $25 an hour. In Case B, your client hires *you* for $100 an hour. On the surface, hiring an employee seems to make the most sense. Right off the bat, your client is going to save $75 an hour — right?

Take a look.

Case A: Hire a new employee to take on public relations chores.

Hourly pay rate	$25.00
Fringe benefits rate @ 35%	+ 8.75
Overhead rate @ 50%	+ 12.50
Total effective pay rate	$46.25
Hours per year	x 2,080
Total annual labor cost	$96,200

In Case A, the new employee is paid a wage of $25 an hour. However, this wage is not the true cost to the organization. The cost of benefits for the employee (health insurance, life insurance, 401(k) plan, college tuition reimbursement, and so on) weighs in at 35 percent of the hourly wage, or $8.75. Overhead — electricity, facilities, computers, and so forth — costs the organization another 50 percent of the employee's wage, or $12.50 for each hour worked and paid. This brings the new employee's total hourly cost to the organization to $46.25 an hour — almost double the wage paid to the employee for each hour worked. When you multiply the hourly rate by the standard number of hours in a work year, the grand total for the new employee comes to a whopping $96,200.

So what happens if the organization hires a consultant to do the same job?

Case B: Hire a consultant to take on public relations chores.

Hourly pay rate	$100.00
Total effective pay rate	$100.00
Hours per year	x 480
Total annual cost	$48,000

Your client actually saves more than $48,000 by contracting with you rather than hiring a full-time employee to do the same work. Although your hourly rate is more than the new employee's rate in Case A, your client saves the cost of the benefits and overhead that would have to be applied to a new employee's wage. Not only that, but because you are presumably more experienced, more efficient, and better connected than the employee, you'll need to devote less time to the project to get much the same results — only 480 hours a year versus 2,080 for the employee.

When your client contracts with your business, *you* bear the cost of fringe benefits and overhead. Your client has to pay only the hourly fee that you agree to. In addition, if things don't work out, your client can terminate the relationship quickly and easily; the client doesn't have to worry about messy employee firings or unemployment benefits.

The net result is that you as a consultant offer tremendous value to a client in this situation. Be sure you price your services accordingly.

Avoiding the commodity trap

Part of the final determination of your value to potential clients depends on whether the service you provide has been reduced to a commodity in the marketplace. By *commodity,* we mean that the services offered by various providers are equivalent in clients' eyes, and that price is the primary factor that determines who is going to get the job.

For example, suppose that an organization is going to hire a consultant to prepare a business plan. If the organization has several business consultants to choose from — all with very good references — it will probably hire the business consultant who offers the best price. In this case, the service that this consultant offers has been reduced to a commodity in the organization's eyes.

Now, say that a unique organization is looking for a consultant who shares its vision and is fully compatible with the owner's personality. The organization interviews a variety of business consultants, but only one consultant shares the organization's vision and meshes well with its owner. This same consultant also proposes to deliver a customized solution that is unique and better suited to this particular business than the other proposals. In this case, the business consultant offers a number of items of value to the client, and price is not the determining factor in making a final selection.

These scenarios reflect the way the consulting business works. If your product is the same as everyone else's, then your clients consistently look for the least expensive solution to their problems. The eventual result of this kind of pressure is that *all* the consultants offering these kinds of services are forced to cut their prices until hardly anyone is making any money at all. You're stuck in the commodity trap, and you'll need to find a way to get out — as quick as you possibly can.

If you find yourself stuck in the commodity trap, there are a number of ways to make the services you offer stand out in a crowd, including:

- ✔ **Add value.** Do more for your clients than they expect you to do, and you add value to your work — the kind of value that sets you apart from your competitors. You don't need to do anything particularly dramatic; all you need to do is consistently give more — even a *little* more — than you promise, and your clients will know the difference. For example, if you promise to complete your project in 30 days, you can easily delight your client (and add value to your work) by delivering early — perhaps in 25 days. The little things *do* make a difference in the eyes of your clients.

- ✔ **Be different from your competition.** When you're caught in the commodity trap, do whatever you can to make the services that you offer *different* from those your competitors offer — especially in ways that your clients value. This means getting to know everything you can about your competition — the services they offer, the prices they charge, and how they deliver services to their clients. What can you do to make your clients realize that you're offering a unique solution instead of a run-of-the-mill solution? Offer free pickup and delivery? Use higher-quality materials than your competitors? Be available 24 hours a day for emergency service? Customize part or all of the products and services you deliver to each client? Provide free educational newsletters or *Webinars* (seminars via the Web) to your clients? Decide how to make your services different from your competition, and then do it!

- ✔ **Focus on customer service.** If you are in a commodity-type business in which most consultants deliver pretty much the same products or services, one of the best ways to stand out from the crowd is by providing unparalleled customer service. Unparalleled customer service starts with something that doesn't cost any money at all: a positive, can-do attitude. Your attitude says that you are making your customer your number-one priority and that you're doing whatever it takes to make your customer's consulting experience the best one possible. Follow up this attitude with action, and you're guaranteed to stand out from the crowd.

✔ **Do great work.** Despite being paid small mountains of money, some consultants simply don't do a very good job. Not only that, but some consultants deliver their products late, if at all. If you do great work and deliver on schedule at the agreed price, your clients will seek you out and will be happy to pay a premium for your work. We know from personal experience that finding consultants who are both talented and capable of following through on promises of quality and delivery can sometimes be a challenge. Therefore, consultants who do high-quality work and deliver it on or before the deadline are well worth the extra money.

✔ **Build long-term relationships.** Nothing sets you apart from the rest of the pack more than developing long-term relationships with your clients. The more work you do for your clients and the deeper your work *and* social relationships with your clients, the less likely your clients are to shop around for other consultants to take your place. And the more work you do for the same clients, the better you understand their operations and their unique needs. This understanding can help you to continue to improve the work you do for them.

Setting Your Fees in Different Ways

When you go about the process of setting your fees, the first question to ask yourself is how much money you want or need to make. Unfortunately, we can't answer this question for you — you have to look at your own situation and go from there. We can, however, provide you with some general guidelines that have worked for many consultants.

When you start out in consulting, you'll probably charge your services to your clients by the hour or day, and your clients will pay you only for the number of hours that you devote to their projects. Your clients also will probably be hesitant to pay you any more than the other consultants who offer services similar to those that you offer. That arrangement may be well and good, but as you gain experience in consulting, keep the big picture in clear sight, and don't get bogged down trying to justify a particular number of hours or a particular rate.

The goal is to move the bulk of your business into a project-based or retainer pricing arrangement. Reaching this goal may be easier said than done — especially if your clients are accustomed to dealing with you on an hourly or daily basis. But believe us; achieving your goal will be well worth the effort as you separate yourself from the very crowded pack of consultants offering the same kinds of services you do — often at lower rates.

As you consider the following options, don't forget that you should base the price you charge for your services on the value that you provide to your clients, not on anyone's preconceived notion as to what a "proper" fee is. The idea is to get the focus off of the price you charge, and onto the value you provide.

Hourly rate

The hourly rate is probably the most common way that consultants price their services. Whether you are proofreading manuscripts, providing legal advice, or designing a client's Web site, you can charge hourly rates. Hourly rates are easy to understand and compare with one another, and clients can buy as many hours as they like. That's the good news. On the other side of the ledger, clients and consultants tend to focus on different issues. The hourly approach means that you're tracking/justifying and billing for every minute of your time. Your client risks that you'll go over the estimated hours and cost them more. Clients generally want to reduce the number of hours that consultants work. Consultants, however, often focus on increasing the number of hours that they work for a client.

If you decide to price your services on an hourly basis, you need to have a basis for developing and supporting your rates. Here are some of the ways in which you can do just that:

✔ **Consider the market for your services.** The easiest way to set a rate for your services is to find out how much *other* consultants — in your area, or nationally — charge to do the same kind of work, and then price your services within the same range. For example, if other consultants in your field charge between $25 and $45 an hour, then you can comfortably set your price within that range. If you step below the range, you may be swamped with low-margin business that doesn't really pay the bills. Step above the range, and you have to convince your clients that you're worth the extra fee.

✔ **Build your rate from the bottom up.** If you've been working in a regular job for a number of years, your goal may be to simply maintain your previous pay rate. If you were being paid $25 an hour at your job, that may be where you want to start. If you add the burden of paying for your own health and dental insurance and other benefits that your previous employer paid — say, $10 an hour — and an additional $10 to cover your overhead, other expenses, and profit, then you end up with a rate of $45 an hour.

✔ **Build your rate from the top down.** You may decide that you want to gross $75,000 a year from your consulting efforts. If that's the case, you first estimate how many hours you can work and bill to clients in a year. For example, if you estimate that you'll work 1,500 hours, then you divide the total amount of money that you want for the year — $75,000 — by the total hours you've estimated that you will work. In this case, you have to charge at least $50 an hour to achieve your goal of $75,000 a year.

✔ **Apply the rule of thirds:** If you're leaving a job to start your own consulting business, a common guideline says that you should take your hourly wage rate and multiply it by three to arrive at the hourly fee you should charge as a consultant. So if you are currently making $25 an hour, as a consultant you should charge your clients $75 an hour. Why so much more than your current job? Because not only are you paying yourself a wage (one-third of the total rate), but you are also paying for the benefits — health insurance, life insurance, retirement plans, and so on — that you want to maintain as a consultant (another one-third of the total rate), plus you need to set aside some extra money for profit (the final one-third of the total rate).

Although you may be a full-time paid employee now, you may not be a full-time paid consultant when you make the move. Many consultants experience downtime between projects, perhaps going for days or weeks without paid work. The higher rate of $75 an hour also helps to cushion that kind of financial shortfall.

When setting your initial fee, remember that you have convinced your client that you are the best person for the task (and we're assuming you have — if you *haven't,* go back to your client-to-be and try again!). The client, therefore, will be relatively fee-insensitive as long as your fees aren't more than approximately 20 percent to 30 percent higher than those of your competitors. Many clients figure that getting the best consultant is worth a 20 percent to 30 percent premium.

Depending on the type of project, you may want to establish a minimum number of billable hours, such as four hours. This protects you from the client who "just wants to get together briefly for a 30-minute meeting." However, by the time you drive to the client's office, meet, and return to your office, you blow half a day — not half an hour. Remember, as a consultant, you are selling time and knowledge. For a consultant, time really *is* money.

And don't forget to bill your client for any and all business expenses you incur on their behalf, beyond those normally incurred in doing your everyday business. For example, a consulting job may require that you fly to a number of client sites nationwide and spend several weeks on the road — incurring charges for airfare, hotels, rental cars, and dining. Remember to add these expenses to your client's invoices in addition to the hours that you are billing for a particular period. Be sure that you fully explain to your clients what expenses you will charge to their accounts and any limitations placed upon them. For example, you may decide to charge a fixed per diem of $125 a day for hotel and dining expenses, or you may want to include an agreement to charge your clients only for the price of economy-class airfare, even if you fly business class.

Per-item or per-project basis

Many consultants price their services on a per-item or per-project basis. For example, if you do image consulting, you might price consultations at $50 each. Or if you are hired to audit a small electronics assembler, you might price the project at a flat rate of $7,500. The beauty of pricing your services this way is that you redirect the focus from the number of *hours* you work to the *results* that you achieve and — ultimately — the value that your client believes he or she receives.

For example, if you agree to conduct a full process review of the purchasing and receiving function of an organization, you might price this project at a total of $15,000. In return for the $15,000, you promise to present a report with recommendations to improve the operation. At the end of the four-week study, you deliver your report and submit your invoice for payment. Now, your client could care less how many hours you spent on the project. Your client cares only about the recommendations in your proposal — and that you performed your work within the $15,000 total agreed to. If the recommendations are good, and you haven't exceeded your agreed price, then your client is happy and doesn't ask you how many hours you expended on the job. If the recommendations *aren't* good, you know soon enough.

Of course, there are some possible downsides to doing your pricing on a project basis. For one, you risk spending more hours on a project with no additional fees — spend too much extra, and you can easily lose money on the job. In addition, your clients may not respect your time as much as they would if they were paying you by the hour, and take longer to provide you the information you need to do the job.

Although you'll do much of your work — especially early in your consulting career — on an hourly or daily basis, pushing your business to a per-item or per-project basis is definitely in your interest. If you set the price right, you'll have plenty of money left over after the job is complete, and you can focus all your efforts on creating the best product possible.

Retainer basis

Sometimes your clients want to ensure your availability to work for them, but they aren't able to define in advance exactly how much of your time they will need or exactly when they will need it. This kind of situation is tailor-made for setting up a retainer arrangement. A *retainer* is nothing more than a guarantee that your client will pay you a fixed sum of money for a particular period of time, most often each month. In return for this guarantee, you promise to be available to work for that client whenever the need arises.

Here's how it works: Say you're hired under an annual retainer of $60,000, giving you a monthly income of $5,000. In January, your client uses exactly $5,000 worth of services. However, in February, your client uses only $2,500 worth of services. Despite this shortfall in usage, your client pays you the fixed sum of $5,000 for February. The shortfall of usage in February is carried forward to March, giving your client a total of $7,500 to work with that month. If, on the other hand, the client *exceeds* the monthly amount specified in the retainer agreement, then you can bill the client for the extra work. At the end of the year, you wipe the slate clean. If the client hasn't used all his or her money by this time, then the client forfeits the unused portion to the consultant.

Retainers are generally win-win situations for both parties. The client has a skilled expert ready to work at a moment's notice. In exchange for this privilege, the consultant gets a steady stream of income each month. And if you are an independent consultant, you know that happiness is a positive cash flow.

But, of course, there are potential downsides as well. The retainer approach has the potential of you receiving demanding "need-it-now" calls at any time. And if you have more than one of these, you always run the risk of having more than one client calling you at the same time! Be careful to plan out the hours you have available and avoid over-committing to multiple clients. If, for example, you have only 160 hours available to work each month, you should not commit to take on another client retainer that will push you to 200 hours a month. Unless you farm work out to other consultants, chances are good that you'll find yourself with more work than you can accomplish while maintaining quality — leaving you with at least one or more unhappy clients.

Making Changes to Your Fees

If you're a consultant, we can absolutely guarantee that you'll eventually decide that you need to either increase or decrease the fees that you charge to your clients. Although you should never make changes to your fees without a good reason, increasing or decreasing your fees definitely makes sense at certain times.

While a client is unlikely to complain when you lower your fees — or to tell you if your fees are too low — this may not be the case when you increase your fees. Who wants to pay a higher price tomorrow for something they're paying less for today? In either case, prepare your rationale before you make the changes and be ready to explain the changes to your clients. The following sections describe the most common reasons for making changes to your fees.

Increases

Most businesspeople would love to pay the same amount — or perhaps even less — for the same service forever and ever. Wouldn't that be nice? But the real world just doesn't work that way. As everyone knows, the costs of doing business continue to increase as time goes on, and as costs escalate, your fees are sure to follow. Although you may know exactly *why* your rates need to increase, you may not be so sure exactly *when* to make the change or whether the change should apply to your current customers in addition to new customers or only to new customers.

The general rule is to pass price increases on to new customers *immediately.* For your current customers, the answer is a bit more complex. If you are contracted to provide your services at a set rate for a defined period of time — say, six months or a year — then you need to wait until you fulfill your commitment before broaching the idea of raising your prices. If you're not bound to an agreement that fixes your prices for a period of time, then give your current clients at least 30 days' notice — or more if you can anticipate far enough ahead — of the impending rate increase before you actually implement it.

Consultants raise their fees for many reasons besides the rising costs of doing business. Here are a few reasons that may compel you to raise yours:

- ✔ **Your expenses have increased.** If your expenses increase and you want to maintain the same level of profitability as you have in the past, then you have to pass the price increase on to your clients.

- ✔ **Your services are underpriced.** You may find that your services are priced too low relative to the high value you are providing your clients. This is especially likely if you are new to consulting. If this is the case, you must act quickly to raise your prices for future jobs so that you don't lose money on the work that you're performing for clients — both current and future.

- ✔ **Your demand is outstripping your supply.** If you find that you regularly have more client work to do than you have hours in the day, then it's time to raise your rates to balance the supply (your time) and the demand (client projects).

✔ **You want to test the marketplace.** Setting your fees is a balancing act. Periodically test the market with higher-priced offerings, and then note how your clients respond. If your supply of prospective clients dries up as a result, it's probably not a good time to increase your rates. However, if your clients don't seem to be very concerned about the increase and they're still clamoring for your services, then you know that you can make the change stick.

✔ **You need to pay for a client's "hidden" expenses.** After you work for a client for a while, you may find hidden expenses that you didn't anticipate and that dramatically increase the amount of work you must do to complete your assignments on time. For example, you may be expected to attend meetings that your client didn't tell you about in advance. Or you may find that obtaining access to the information you need is more difficult and takes more time than you first anticipated. If you must take on unexpected work, you may have to increase the fee that you charge your clients to cover the extra time required to complete the project.

✔ **You don't really want to do the work.** Sometimes you just don't want to do the work. Yes, at times you would rather turn down a particular client or job than suffer through it. When a client offers you work that you don't want to do, you can price your proposal significantly higher than you normally would. If the client turns down your proposal, fine; you didn't want the work anyway. However, if the client accepts the proposal, then you'll be paid enough to make up for the pain and agony of doing the job or for working with that particular client.

Regardless of the reason for increasing your rates, take the time to carefully consider *how* you're going to implement your increase. Your goal is to keep your very best customers (the ones who pay you the most and the ones with whom you most enjoy working) while continuing to attract new business. As you attract and do business with clients who are willing to pay you higher fees, letting go of your marginal clients — the ones who aren't willing to accept fee increases — is definitely in your interest. As a rule, after you have your business firmly established, you should always strive to lose the bottom 10 percent of your business to make room for a new 10 percent of business to move in at the top of your client roster.

Decreases

Yes, believe it or not, sometimes you may actually find it advantageous to *decrease* the amount that clients pay for your services. However, because price decreases have the potential to reduce your revenues and profit, you must carefully consider any price decrease before you implement it. You also have to be careful not to set a precedent for continued price decreases (unless you *want* to) that your clients may expect in the future.

Several reasons to decrease your fees are

> ✔ **Because your services are overpriced.** You should always suspect that your services are overpriced when, despite advertising, networking, and making plenty of personal contacts, your only customer is Uncle George. If you're not getting the level of business that you expected when you started your business, look closely at your rates. If they're too high, you need to bring them down to a level that is more consistent with your perceived value. Either that or improve the value that you offer to your clients so that the value matches the fees you charge.

> ✔ **To reward your long-term clients.** Everyone appreciates getting an occasional bargain, and this is certainly true for your clients. The most common ways of decreasing your pricing for long-term clients are either by giving them special premiums from time to time — such as reduced rates for a month — or by holding your fee constant. (You can still increase your fees for short-term and new clients.)

> ✔ **To get your foot in the door.** Although you run the danger of setting a precedent that will be difficult to change for future work, you may find that lowering your fees when you're trying to break into a new industry or line of business is advantageous. The simple fact is that if you can't get anyone to hire you at the rates you've set — no matter how fair they may be or how much value you deliver — you're not going to make any money. And if you don't make any money, you're out of business. When you're trying to break into a new market, dropping your fees to give your prospective clients an incentive to give you a try can often pay off in the long run. Just be sure to let your client know that you are making this exception on a one-time-only basis and that you will bill any future work at your normal rates.

> ✔ **As a professional courtesy.** Doctors, lawyers, and other professionals often lower their fees as a courtesy to others in their profession. As a consultant, you may decide to extend a similar favor. Why? Because it can help you to develop better relationships with other consultants — consultants who may refer work your way someday or who may want to partner with you on a particular project.

One technique to address the fee issue for a new client is to quote rates as follows:

> ✔ Normal professional fee: $75 per hour

> ✔ New-client discount to demonstrate performance and build goodwill: $15 per hour

> ✔ Net fee for this project only: $60 per hour

This approach establishes your normal fee in the client's mind for future projects while positioning you as a vendor who really wants an opportunity to show your stuff.

Taking a Stand

Every consultant can tell you at least one or two stories about clients who wanted them to reduce their rates — on either a short-term or a long-term basis. No doubt, as a consultant, you will have your own stories to tell. But, don't forget that this is *your* business, and *you* are ultimately responsible for deciding how you're going to run it. If you decide to reduce your rates or make other concessions to your clients in exchange for their goodwill (and business), that's fine. Just be sure you have a good reason and definite goals in mind for doing so.

If you'd rather stick to your guns and not cave in to clients' requests, then by all means do so. Not only do you earn the respect of prospective clients (this reason alone often earns you their business), but marginal clients who are more worried about fees than the results and value you provide to them stay away. And that's really not so bad, is it?

As you prepare to (politely) tell your clients what they can do with their demands to drop your fees, keep these tips in mind:

✔ **Just say no!** When you're in business, telling your clients no isn't fun, but sometimes you just have to. When you have to say no to your clients' requests to lower your fees or make other concessions, do so promptly and be firm. When done firmly and with confidence, saying no can often be strangely reassuring to your client. They feel better because they perceive they're getting value and not leaving any money on the negotiating table. If you drag your feet or beat around the bush, your clients may be angered that you weren't forthright to begin with. And if you aren't firm in your response, then your clients may believe that you've given them an opening to negotiate with you — even when you really haven't.

✔ **Be prepared with good reasons.** When you tell your clients no, you should be prepared to explain exactly why you're doing so. Explain to your clients, "Those rates don't allow me to cover the expenses of doing business," or "I can't deliver the kind of high-quality results that I demand and that you expect if we compress the schedule as much as you have proposed." Clients may not particularly enjoy being told no, but if you have a good reason for it, then at least they may understand *why*.

✔ **Be prepared with a counterproposal.** Although you may not be able to accept a client's proposed terms, you may be able to propose alternatives that you both find acceptable and that result in a win-win situation. For example, say something like "I absolutely can't reduce the price I proposed to complete your project, but I *can* get you your results faster if you like." The more alternatives you can muster for your clients to consider, the better.

✔ **Don't forget: "It's not personal; it's only business."** Avoid, at all costs, the temptation to get caught up in arguments about your fees and prices or about why you have to decline your client's requests to decrease them. These decisions are, first and foremost, *business* decisions, and you should never allow them to devolve into personality clashes or conflicts. If your discussions with a client take a turn for the worse, politely cut the conversation short, tell the client again exactly where you stand, and ask the client to call you if he or she has a change of heart.

When a client brings up reducing your rates, it may be an opening to change the structure of your pricing arrangement. A little probing into why they want or need you to reduce your rates may give you an opening to move to a different fee approach. For example, they may ask that you reduce your hourly rate but what they really want is to reduce the total cost of your services. This may be the time to explore a retainer which could reduce their total cost while letting you do less work for them. Or perhaps you've been charging by the hour but they'd prefer a project-based arrangement.

Although setting your fees can sometimes seem like a random act, there really *is* a rhyme and reason behind the rates that you establish and the decision to change them from time to time. Regardless of your feelings about how you set your own fees, don't forget that you're running a business: You have to *make* money, not *lose* it. Otherwise, you're pursuing a going-out-of-business plan. Set your fees so that you meet the financial goals of your business and can afford to take a few days off every now and then.

Part III
The Short Course in Consulting

The 5th Wave   By Rich Tennant

@RICHTENNANT

BILL BLOWS THE SUMMATION

PRODUCT EXPANSION

"Well, I think this proposal meets all of your business needs. For the rest of your needs, I'd recommend a competent tailor, a low-fat diet, and regular flossing."

In this part . . .

All consultants — whether they're experts in planting organic gardens or in managing organizational change — apply a uniform process for determining what their clients' problems are and what needs to be done to fix them. In this part, we take a look at the consulting process: defining the problem and writing winning proposals, collecting data, problem-solving, presenting recommendations, and implementing solutions. Become an expert at this process, and you'll be a consulting force to be reckoned with!

Chapter 7

Defining the Problem and Writing a Winning Proposal

• •

In This Chapter

▶ Meeting your client prospects for the first time

▶ Creating partnerships with clients

▶ Writing great proposals

• •

*E*very business process has a beginning, a middle, and an end. The consulting process is no different. It begins with defining the problem, moves through the stages of collecting and analyzing data and making recommendations, and then ends with implementation. Because the first step — defining the problem — sets the stage for all the other steps that follow, it is particularly critical.

For most consultants, this initial assessment takes place in a one-on-one meeting with the client-to-be. Although this meeting is usually in person, it can take place over the phone or even in writing, through letters or e-mail. For most purposes, a face-to-face meeting is best because it allows you to develop a much stronger relationship with your client and a much deeper understanding of your client's problems than you can get from other methods of communication. However, a face-to-face meeting may or may not make sense depending on the value of the work, how far away your client is located, and the prospects for future work. Regardless of which method you ultimately choose, your meeting has three key purposes:

✔ To identify your client's problem

✔ To determine whether you can be of help to your client

✔ To develop rapport with your client

Note that this simple list of purposes for your first meeting with your client is appropriate for *any* kind of consultant. Whether you teach homeowners how to recycle their trash (and sell them the sorting systems to do it) or conduct management audits for a huge, multinational consulting firm, the purposes underlying your initial client meeting remain the same.

In this chapter, we identify specific goals for your initial client conversations, as well as some things you should do and questions you should ask. We discuss building a partnership with your client and, finally, how to put together a winning proposal that summarizes the understandings that you reach as a result of your client meeting.

Making the Most of Your Client Conversations

At first blush, you may think that you have only one goal when you talk with potential clients about a new project: to sell them on hiring you to do the work. This may very well be your overall objective. However, you need to know much more about your clients and the problems they face before you can be sure that the work fits well within your base of experience and that you can develop the kind of partnership with your clients that is so important for ensuring a successful project.

Discovering the nature of the problem — and your client

Conversations with your prospective clients are ones of discovery: developing a basis for a strong business relationship, learning about your client's organization and its successes and challenges, and deciding whether you and your prospective client are a good match. To help yourself through this discovery process, think of the following as the goals of your initial discussions:

- **Develop rapport and build a partnership.** Consulting is very much a business built on people and relationships. If you have a talent for developing rapport with potential clients quickly, you are well on your way to building strong relationships and, ultimately, partnerships with your clients. If it's difficult for you to develop rapport with your prospects, you're going to be an awfully lonely consultant. Work hard at breaking through the first-meeting jitters and establishing the kind of rapport that helps develop the foundation for long-term, fruitful relationships.

✔ **Assess your client's personality type and adjust your style accordingly.** If your client has an assertive, take-charge style, you want to get to the business at hand sooner than if the client is more social and personable. With the latter style, the client may need to be comfortable with you personally before he can devote full attention to your abilities.

✔ **Help identify the challenges and opportunities and get a feel for your client's desire to change.** Clients agree to discuss consulting projects with you because they believe that you may be able to resolve signifi-cant organizational challenges or problems in their organizations or that you're in a position to help them take advantage of opportunities in the marketplace. Most likely, your clients already have some idea of what they need, and they may very well have decided how that need should be met. You should also already have some idea of the client's problems and opportunities, gained through your own research on the company. Your goal is to identify the *real* nature of your client's problems and then determine whether you can be of value in helping to fix those problems.

For example, your client may be convinced that the organization's high rate of employee turnover is related to the low wages paid to employees. You may suspect, however, that the turnover problem is actually a result of poor management skills. Through your prior research, you may have discovered newspaper articles on the Internet indicating an ongoing exodus of key employees from this company who all worked for the same executive. Although your client may be willing to address the *perceived* problem by giving employees a pay increase, the client may not be willing to address the *real* problem of poor management. We have known many consultants who feel that clients initially almost never report the real problem but only a symptom of their true problem. You'll get the opportunity to test your client's perception of the problem versus the real problem after you collect data, the second part of the consulting process.

✔ **Define project objectives and deliverables.** After you determine that your clients indeed have problems that need to be solved and you have a good idea what they are, you need to work with your clients to define the objectives of the project and the products that you will deliver at its conclusion. Your clients typically know the results that they want; they just don't know how best to achieve them. When you talk with your clients, help them translate their desired results into objectives that are concrete, measurable, and realistically achievable. A good exercise is to ask clients to define "what it looks like" when the problem(s) is solved. After you define your objectives, decide which "deliverables" you will include in your proposal — perhaps a final report containing recommen-dations for top management, a customer perception survey, training for the client's employees, or an advertising campaign.

This is a great time to listen for the cost of the problem to the client. In other words, how is the client measuring the cost of the problem? You may hear him say, "This problem is burning up an extra 100 man-hours a month," which gives you a sense of how much money it's costing them. Knowing this cost gives you an inside view on the value of solving the problem — and a sense of the value (read, the price) of your services.

✔ **Get a handle on the client's budget.** Remember, your time equals money. If your client-to-be has a budget, you should know it. If they don't, you should know that too. No use in developing a million-dollar proposal when the budget is clearly no more than a hundred thousand dollars — or less.

✔ **Decide who does what.** To ensure that possible confusion due to overlapping (or *dropped!*) responsibilities doesn't come back to haunt you during the project, take time during your initial meetings to sort out exactly who is going to do what. Will you distribute surveys to your client's employees, or will your client take care of that? Will you be responsible for scheduling and setting up employee training sessions, or will your client take care of those details? Who is going to be responsible for implementing your recommendations — you or the client? Now is the time to resolve these issues — not after the ball gets dropped.

✔ **Determine the information and client support that you'll need.** During the course of your initial client conversations, try to determine the information and support that you're going to need from your client and get the client's buy-in to provide it. For example, suppose that you propose to redesign a client's headquarters building ventilation system to incorporate improved air circulation as well as better filtration and absorption of mold spores and other particulates. Then you certainly need your client to provide a set of blueprints that shows you the exact location and measurements for the existing system. Work with your client to mutually determine the information and support that you'll need during the course of your project and from whom, specifically, you can get such assistance.

✔ **Define the project schedule.** A lot of things depend on your clients' desired project schedule and your ability to meet it. When clients decide they have a problem that is serious enough to require them to hire an outside consultant, they're usually in a rush to get the work done. For example, if you're an engineering consultant brought in to recommend actions to repair a leaking dam, your client isn't going to be very receptive to a completion date that is a year away. A week may not be quick enough in a situation where people's lives are at stake. Work with your clients to define a project schedule that meets their needs but that, in your best judgment, allows you sufficient time to do the project right.

✔ **Know who makes the final decision.** You may have already figured this out in the lead-up to the first meeting, but this is still a good time to confirm your understanding. If others are going to be involved, say the

CFO or the IT department director, then this is a good time to find out. If you're meeting at the client's offices, this is a great time for a personal introduction to the others involved in making the decision to hire you. (This also begins building your rapport with the troops — which can sometimes be more critical than rapport with the boss!)

✔ **Decide whether to proceed.** Despite the impression that some consultants (and clients, for that matter) may have about who decides whether a project goes forward, it is *not* the sole province of your clients to make that decision. In reality, the decision whether to proceed with a project is very much mutual. Just as your clients can decide that you're not the best consultant for the job or that your personality doesn't mesh well with theirs, *you* can decide not to work for your clients for a variety of reasons, including your belief that they're not prepared to make the changes necessary for your solutions to work or that you just don't like something about your clients' personalities. It takes two to tango, and this is just as true with the consulting process as it is on the dance floor. If you decide to proceed, your next step is to develop and submit a project proposal to your clients.

As you can see, your client conversations are much more involved than simply trying to sell the merits of hiring your business to do some work. If you conduct these conversations in the manner we describe, you set the stage for submitting a winning proposal and for completing your project smoothly and successfully.

Preparing for client meetings

Some consultants never meet with their clients face to face, while for others meetings are an essential part of the consulting process. In some cases — where the issues are simple and your solutions are straightforward — you may go directly to creating a proposal without meeting. However, when the problem is more complex or your solutions are yet to be completely defined — or when a personal touch may be needed to help you develop a relationship and rapport with a prospective client — you may find it advantageous or necessary to meet with your client face to face.

With potentially so much riding on meetings with your client, you may be nervous or apprehensive about them. Our advice is to take a deep breath and relax. Even if you're relatively new to consulting, you undoubtedly have a lot to offer your clients, and they'll be glad to hear what you have to say.

Make the best possible impression

Here are a few tips to help boost your confidence in your client meetings and leave your client with a positive impression of you and your abilities:

✔ **Relax!** Sure, meetings with your client are always critical. If you want to build rapport quickly with your clients, you must put them at ease right away. This means that you need to be confident and at ease yourself. Relax! As long as you're prepared for the meeting and you're confident in your ability to do what you do best, you shouldn't be nervous or apprehensive. In fact, if you've done your homework, you should be positively overflowing with the excitement of having the opportunity to help your clients solve their problems. Channel your anxiety; it can inspire your best thinking.

✔ **Know who will be there and why.** Before you meet with your client, find out who will be attending from your prospective client's organization and what their roles are in the proceedings. You can then prepare yourself to address any topics that may be of particular interest to individual attendees. For example, if you find out that the company's chief information officer (CIO) is planning to attend, you can mention that you have extensive experience working with computerized management information systems — a topic that is sure to cause the CIO to pay attention to what you have to say.

✔ **Make your best impression.** You only have one chance to make a first impression, and this is the time and place that you want to make a *great* first impression. The way you greet your client, the way you dress, the way you speak, and the way you carry yourself should all lend weight to the fact that you are a professional. If you do financial consulting for banks, you had better look like a banker. If your expertise is squeezing an extra knot or two of boat speed out of a 12-meter racing yacht, then shorts, a polo shirt, Top-Siders, and a windbreaker are the uniform of choice. Without boasting or resorting to name-dropping, tell your client about some of the successful projects you've worked on in the past and about some of the better-known clients you've done work for. If you provide a formal reference with contact information, make sure that you get permission from your previous clients first. Be energetic, attentive, and sincerely interested in helping your clients solve their problems, and your clients will have little choice but to be impressed with you.

✔ **Be prepared.** In an effort to test your knowledge and see exactly how you will respond to questions as they arise, your client may ask you highly technical questions or questions that require good judgment and expertise to answer well. The best way to handle these kinds of situations is to prepare fully for your meeting before you show up. If your client is new to you, you should find out everything you can about the organization: its markets, its technology, its people, and its successes and failures. Your client will be impressed that you took the time to find out about the organization. This gives you an opportunity to wow them.

✔ **Listen.** To get an exact understanding of your client's problem and some idea of how best to address it, you have to *listen* to your client. Some consultants mistakenly believe that they have to do all the talking in order to show their expertise. This is simply not the case. In fact, in any meetings with your client — except, perhaps, ones where you are making a presentation of some sort — you should do more listening than talking. This is the *only* way that you can hear what your client is really saying and understand what is really needed.

✔ **Take notes.** During the course of your client meetings or phone calls, you will discuss a multitude of ideas, concerns, concepts, approaches, and understandings. Taking notes of these critical discussions is invaluable to you both when you develop your project proposal *and* during the course of project performance. Not only that, but your client will be favorably impressed by the importance that you accord what he has to say. Right after the meeting, you should make additional notes of your impressions while they're still fresh in your mind.

That wasn't so bad after all, was it? The more client meetings you participate in, the more your confidence will increase, and the less reason you'll have to be concerned about them. Before you know it, these meetings will become second nature to you, and you'll handle them like a pro. Until then, keep working at these skills and keep meeting with your clients.

Ask your clients lots of questions

If you want to create great proposals — ones that have your clients reaching for their checkbooks minutes after they receive them — you need to know the answers to a *lot* of questions. And after your client selects you to do the work, the answers you receive in this preliminary stage of the consulting process will help to guide you through the rest of the consulting process.

Your job, therefore, is to ask the questions that get you the answers you need. Here are several different questions for you to try. Feel free to add others that have provided you with good information.

✔ What is the problem that you would like me to address?

✔ Why do you think that the problem is occurring?

✔ How long has your organization had this problem?

✔ Have you tried to solve the problem? How? What happened?

✔ What suggestions do you have about how I should approach this problem?

✔ What are your objectives for this project?

✔ Are there any organizational obstacles in the way of a finding a solution?

✔ Are there any organizational obstacles in the way of implementing my recommendations?

✔ Is your management team committed to making the organizational changes needed to make this project a success?

✔ What measurable outcomes do you want to see at the end of the project? (This gives you a clue as to the cost of the problem to the client.)

✔ When would you like this project completed?

✔ How do you see your role during the course of the project? After project completion?

✔ What kinds of information and other support can your organization provide?

✔ Will I be responsible for helping to implement the project recommendations?

✔ Do you have a budget in mind for this project?

✔ Do you have any personal concerns about this project?

✔ How soon would you like me to start?

You may already know the answers to many of these questions as a result of the research you've done in advance of your meetings. However, it's a good idea to confirm the accuracy of these answers by asking your client anyway. Asking questions now will save you lots of time and anguish down the road. Make asking questions a central part of your client conversations and meetings.

Building Partnerships with Your Clients

You have a choice: You can either work *with* your clients or work *against* them. We're going to let you in on a little secret: The wonderful world of consulting isn't always a bowl of cherries. In fact, if you have to deal with hostile clients or with uncooperative, troublesome employees, you may wish that you had followed a different career path — taxidermy, perhaps. The problem with working against your clients is that *nobody* wins and *everybody* loses. You lose because you waste your time on a project that no one appreciates or even wants, and your clients lose because the original problem remains unresolved.

If something doesn't feel right or you're getting bad vibes, you may want to terminate the relationship and find clients with whom you are more compatible. If the client-consultant chemistry isn't right at the beginning, it's not likely to get better farther down the road.

Clearly, building strong partnerships with one another instead of working against one another is in the best interest of you and your clients. Your clients win and you win, too. Here are some dependable ways to build partnerships with your clients:

✔ **Collaborate, collaborate, collaborate.** Collaboration between consultant and client is an absolutely essential element in any successful consulting project. If the so-called "expert" consultant sits up in an ivory tower — remaining aloof from the organization and the people who work within it — the client may decide that the consultant is out of touch with the organization and quickly discard the consultant's reports and recommendations. Conversely, if the client decides to treat the consultant as just another employee — directing everything the consultant does and approving (or disapproving) every move the consultant makes — then the credibility of the consultant's results and recommendations will be compromised. The solution is for consultant and client to work together — *collaboratively* — and build a partnership to ensure that the project is successful.

✔ **Make all communication two-way communication.** Good communication is not a one-way street. You can't do all the talking and expect to understand your clients' problems or what outcomes they want to achieve. The strongest partnerships are built on a firm foundation of trust and mutual respect, where each party can speak openly and the other party listens. In a real partnership, the opinion of one partner is just as important as the opinion of the other, and all communication is open, honest, and moves freely in *both* directions.

✔ **Discuss and negotiate the tough issues.** In any meaningful partnership — including ones between consultants and their clients — tough issues have to be addressed and dealt with head-on. Dancing around issues or avoiding them to keep a relationship pleasant doesn't allow you to resolve the issues that need to be resolved, nor does it result in a better set of conclusions and recommendations. In fact, your conclusions and recommendations will be incomplete and, quite possibly, inaccurate because you failed to address crucial issues. Discuss and negotiate the tough issues with your clients *directly.* Be frank and straightforward. Though you can and should be diplomatic and respect your clients, you should attack tough issues without hesitation. The result is a real partnership — not a fantasyland version that is handicapped from the start by its artificiality.

✔ **Make mutual decisions.** Whenever possible, include your clients in making the big decisions that have the greatest effect on your project. Making them feel like part of the team can help build your partnership while preventing them from feeling like they're being left out of the problem-solving process. In the same vein, encourage your clients to include you in the decision-making process for issues pertaining to your project. Doing so will help you to build and strengthen your partnerships with your clients while leading to better project results and recommendations.

✔ **Deal with the people problems, too.** In some organizations, the consultant may be pressured to ignore people problems — weak or overbearing managers and supervisors, employees who consistently show up late for work, executives who have a habit of taking long lunches — and focus only on technical issues. This is a mistake. If you are to reach your goal of successfully solving your clients' problems, you can't leave people out of the equation. Although faulty policies, systems, and procedures can wreak havoc in an organization, so, too, can faulty employees. For the consultant-client partnership to be successful, artificial boundaries and fears have to be left behind, and the consultant must have free and unfettered access to the entire organization. Be sure to discuss this issue with your clients at the beginning of your projects — not after you've already gotten them underway.

Although establishing partnerships with your clients won't necessarily solve *all* your problems and challenges, it sure makes your relationships much easier to live with, your work more productive, and your results more meaningful.

Crafting Winning Proposals

After you wrap up your initial contacts with your client, you next need to write and present an out-of-this-world, bang-up proposal. A *proposal* is a document that is specifically designed to provide your client-to-be with all the information he or she needs to make a decision to move forward with you — and to do so in a very compelling way.

A proposal can be anything from a one-page e-mail message to a more formal letter proposal to a multivolume tabbed, perforated, and indexed extravaganza. In this section, we discuss the logistics of various proposals and give you lots of tips to ensure that yours are top-notch.

Considering popular proposal types

The length, depth, and breadth of your proposal greatly depend on the nature of your business, as well as your client's expectations. For example, suppose that you are a computer consultant and you're simply going to install a new hard drive in someone's computer. You certainly don't need to present your client with a 35-page proposal describing all the benefits of the hardware upgrade and the reasons for selecting you over the competition — heck, your client will probably give you the go-ahead after briefly discussing your experience, your price to do the job, and how soon you can do it. However, for a complex, multiyear proposal to do some serious management consulting that will result in significant organizational changes, 35 pages may not be enough!

For most situations, you submit either a short, letter-type proposal or a longer, narrative-type proposal. In the following sections, we check out each approach.

The letter proposal

In many consulting situations, all you need is a brief, one- or two-page proposal that concisely and simply presents the most important information that your prospective clients need to know. This can be submitted to your clients via e-mail, fax, or an actual printed and signed letter. Letter proposals are particularly useful for projects that are simple, are short in duration, or don't cost your clients very much money.

At minimum, your letter proposals should contain the following information:

- ✔ **The point:** After a word of thanks for meeting with you or requesting your work, get directly to what you have to offer, focusing on results and on the advantages of working with you and your firm.

- ✔ **Proposed project:** What are you planning to do for your client? Make sure you include a brief description of your project in your letter proposal.

- ✔ **Anticipated outcomes:** Summarize your anticipated project outcomes. If your recommendations will save your client $1 million, tell him so here. If you're going to train your client's employees to use a new software program, this is the place to present that particular bit of information.

- ✔ **Action plan:** Briefly outline the steps you will take to reach your anticipated outcomes, along with any assumptions that you are making and any other details that your client should know.

- ✔ **Price:** Provide your client with the bottom line, which may include your fees and reimbursable expenses.

- ✔ **Payment terms:** It's wise to break up your payments so that you're paid pieces of the overall total during the course of project performance instead of one lump sum at the very end. Not only is this payment schedule better for the health of your bank account, but it also helps to ensure that you don't complete and deliver a project to a client only to have the client refuse to pay for it. Although you may have provisions in your contracts to protect you legally from this eventuality, collecting may take you months or even years if you have to take your client to court.

- ✔ **Next steps:** Put the ball in your prospective client's court — explain what the client needs to do to initiate the project and get you working. The simplest way is to ask your potential client to accept your proposal by signing it at the bottom and mailing the original, signed proposal to you, along with the first project payment. Alternatively, the signed proposal can be faxed or scanned and e-mailed to you with the payment to closely follow via regular mail or express delivery. As soon as the client signs and returns the proposal to you, you have a contract binding both parties.

To give you an idea of what we're talking about, Figure 7-1 shows a sample proposal for a consultant who does freelance software development and troubleshooting for a living.

September 28, 20xx

Ms. Stella Bella
The Nova Corporation
33 Rue d'Orleans
Shreveport, LA 71103

Dear Ms. Bella:

Thanks for taking the time with me today to discuss your forthcoming software program. As I mentioned at our meeting, I honestly believe that millions of computer users around the world are ready, willing, and able to pay their hard-earned cash for a Windows version of the popular children's game "Hula-Hoops." As I looked over what you have done to date, however, I noted many areas where I can help improve the program's functionality. Beyond the simple issues of color and graphics, I will be able to help you bring your entire presentation into sharper focus and tighten up its response to user input. I also have questions to ask you regarding your overall vision for the program, your intended audience, and the graphic look that will best meet the needs of the audience.

As a result of my initial review of your beta program, I propose the following:

- Conduct an initial telephone interview with you to discuss your overall vision of the program. This interview will be conducted within one week of execution of an agreement and payment of the first installment.

- Based on the telephone interview and a further review of the beta program, provide creative input to you in the form of a written report. This task will be completed within one week after the telephone interview with you.

- Completely troubleshoot your beta program for functionality and aesthetics and incorporate any changes that you may approve from the previous step. I will provide the revised program to you via e-mail within two weeks of receipt of your go-ahead.

- Provide online support and answers to your questions (limited to the scope of this project) via telephone and e-mail.

The price for this project is $10,000. Payment will be as follows: $2,500 upon execution of this agreement, and $7,500 upon delivery of the final program. If you would like to proceed with this project, please sign both originals of this letter and return one of them to me by U.S. Mail with a check for $2,500.

I'm looking forward to working with you on this project. I know that you will be happy with the final product. Please don't hesitate to call me if you have any questions.

Sincerely,   Accepted:

J. Edgar Gerber   Stella Bella

Figure 7-1:
A sample
consulting
proposal.

The narrative proposal

When you make a proposal for a job that is complex, that you anticipate to run for a long time, or that requires a substantial investment on the part of your client, you'll most likely be required to submit a narrative proposal. In a narrative proposal — which can run anywhere from ten pages to hundreds of pages — you generally address the same kinds of information that you do in a letter proposal, but in much greater detail. For example, while the anticipated outcomes take up all of a sentence or two in the preceding example letter proposal, the section of your proposal describing anticipated outcomes could take five pages or more in a narrative proposal.

Because we don't have enough pages available in this book to provide you with a complete sample narrative proposal (sorry, but our editor says *no way!*), we instead summarize a typical approach to putting one together:

- ✔ **Cover letter:** The cover letter contains a brief overview of the proposed project, along with your name, phone and fax numbers, and e-mail and Web site address. For some projects, you can also put expected benefits in the cover letter.

- ✔ **Title page:** As you may expect, the title page contains the title of your proposal, along with the date, the name of your business, and the name of your client's organization.

- ✔ **Table of contents:** We warned you that this proposal would be big. Your clients need a table of contents keyed to page numbers just to find their way around this monster!

- ✔ **Executive summary:** For the client who is too busy to read the 75 pages that you labored over for three weeks or more, this paragraph summarizes the entire proposal in a quick, 30-second reading.

- ✔ **Anticipated outcomes:** As in a letter proposal, you present the anticipated outcomes here — albeit in a much more complete fashion.

- ✔ **Detailed scope of work:** A scope of work is a presentation of every task that you will perform as a part of the project. For some narrative proposals — especially those for the government — a proposal's scope of work can easily consist of 25 pages or more of highly detailed tasks and subtasks. We hope you have lots of toner left in your laser printer cartridge to print this one out!

- ✔ **Schedule:** In a narrative proposal, your schedule is likely to be much more complex than a simple, "The project will be completed six months after go-ahead by the client." In complex, long-term projects, you may assign each task presented in the statement of work a start date, a duration, and an end date. If your scope of work contains lots of tasks and subtasks, you should present your schedule in the form of a chart or graph that shows the information visually for greater understanding and impact.

✔ **Fee:** The price to your customer for the work you plan to do. You should first propose your fee in the way *you* prefer it to be, for example, a monthly flat rate or an hourly fee. You can modify it later if your client wants you to price your work in some other fashion. In some cases, your client may want you to break down your price by task, by outcome, or by deliverable (for example, your interim or final report). If so, your pricing is going to get awfully complex very quickly. Keep in mind that your project may have reimbursable expenses. Make sure you and your client agree on which expenses will be approved, and how they will be reimbursed.

✔ **Qualifications and experience:** Here's where you can go to town about all the great experience you have and all the years of training you underwent to get where you are today, as well as that great high school or college you attended. If it's okay with your present and former clients, you can even mention their names if you want to augment your credibility.

✔ **Resumes:** If you feel it will help support your proposal, include a copy of your resume along with the resumes of other key project personnel. One caution: Make sure to tailor your resume to the kind of work you're proposing!

✔ **Letters of reference:** If any of your clients were so overwhelmed by the work you did for them that they were moved to write you letters of thanks or reference, include those letters here if your prospective client asks for them.

After you submit your proposal, follow up with your clients to be sure that they received the proposal and that they have what they need to make a decision. And don't forget to ask when you can expect a reply. But don't pressure your clients too much, or you may not like the answer you receive — *no!*

Proposal success secrets

Because proposals are so important to the financial well-being of your consulting business, they deserve your utmost attention and care. This section gives you our favorite (and most effective) proposal success secrets.

Know your competition — inside and out

If you're competing with other firms for the same business (and what firm isn't?), you have to become very familiar with your competition. However, not only do you need to know how many competitors you have and who they are, but you must also become knowledgeable about your competitors' pluses and minuses relative to your own business if you expect to survive and prosper. Ask your clients what they like and dislike about your competitors. Scour the Internet for information about your competitors, pro and con. Get to know your competition inside and out.

Hint: Set up a file folder for each competitor. When you get some information or an article about a competitor, file it. If you review the file every few months, you'll see a picture begin to emerge.

Help your client develop the specs for the job

Salespeople have known for eons that if they can help you develop the specification for the product you want to buy, you're more likely to buy the product from them. Why? Because they define your problem in ways they can address. Few of your clients are expert in your area of technical specialty — that's why they hired you. The wealth of knowledge and experience that you possess can save your clients time and money in trying to figure out how to describe their problem and what needs to be done to fix it. Volunteer your services freely — and for free — when asked; that small investment of time will undoubtedly pay off in a big way down the road.

Talk through the proposal with your client first

Before you submit your proposal, talk through your concepts with your client. Drop in for a visit, make a phone call, or send an e-mail to communicate your ideas. Although you may be certain that your proposed approach is the right one for the particular situation, you may be surprised to find out that your client doesn't agree. Discovering this before you submit your proposal is better than finding out after you submit your proposal. Not only that, but whether or not you get the work, you begin to develop a relationship and rapport that make you a welcome bidder in the future.

Include great references

If you were going to hire someone to advise you in some aspect of your business — say, a certified public accountant to help you do your taxes — wouldn't you prefer to hire someone who had years of experience and a list of satisfied clients about half the size of your phone book? Your ability to show prospective clients in a proposal that you have an established and successful track record in your field goes a long way to prove that you can do the proposed work. A successful track record can directly result in your being hired for a job; this is especially the case when clients you have worked for in the past are in the same line of business as your prospective client. Make a point to include the names of your best clients in your proposal — after getting their permission to do so. Asking satisfied clients to call new clients on your behalf is often a good idea.

Submit your proposal in person

Mailing or overnighting a proposal to a client is okay. Your client will most likely get it on time, and everyone will be happy. Delivering your proposal in person, however, is much better. Why? Because you not only ensure that the proposal is delivered promptly and accurately, but you also demonstrate to your client that his or her business is important to you. Delivering a proposal in person also allows you to answer your client's questions on the spot and to leave a good parting impression. Unless the cost is prohibitive, or the job too small to merit it, always try to deliver proposals in person.

Be prepared to answer every question

When you develop and submit a proposal to a prospective client, you must be prepared to answer any question that the client may ask you. This requires you to know what you wrote in your proposal (don't laugh; we both have met with consultants who hadn't read their own proposals). By knowing what's in your proposal, you're prepared to address your clients' needs and concerns with thoughtful responses tailored to their specific situations. Don't forget: You are the expert. Don't be unprepared when your clients expect you to act like one!

Be sure to follow up

After you deliver your proposal to your prospective client, set up a definite time and process for follow-up. First, call your client within two days after you deliver the proposal to ask whether you can answer any questions and when the client expects to make a decision. When the decision date arrives, call your client again to ask whether he or she has made a decision. Continue with this approach until your client makes a decision. If the decision is favorable, congratulations! If it's not, ask if there is some change you can make to your proposal to win the business. A new approach? A tighter schedule? An extended payment plan? Whether you win or lose a job, be sure to ask your prospective clients what led to their decision and what you can do to improve your proposals in the future. Then fine-tune your approach accordingly.

A few more tips

Your proposals should always be easy to understand, attractive, and concise. Here are a few more tips for your next proposal:

- ✔ **Respond directly to your clients' needs, questions, and concerns.** Listen to your clients and determine exactly what their needs, questions, and concerns are. After you figure them out, respond to each one with a solution.

- ✔ **Place your clients' perceptions above your own.** When it comes to proposals, your clients' perceptions count, not your own. If your clients absolutely love color photographs in their proposals but you hate to use photos because you think they detract from your image, you better use lots of color photographs in your proposals, regardless of your own opinion.

✔ **Don't wait until the last minute to start working on your proposals.**
Get to work on your client proposals as soon as you decide to do them;
avoid the temptation to put them off until the last minute. Not only are
you more relaxed when you write them — resulting in a better, more
thoughtful product with fewer errors — but you improve your ability to
get them in on time (or even early!).

✔ **Take time to review your proposals before submitting them to your
clients.** Always set aside time after you write your proposals to review
them before you submit them to your clients. If you submit sloppy
proposals, your clients-to-be will probably assume that your work will
be of similar quality.

✔ **Don't ignore your competition.** Your proposals should be at least as
good as theirs, or better. Keep an eye on your competitors, and don't
get too complacent or settled in your ways. Plenty of competition is out
there, and in most cases, your competition isn't standing still. Always
strive to make each proposal better than the one that preceded it, and
stay up-to-date with your competitors' innovations.

✔ **Create a database of proposals.** Our experience is that after a while,
50 percent of any proposal becomes boilerplate; that is, content that
is used time and again. For example, resumes of key members of your
consulting team will likely only need minor updates from time to time.
And this also goes for your listings of client references and project
experience. Take advantage of this fact and recycle your proposal
material whenever you can.

Chapter 8

Collecting the Client Data You Need

. . . .

. . . .

*A*fter you meet with your clients to help determine whether they have a problem and, if so, what that problem is (see Chapter 7 for more information about this step), your opinion of what your clients' problems are and why they're happening is preliminary. Imagine being a doctor who's examining a patient complaining of chest pain: The patient (the client) may be convinced that a heart problem is causing the pain, and you, the doctor (the consultant), may suspect that something else is actually at work — perhaps heartburn or acid reflux. But until you run some tests and gather further data, you can't really know for sure what your patient's problem is. The heart problem could turn out to be a simple case of indigestion! You use the data you gather to test your assessment of what's wrong or determine the best approach to achieving your clients' goals. The data could prove you right or wrong, but whatever the results, you need complete, accurate, and timely data to diagnose your client's problem and know one way or the other.

In any data-collection exercise, you face a dilemma. Every organization generates an incredible amount of information — internally in the form of memos, reports, contracts, plans, graphs, and more and externally in the form of investor relations materials, marketing materials, newspaper and magazine articles, and other documents. When deciding what information you need, you can easily get bogged down in a flood of information, much of it irrelevant to the problem. On the other hand, if you are too selective in your approach, you may miss an important source of information. The challenge is to obtain just the information you need — no more, no less. This is often much easier said than done, but you should always make it your goal.

Another problem with collecting data is that you often have to dig deep into the organization — and into its hierarchy — to get to the real answers. As you speak to people in an organization, their awareness of a problem moves from an external focus to an internal one. When you first question your client, for example, she may perceive that the "payroll system is all messed up." If you press her a little bit, she may move down one level and focus on external causes for the perceived problem: "If those lazy payroll clerks would stop taking those long lunches, maybe we wouldn't have this problem!" If you continue to press your client, you may get to the heart of the issue: "Well, I guess I did forget to turn in my time sheet on time a few weeks ago, but I don't see what the big deal is about that." Questioning a variety of people throughout the organization — employees on all levels and with all types of work assignments — invariably leads you to the truth.

Collecting the kind of data from your clients that is useful in your efforts on their behalf is an art. In this chapter, we describe the most common and reliable sources of client data, and we tell you how you can involve your clients in helping you get that data. Finally, we consider some of the most dangerous data disasters and explain how you can take steps to avoid them.

Identifying Key Data Sources

Selecting the sources of data you need and then obtaining that data in an accurate and timely manner is a critical step in the consulting process. The secret to knowing what data to gather is simple: You must have an analytical model — a hypothesis — to explain the problem or demonstrate your preferred approach. (If you don't have a hypothesis, don't worry — we can guarantee that everyone you talk with in your client company will have an opinion about why things aren't working!) Start by gathering data that can prove your idea or model true or false. The initial identification of the problem or approach gives you a starting point for which specific data to gather.

For example, say you've got a client whose salespeople can't meet their monthly sales goals to save their lives. Your client wants you to figure out why. After some initial discussions with your client — and preliminary observations of the sales organization, you may have a hypothesis in mind about the problem. Perhaps in this case you suspect that the organization's client relationship management (CRM) software is out-of-date and, therefore, the salespeople aren't using it. By gathering data of the right kind from the right places, you can test your hypothesis and prove it right or wrong.

Pulling together a large quantity of complex data from a variety of sources can be an incredibly difficult job. Fortunately, the number of sources for gathering data is not unlimited. The six categories we discuss in the following sections pretty much sum them up.

Of course, gathering data from all these different sources, depending on which ones you finally settle on, can involve an incredible amount of time and effort. Fortunately, there is a solution: You can have your client help gather the data for you! Not only do you save time and money, but you also have the opportunity to better cement the relationship with your client. Why? Because you and your client will naturally work together more closely as you strive toward a common goal: obtaining the information that you seek. Thus, you strengthen your relationship with your client while you reduce your own effort. That combination is hard to beat as we discuss in the section "Getting Help from Your Clients in Collecting Data," later in this chapter.

Direct observation

One of the best ways to gather data — especially when you want to know how people really carry out a job, task, or procedure (not how they say they carry it out) — is to actually watch people do their jobs. It's amazing how people's perceptions of how they do their jobs can differ from the reality of how they do it. The only way to get past the discrepancy is to directly observe them in the business environment.

Internal documents and records

Every organization — no matter how large or how small — has internal documents and records that prove the way it does business: accounting records, purchase orders, internal company memos, policies, procedures, product marketing plans, vision statements, and more. As a part of your data-collection efforts, you need to determine exactly which internal documents and records are most useful for your project, and then work with your clients to obtain those items. For example, if you believe that your client's security problem is a result of security guards who aren't performing their duties in accordance with prescribed policies, then you can seek security logs and similar data that indicate the daily activities of the security guards.

External documents and records

Every organization distributes numerous external documents and records outside the company, including such things as press releases, marketing materials, magazine and newspaper articles, radio and television interviews, licenses and permits, health inspections, and tax records. In your search for external data, you'll find libraries, government offices, and research services to be invaluable assets. And as you likely know if you have ever logged onto the Internet, a heck of a lot of information is out there in cyberspace just waiting to be grabbed. You may be surprised at what comes back when you do a global Yahoo! or Google search on the names of your clients' organizations or the names of the people in charge.

Surveys and questionnaires

Surveys and questionnaires — especially anonymous ones — offer a structured and confidential way for an organization's employees, and for your client's customers, vendors, bankers, and other business associates, to provide you with data. As with interviews, you get to decide exactly what information you need and what questions you need to ask to get the information you need. And because you control the way the questions are asked, you can direct the response — from a simple yes or no to an expansive, essay-type, multipage response. For example, if you are trying to find out how your client's customers rate your client's efforts at customer service, you can design a survey with questions that help you gauge the opinions of your client's customers. To conduct the survey, obtain a list of your client's customers, call them — using either the entire list or a sampling of the list — and ask them to answer your questions. Their responses can provide valuable data for your investigation.

Interviews and group meetings

Any data-gathering exercise worth its salt includes interviews with people in the organization as a basic foundation. Interviews can take the form of one-on-one question-and-answer sessions ("What do you do after you weigh the package on the postal scale?") or small group meetings ("Do you have any idea why so many accidents are occurring on the night shift?"). Interviews should always include the people who are directly involved with the problem, as well as others who aren't directly involved but who may have a good perspective on it. One-on-one interviews are often better than group meetings because the participant can tell you what's on his or her mind without fear of retribution from management or co-workers. However, group meetings often offer their own insights — especially when they reveal rivalries between individuals or departments or expose raw nerves in the organization. One method of dealing with extensive data is to use these sessions as opportunities to get the participants' interpretation of the data. For more information about these and other potential land mines in the data-collection process, check out the section "Watch Out! Avoiding Data Disasters" at the end of this chapter.

Personal experience

The longer you have worked in your field of expertise — whether as a consultant or as an employee — the more personal experience you have to draw on. For example, you may have 15 years of experience in building composting bins for organic farmers and gardeners and may have written scores of articles on the topic. Your own opinions and experiences can be important sources of data, supplementing the other data you gather directly from your clients. In some cases, you may have seen identical problems in other organizations. If you have extensive experience in a particular field, take advantage of it!

Getting Help from Your Clients in Collecting Data

Collecting client data is an important part of the consulting process, but it's often an incredibly time-consuming part of the process as well — for both consultant and client. If you allow it, you can quickly get bogged down in your data-collection efforts — slowing or even halting your progress on a project. Not only is this outcome potentially frustrating for you, but it also can make your client question whether you are the right consultant for the job.

One way to avoid getting bogged down in the data-collection process, while improving the quality and timeliness of the data you collect, is to enlist your client's help. The old adage that many hands make light work applies in consulting, too. If you decide that getting your client involved is in your best interest — and in the best interests of your client (and it generally is because you get better access to the data you seek) — then ask your client to do the following to help you through the process. If you are concerned that your client may tamper with the data, then you may not want to ask your client to help you collect data.

> ✓ **Mutually decide what data is best.** After you have a general idea of the data that you need to get, meet with your client to decide the kinds of data and the sources that are the best for what you are trying to accomplish. For example, you and your client may determine that the organization's weekly sales reports are a better source of near-real-time data than the quarterly financial reports released to shareholders. After you determine what data is best, you can turn your attention to finding it.

✔ **Identify where the data you need is located.** Who better to know where the data you seek is located than your client? You can play detective all you want and try to track it down yourself, but you can save yourself (and your client) a great deal of time and money if you ask your client to help direct you to the data you need. If, for some reason, the data is not what you expected or is incomplete, then you can dig in more deeply in your own search for it. However, getting your client to direct you to the right source to begin with is certainly worth a try.

✔ **Prioritize your effort with employees.** If you are an experienced consultant, you probably already know that many employees (that is, anyone in the organization besides the person or persons who hired you) look forward to dealing with consultants about as much as they look forward to trips to the dentist. As an outsider, you can be stonewalled, misled, obstructed, and otherwise thrown off track by employees who not only don't want to cooperate with you but also may be actively fighting your efforts. Your client can help to smooth out these little bumps in the data-collection road by explaining to employees that their cooperation is not only encouraged but also expected.

✔ **Help you physically obtain the data you need.** The data you need may be archived in an organization's warehouse, or it may be squirreled away at a variety of sites scattered around the country. After you know exactly what information you need, your client can pull it together for you. All it takes is a simple memo or a phone call to your client, and before you know it, you have everything you need, when you need it. Not only do you save the time and money that it would have taken you to physically gather the data yourself, but you avoid organizational red tape and employee resistance that may otherwise have caused you problems.

✔ **Grant the ongoing support of the keepers of the data.** Sometimes you need one or more of the keepers of an organization's data to, in essence, act as your guide and translator as you review the many different pieces and sources of data that you uncover during your project. This person can be an invaluable resource as you try to understand the context of the data that you're reviewing. When was this policy last updated? Why was it updated? Was it intended to address some sort of organizational problem? Find the individuals and departments responsible for generating the data and have them tell you two things: what it means and how it was used. If necessary, your client can grant you the help of one or more employees on a part-time or full-time basis.

If there are any areas of data that will be out of your reach, you must know this at the beginning of your project. For example, if the client doesn't want you talking with customers (due to concerns about what you may say or what his hiring a consultant may indicate to the market) and you've determined that talking with key customers is critical to the project's success, you need to know about this restriction upfront. You will have to negotiate a work-around, redefine the deliverables of your work, or — regrettably — decline the project.

In some cases, your clients may be very willing to help you collect the data you need — perhaps even undertaking the entire effort. Alternatively, your clients may expect you to take responsibility for data-collection yourself. Which is the better approach? It depends.

If it is important for the data to be collected by an independent, outside party, then you should collect it. This would be the case when administering employee-opinion surveys where employees may not provide candid answers to their own managers or human resources department for fear of retribution, or when collecting financial or other data for auditing purposes. If it doesn't matter who collects the data — or if the process would be particularly cumbersome for an outside party to collect — then consider asking your client to collect it. A very important and valuable result of having clients help in the data gathering is that it begins to build buy-in. They have a difficult time disputing the data if they gave it to you. Of course, there is still the interpretation of the data (see Chapter 9), but often it helps to have them involved in that too.

The best way to solicit the assistance of your clients in the data-collection process is to include this discussion in your initial client meetings and sell your clients on the benefits of involving them in the search. You can encourage your clients' involvement by pointing out two benefits to them. First, the quality of the data-collection efforts is enhanced (thus enhancing the quality of the results of your efforts). Second, you can pass on the savings that result from the reduced number of hours that you devote to collecting data. You'll have much better luck getting your clients signed up if you make data collection a part of the original contract instead of springing the request for help on the client during the course of the project. Be sure to include in the contract a section listing the exact support that the client is to provide. A specific clause in the contract calling this out is critical to establishing the client's role in the process and its impact on costs.

Watch Out! Avoiding Data Disasters

If you aren't careful, you may conduct an involved data-collection effort only to find that key data is missing, incomplete, or suspect because the source was biased. These data disasters not only can cause you additional work and heartache, but when they become a part of your project assumptions, they can also destroy the validity of your work as well as your credibility as a consultant. For these reasons, it's especially important to validate your sources and to examine them closely for problems that could lead to data disaster! The following sections describe the most common data problems and suggest ways to ensure that they don't cause *you* problems.

Overlooking key data sources

It's easy to overlook a source of data — perhaps a disgruntled employee who has been moved to an offsite location or a disheveled box full of audio-tapes recorded at executive team meetings. Sometimes it's easy to ignore answers that bubble up from the lowest levels of the organization. Such over-sights may occur because your clients direct you to information sources that are less embarrassing to them, there's a bias that people on the shop floor can't possibly understand the complex issues you're addressing, or simply because you inadvertently omitted some information. Unfortunately, the data you overlook may be a crucial link in the success of your project. Be exhaustive and relentless in your search for the data that you need to complete your project successfully.

Missing client biases

Regardless of what they may say or think, every employee — from the mail-room clerk to the chairman of the board — comes with a unique set of biases. For example, a design engineer may tell you that the problem with product development is absolutely, positively the result of late input from the market-ing department. But you may not be aware (and you won't be aware until you start digging into the problem more deeply) that he harbors a personal grudge against the head of marketing because she got a bigger bonus than he did last year. The secret to gathering accurate data from interviews with employees, group meetings, and questionnaires is to recognize that bias is a part of most data gathered directly from employees, understand the source and nature of the bias, and filter the bias out of the data that you have gathered.

Ignoring personal biases

Believe it or not, you may harbor a bias or two yourself. Perhaps your client is from Tierra del Fuego, and you've never trusted anyone from Tierra del Fuego. Or maybe you don't think that your client knows what he's talking about, and you think that you have all the right answers. Take a close look at yourself and any biases that may color your data-gathering efforts; work to overcome them and make your approach as balanced as you possibly can.

Accepting incomplete data

Sometimes you know exactly what information you need from someone and ask for it, but what you get in return is incomplete or not what you asked for. You may be greatly tempted — especially when you are under a lot of pressure to complete your project or you have tons of data to analyze — to simply let it go and accept what you are given. This can be disastrous to the successful outcome of your project. When you get incomplete data — or no data at all — follow up with your source and insist on getting what you need. If you meet with continued resistance in obtaining necessary information, ask your client to help prioritize the effort with the difficult employee.

Failing to fully document data

When you are in the middle of fast and furious data gathering, the sheer amount of data that comes your way can be overwhelming. Before you know it, you can find yourself focusing your efforts on data that is already documented for you — reports, policies, staffing plans, product schedules, and the like — at the expense of data that isn't documented, such as employee interviews and surveys. Often, the data that you gather from *your* sources turns out to be the most useful in getting to the heart of an organization's problems. Don't let these important sources of information slip through your fingers; document your conversations, interviews, and other interactions with client personnel as soon as you can after they occur.

Receiving intentionally false, misleading, or fraudulent data from your client

Not only can this cause you to draw the wrong conclusions in your analysis, but your consulting firm may become entangled in the fraud too. You may recall that not too many years ago, a company by the name of Enron made a fine art of regularly providing misleading financial information to its outside auditor, Arthur Andersen — at the time one of the top-five accounting firms in the United States. When this approach to doing business was eventually revealed, it led to a number of events, including a drop in the company's stock price from more than $90 to just pennies a share, and Enron's eventual bankruptcy. Not long after Enron filed for bankruptcy, Arthur Andersen — which was being prosecuted by the Department of Justice for its role in the Enron disaster — surrendered its license to practice as a Certified Public Accountant (CPA) firm, and was forced to terminate 85,000 employees.

So, the lesson is this: There are times when a client may give you false, misleading, or fraudulent data. If you can determine that such data was given to you unintentionally and with no intent to mislead you, then you may decide to continue your project with this particular client. If, however, it seems clear that your client is intentionally trying to mislead or lie to you, you're being used and you should then run — don't walk — to the nearest exit. If your contract agreement has a termination provision, then seriously consider invoking it.

Chapter 9

Problem-Solving and Developing Recommendations

. . . .

In This Chapter

▶ Organizing client data

▶ Problem-solving and weighing alternatives

▶ Developing, prioritizing, and selecting your recommendations

. . . .

*T*he first step in the consulting process is defining the problem. The point of collecting data, which is the next step of the process, is to test your assumptions of what the real problem is. For example, if you and your client make a preliminary decision that the organization's problem is a lack of training for line supervisors, the data you collect should either support that conclusion or point you in a different direction.

Now, what are you going to do with all that information you gathered? Before you can tell whether the data supports or refutes your conclusions, you need to organize it and make sense of it. This means sorting it into recognizable categories and then looking for commonalities and trends. Through this process of sorting data — discarding irrelevant data along the way — and then focusing on the data that is most compelling, a range of possible alternatives for problem-solving naturally opens up.

The point of this exercise is to arrive at the very best recommendations for your client. By considering your client's needs, the cost of your recommended courses of action versus the benefits to be derived from them, and the organization's culture, you can arrive at recommendations that not only solve your client's problem but also are right for your client's organization. In our experience, if your recommendations don't mesh with the organization — its culture *and* politics — then your report gets filed away and is soon forgotten.

In this chapter, we consider how to take a flood of data and organize it so that it makes sense to both you and your clients. We explain how to apply an effective model for problem-solving and discuss the best way to go about deciding which recommendations to present to your clients.

Making Sense of All That Information

After a week or two (or three) of collecting data, most consultants find themselves up to their ears in data of all kinds, sizes, and formats. Surveys, interviews, focus groups, archives, management reports, and much more are available to you. This is good because the more data you have to draw from, the higher the probability that you're going to get to the bottom of your client's problem. However, all this information can be overwhelming. If you don't have a good system for organizing it and separating what's important from what's not, you're going to find yourself bogged down in a flood of data. And if you can't pull yourself out of the flood, your project progress is going to slow to a crawl, and your client is going to begin to wonder whether hiring you was the wrong choice. This is not the best outcome for you or your client.

It's up to you to make sense of all that data and identify the trends and patterns that point you to solutions. Here's a hint: Just follow the steps listed here, and before you know it, you'll have the right information at your fingertips.

Sort and consolidate the data

After you pull together all the data, you're likely to be faced with a stack (or perhaps a small mountain) of information from many places: project status reports, computer diskettes and printouts, sales forecasts, promotion plans, internal memos, discs full of e-mail messages, and the like. Your first task is to synthesize all this data by sorting it into collections of similar _kinds_ of information. For example, you may organize a year's worth of data on an organization's financial performance into monthly categories. Within each month, you may further organize the data into the categories of sales, expenses, and so on. Such categories may include company departments, locations, products/services, markets/customers, capital equipment utilized, internal/external, and so forth. Other categories may include the types of issues you're discovering, such as quality, safety, cost, communication, or leadership. How you decide to organize your information is up to you; you should base your decision on the nature of your project and your personal preferences.

After you sort your data into collections of related items, you can consolidate it. You may have multiple copies of the same data or the same data from several sources; if so, toss the duplicates.

If you use surveys to collect data, first read the ones on which the respondent made numerous comments. Because those respondents cared enough to take the time to give you additional information, you'll undoubtedly get the most productive and thoughtful feedback from them.

Put steps and processes in time sequence

When people take on a task, they normally do so in a logical and stepwise fashion. Part of organizing and synthesizing your data is to figure out the sequence of the steps your clients take to carry out tasks and processes. What do employees say they do first, second, third, fourth, and so on? Now, what do they *really* do first, second, third, fourth, and so on? What then are the differences between what employees say and do, and why is there a difference?

For example, a mailroom clerk may claim that he delivers all incoming overnight mail to employees first, processes and routes incoming regular mail second, and then prepares all outgoing mail third. However, upon personal observation, you may discover that incoming overnight mail is actually handled second, causing delays in the receipt of important correspondence.

A great way to work out time sequences is to draw the steps and processes on flowcharts or write the steps on stick-on notes and then stick them on a wall in sequence. This technique is commonly known as *process mapping*. Using computerized flowcharts or stick-on notes makes it easy to rearrange the steps as you enter the problem-solving and recommendation phases of the consulting process.

Look for patterns, trends, and themes

As you pore through all the data you pull together, you may soon begin to notice certain patterns and themes emerging. For example, if you're reviewing the attitudes of a company's employees, you may notice that employees are happier towards the end of the calendar year — when the holidays arrive and bonuses are traditionally given out — but then consistently dip at the beginning of the next calendar year. Or you may notice that more accidents occur on an assembly line during the night shift than during the day or swing shift. These emerging trends tell you where to delve deeper when it comes time to problem-solve.

Ignore and set aside extraneous data

As you begin to refine your data further — noting which information is starting to point to recurring themes and possible solutions — you notice that some of the data you collected is extraneous to your efforts. Set that data aside and remove it from further consideration. Doing so allows you to focus your efforts and attention on the most promising data while ignoring the information that has little or no bearing on your recommendations.

You may find you've collected data that is extraneous to your particular project but important for your client to know. You might choose to offer a "freebie" to your client by handing over this data without comment/recommendation. Who knows, it may lead to additional work.

Focus

Concentrate your full focus on the most relevant data, and consolidate it to the lowest common denominator — that is, the information that keeps coming back to you as a possible solution. For example, suppose you're investigating the reasons for the poor morale of an organization, and a large amount of the data that you collect through employee interviews and one-on-one meetings points to uncaring managers as the source of the problem. In that case, you focus your efforts on the information that tells you exactly which managers are at the root of the morale problem and what they are doing to cause it. Focused information forms the basis of your problem-solving efforts, which are at the heart of this process.

This process of compilation and synthesis is ultimately what gives the consultant the unique position of expert for the problem at hand. No one else will have seen all the information in this form in this way — not the owner, not the CEO, and not the managers or line workers. In many ways, it really is at the heart of the consulting process.

William Eastman on developing client partnerships

Bill Eastman is executive vice president for knowledge management at the training firm ISB Worldwide (www.isbworldwide.com), and chairman and president of Content SourceWare and its delivery organization Applied Knowledge Laboratories (www.appliedknowledge labs.com), an intellectual property company commoditizing the consulting and training industry. We spoke to Bill about how to develop client partnerships and the secrets of running a successful consulting business.

Consulting For Dummies: What do you do to develop partnerships and long-term relationships with your clients?

Bill Eastman: We're convinced that for an organization to make change, most of the recommendations we provide cannot be created inside the organization. Why? Because our clients are too busy, there's too much on their plates, or they are up against entrenched forces. To solve this problem, we create a temporary and joint organization from our operations plus key players from the client's organization. The joint project is run independently, and as a beta operation for the duration outside the boundaries of the client organization. What this allows is the testing of new ideas: bringing the best inside the organization and integrating them with current operations. Consulting is not about staying around; it is about transferring technology — the temporary organization should cease to exist as soon as its mission has been accomplished.

CFD: That's an innovative approach. Many projects conducted *within* organizations are subject to all kinds of employee resistance.

Eastman: Definitely. And if your client is resistant, then you've really got to ask yourself whether or not partnering is appropriate. You may still want to work with them and sell them your expertise, or sell them the products and services that they need, but clearly understand that you're not dealing with a partner; you're much more into a customer-vendor relationship as opposed to a true partnership. And that's okay, because every client is different. What we try to do is focus on those companies to whom we don't have to explain that concept twice — they get it. Their issue is not resistance to change as much as it is "My plate is full. I know I've got to do this, but I can't because I don't have time; so I commission you to do it."

CFD: Most successful organizations have a plan. What's yours?

Eastman: We have a five-part business plan for running our business. The first thing we do is attempt to gain visibility and exposure — *visiposure* (a word that I got from somebody about 25 years ago) — in our targeted industries. This includes membership in trade organizations, writing articles, being present in newsgroups and user groups on the Internet, and executing a number of other promotional strategies. However, we focus on only a couple of industries that we want to own.

CFD: So what's the second part of your business plan?

Eastman: The second step is the gathering of mindshare. In other words, by creating an image in the marketplace, we're trying to get mindshare for integrated solutions. And we focus predominantly in the service arena. Although we know a lot about product quality, we don't work in that particular arena — the competition is brutal.

Service quality is a lot more difficult for organizations and consultants to handle, and that's the arena that we want to play in. We look at companies that live or die on the quality of their customer service — that are in very complex types of businesses and that have incredibly rapid rates of change — a perpetual state of white water.

CFD: What do you mean by "perpetual state of white water"?

Eastman: It used to be that being in business was much like riding the Mississippi — for the most part, the ride was slow and wide. In business today, it's much more like shooting a river that's got an incredible drop; lots of rocks, currents, and eddies; and almost no flat water whatsoever to rest and catch your breath. It's all white water. So, although you can put together plans to run your business, those plans can only be put together strategically. Tactically, you need to, as you approach a rapid, have the people in your organization standing on the rocks *in the river* figuring out how to shoot it. It's an immediate decision made at the front line.

CFD: And as soon as you get through that first rapid, there's another right behind.

Eastman: Right. The best thing that management can do for people is to walk the rim of the canyon so that they can inform their team that there's another set of rapids coming.

CFD: How about the third step in your business plan?

Eastman: The third step is to create a temporary organization where the project that we're engaged in — in terms of both strategy and implementation — is run as a beta. We briefly discussed this concept earlier in this interview. Not only do we feed the information that we learn back into the organization so that they can incorporate it as we go, but we train the people from the company who join us how to handle it. The one thing I would like to add is the development of project metrics. Under the right circumstances we offer a guarantee on ROI (return on investment). Working closely with the client and using their metrics to identify potential revenue increases or cost reductions that the change will drive. An ROI of 3 to 1 or higher is not a reach for a well-designed and -managed project. Our goal is, at a minimum, for the client to break even on the project!

CFD: And what's step number four?

Eastman: The fourth step is re-integration. This step allows our clients to re-integrate our findings from the third step back inside the organization. We can then shift our role to an expert provider, where we provide expertise to upgrade and update them on what's happening. Once clients pick up our technology in the third step, for a small fee they get a download of the latest technology. So we're now selling information to our consulting groups who are internal to the companies that we sold contracts to.

CFD: Once a client, always a client?

Eastman: That's certainly our goal. In the fifth and final step of our business plan, we publish what we've learned — the successes *and* the failures. That information then goes back to step one and gives us added visiposure.

CFD: What's the key to the future for consultants?

Eastman: You've got to be able to find a way of providing new, identifiable, and significant value. For example, I used to subscribe to *Business Week* magazine, but that's not where the *future* is. We now have a full-time Market Intelligence business unit that researches targeted industries This future is a dynamic Web site that people can customize to fit their own needs, one they can interact with. We work hard to stay ahead of what's happening in our clients' industries in regard to how technology is going to alter them, and then we help them integrate this information so they can run more efficient and effective business operations. The net result is that our clients *win*. And when our *clients* win, *we* win.

Problem-Solving the Right Way

In consulting, problem-solving is really where the rubber meets the road. While problem-solving, you review the data that you sliced, diced, and otherwise processed to develop a set of solutions, one or more of which will ultimately become the recommended course of action that you present to your clients. Because of this, you want to open the net as wide as possible at the beginning of the problem-solving process — sucking in as many possibilities as you can. Then you need to throw some of your catch back into the sea (and keep the good ones for yourself) by weighing the alternatives until you are left with the best possible courses of action. At this point in the process, you aren't narrowing the field down to one possible course of action, but only down to the few *best* ones.

There's a right way and a wrong way to problem-solve. Fortunately for you, we present the right way here:

1. **Brainstorm possible solutions.**

   The first step in the problem-solving process is to take the data that you collected and consolidated and to brainstorm possible solutions to the problems that the data raises. Although you can brainstorm by yourself or only with other members of your firm — if there *are* other members of your firm — you get a much wider variety of options when you include your clients in your brainstorming sessions, and you begin building client buy-in to your recommendations.

The secret to conducting productive brainstorming sessions is to encourage *every* possible idea — no matter how far out it may seem. This means suspending judgment for the duration of the session and welcoming everyone's input. Record every idea on computer, paper, flip charts, or a white board so that you don't lose track of any of them.

2. Consider the implications of each possible solution.

Isolate each alternative that was generated during your brainstorming sessions and follow it to its logical conclusion. For example, if a client has a problem with the quality of the circuit boards leaving the factory floor, one possible cause is that workers are not using the correct soldering techniques. If you follow this possibility to its logical conclusion, a solution may be to provide more training to employees on soldering correctly or to provide better supervision and monitor employees' work more closely.

3. Weigh alternatives and narrow your focus.

After you work through all possible alternatives, weigh them against each other to determine which ones are most likely to be relevant to the outcome and which ones are least likely to be relevant. As a part of getting to your final recommendations, you have to focus your efforts more sharply at this point and move ahead on a few fronts instead of many. Discard the alternatives that are *least* likely to become viable recommendations, and continue to narrow your focus to those that are *most* likely.

4. Pick the best courses of action.

By this time, you should have your list of possible alternatives narrowed down to a manageable number. Continue to work through this list with your client until you whittle it down to no more than five or so of the best courses of action. If you look up for a moment, you should be able to see the light at the end of the tunnel. After you complete this step, you are ready to go on to developing your recommendations.

So you've managed to wade through all your data, problem-solve, and arrive at a reasonable number of alternatives from which to draw your recommendations. This is the reason your clients hire you: to take advantage of your expertise by obtaining your advice and recommendations on ways to solve their problems. Don't worry — you're almost there!

Determining the Best Recommendations

Your clients hire you to get your recommendations on how they can solve their problems. However, you have to test every set of recommendations to ensure that they are in the best interests of your clients and that your clients will readily accept and implement them. All the most wonderful recommendations in the world — bound in attractive report binders and accompanied by lush PowerPoint presentations — aren't worth a hill of beans unless they are heeded and implemented.

The best client recommendations are effective and honest but take into account clients' budgets, needs, resources, and culture. The following sections provide some guidelines to help you develop recommendations for *your* clients.

Evaluate the best courses of action

At this point, you have approximately five possible best courses of action from the problem-solving phase of your effort. Take another look at them in light of the following criteria:

- ✔ **Cost versus benefit:** Before settling on your final recommendations, consider each recommendation in terms of its cost versus its ultimate benefits. Don't forget: There is also the cost of *not* doing something to consider. If a recommendation is potentially very expensive for your client and the benefits are marginal at best, it may not deserve a position at the top of your list. However, if a recommendation costs your client relatively little and the payoff is great, it should make a speedy trip to the head of the class.

- ✔ **Client needs and resources:** Your best recommendations not only address the very real and concrete needs that your research and brainstorming uncover, but they also address the unique situation that your client's organization and employees are in right now. Each client has particular needs and can muster differing amounts and kinds of resources. Whereas some companies may be short on cash and long on employees, other companies may have plenty of cash to throw at their problems but have no excess personnel to assign to the needed repairs and solutions. Be sure to account for these kinds of differences as you finalize your recommendations.

- ✔ **Client's organizational culture:** Every organization has a unique culture, and your client's culture is an important consideration in molding your final recommendations. You may have the greatest recommendations in the world, but if they run counter to the organization's culture, at best they will be adopted only grudgingly. Much more likely, they'll be discarded altogether. For example, if you recommend laying off half of a company's workforce but the founder is rightfully proud that throughout the company's history no employee has ever been laid off (and layoffs are not about to start now), your recommendation will be quickly discarded.

✔ **Client's people and politics:** Politics plays a major role in how things are done in every organization. Your recommendations have to take into account your client's political landscape and the way that people relate to one another to get things done. If they don't, your recommendations may *look* great but be unworkable in the organization. For example, you may determine that an organization needs to get its employees *much* more involved in the decision-making process. However, if the middle managers in charge of implementing this change are dead set against it and they have the political power to block it, the recommendation will die a quick death. And politics can trump everything!

You should constantly test your recommendations with your client and the key people in the organization. This testing can be in the form of simply asking for feedback on your evolving perceptions and ideas, or actual rigorous testing of budding recommendations (for example, actually adjusting that new packaging procedure you think will solve the problem). This gives you insights into your client's response to your recommendations, it may uncover a fatal flaw of your recommendations before it's too late or, best of all, it may start to build acceptance and momentum behind your recommendations.

Draft recommendations

After taking the preceding criteria into consideration, the next step is to draft the recommendations to present to your clients. Although you still have a *little* bit of time to rework them before you make your client presentation, they should be fairly definite, settled, and stable. At this point in the process — before you actually present your final recommendations to your client — you can and should be informal. A simple bullet list of recommendations should be sufficient for most purposes.

Rank your recommendations

After reviewing all the potential recommendations and running them through the gauntlet of criteria such as cost versus benefit, client needs and resources, and organizational politics and culture, you're ready to take the last step: ranking your recommendations in order of practicability. After you do that, you're in business. Provide options for your client. Let the client choose among lower price, faster completion, and higher quality. It's best to use a min-max strategy: Build a first-class, top-note strategy, and then build a bare-minimum strategy. Doing so tells you when to walk away and helps your client build a solution between your two viable ends of successful solutions.

After you rank your draft recommendations, you're ready for the next step: presenting them to your client. Coincidentally, we address that very topic in Chapter 10.

Chapter 10

Tell It Like It Is: Presenting Your Recommendations

In This Chapter

▶ Giving feedback to your clients

▶ Designing your feedback meeting

▶ Building client ownership of your recommendations

▶ Making great presentations

*A*t some point in your consulting project, you're going to develop a set of recommendations for your client. This, after all, is what your clients pay you the big bucks for. So how do you go about presenting your recommendations to your clients? Should you write them a letter, or drop them an e-mail message? Although those are certainly options you can pursue, you'll more likely communicate your recommendations in the form of both a written report and a presentation. As a rule, you should always give your clients a tangible product of some sort at the end of the project — in most cases, at minimum, a written report. And to ensure that your clients understand and ultimately act on the recommendations in your report, presenting your recommendations personally — whether directly to your client or to a group of managers or other members of your client's organization — is definitely the way to go.

Your primary goal in this phase of the consulting process is to get your clients to accept your recommendations. Bringing your clients around to the point where they are ready to embrace your recommendations is very much a selling process; running through a few charts is usually not enough. You should be passionate about your recommendations and feel strongly about your clients' need to adopt them.

In this chapter, we consider the importance of presenting your recommendations to your clients, plus we give you some tips for making the feedback meaningful and lasting. We also review the steps involved in presenting your recommendations in an effective and successful client feedback meeting and discuss ways to help your clients take ownership of your recommendations to build the momentum necessary to carry them out.

Giving Client Feedback: Setting the Stage

You can have great impact on whether your client ultimately accepts and implements your ideas. Keep these tips in mind as you prepare for your presentation; they'll pay you back many times over in the form of happier clients and a greater probability of implementation of your recommendations. And don't forget, a happy client is a client who is likely to contract with you again — and refer you to *new* clients.

✔ **Don't forget your selling cap.** Sure, the point of communicating your recommendations to your client is to explain exactly what the organization should do to solve its problems, whatever they are. However, making your recommendations involves more than that. In most cases, presenting your recommendations to an organization is as much (or perhaps even more) a *selling* job as it is a *telling* job. No matter how much an organization wants to solve its problems, you always run across at least some resistance from some of the people within it. As you present your recommendations, keep this in mind and be consistent in highlighting the benefits to be gained by the organization and the people who are part of it. Your case must be compelling!

✔ **Keep your clients involved.** If you've been playing your cards right throughout the consulting process, your clients are very much a part of your presentation and the recommendations you make. They're involved because you keep them abreast of your findings as you encounter them, and you ask for their feedback and input. Not only do you gain great insight from their feedback, but you give your clients the opportunity to begin to buy in to your recommendations before you formally make them. By keeping your clients involved — and, actually, an integral part of the process — your recommendations are better suited to the organization *and* more likely to be accepted and implemented than those that are created in a vacuum and announced to a resistant audience. You can anticipate objections and have information designed to counter them incorporated into your solutions.

✔ **Unleash no surprises.** You may like surprises, but chances are your clients don't — especially when it comes to your recommendations. If your recommendations will shatter your clients or embarrass any of the principals of the firm, you haven't involved your clients enough in the consulting process. A good sign that your clients *have* been adequately involved is that not only are your clients not surprised by the recommendations, but they're already sold on them before you make your presentation. Make that happen by involving your clients closely in the problem-definition, data-collection, and problem-solving phases of your work.

That said, if, for some reason, you *do* have a surprise or two up your sleeve, first present it privately to your client or to a key member of the client's organization.

✔ **Be honest and frank.** Sometimes the truth hurts. Despite the fact that you probably would much rather give your clients good news than bad, you're getting paid to lay it all on the line. Be sure that your client gets the *complete* benefit of your expertise — not just the parts that make your client feel good, are politically correct, or are easy for you to communicate. This will go more smoothly if you reinforce this point during your initial client meeting: "You may not like everything I'm going to tell you, but being candid is what you are paying me for."

✔ **Don't insult your clients.** Avoid insulting your client by criticizing the decisions he or she made that got the organization into its current mess. Opening your presentation by saying something along the lines of "In all my years of consulting, I have never seen such a mess as this!" is definitely not the way to build more business with your client. Not only are you likely never going to work for *that* particular firm again, but your recommendations also will find their way into the wastebasket sooner than you can say, "Oops!" Maybe the management team has some problems, but you have a much better chance of helping if you present your findings in a way that doesn't insult your client.

✔ **Support your client.** Change is tough for any organization, and the recommendations that you present may set the stage for tremendous change in your client's organization. Reorganization, downsizing, streamlining, and more are often inevitable results of consultant recommendations. Be prepared to support your client — both emotionally and organizationally — as the organization prepares to confront the need for change.

Now that you know some things that you should definitely do when you present your recommendations to your clients, the next step is to plan and conduct your client feedback meeting. We review each step of this very important meeting in the following section.

Conducting a Feedback Meeting

Hours and hours of work — defining your client's problem, collecting data, and problem-solving — bring you to this point: your client feedback meeting. In this meeting, you present your results to your client, and you plant the seeds for the eventual acceptance or rejection of your recommendations. If the meeting goes well, your client is likely to implement your recommendations. If not, your recommendations are most likely to end up on the proverbial dust heap of history.

Client feedback meetings are first and foremost *your* meetings — you set the agenda and control the pace and flow of your presentation. Sure, you can and should be responsive to your client's needs and allow for some flexibility in the agenda, but be sure to get back to the topics that you planned to discuss. You should also do what you can to influence which members of your client's team will attend. More than a few projects have stumbled when the wrong people were in attendance (for example, they didn't have a sufficient understanding of the subject, or they were not in a position to implement the consultant's results) or the right people were left out of the meeting (for example, managers directly impacted by findings or executives with the authority to implement the recommendations). Be sure you have the right people at the table and, while you're at it, identify in advance who is going to oppose your recommendations and why.

Here are five steps aimed at conducting a successful client feedback meeting:

1. **Present project background, goals, and methodology.**

   The first part of your presentation consists of a brief description of the project, including the problems you were hired to tackle, your project goals, and the methodology you applied to arrive at your recommendations. Be sure to highlight your client's role in the problem-solving process and in helping you arrive at the recommendations you are presenting. Everything here must have been agreed to beforehand.

2. **Present your recommendations.**

   Getting to this point has taken a while, but, finally, here you are. At this point in the presentation, you give your key recommendations along with the reasons why they are the most likely solutions to the problems your client faces. Be sure to have an array of alternative recommendations for your client to consider (including options that offer a lower price, faster completion, and higher quality), and explain why you didn't select them as your primary recommendations. Check out the next section, "Making Great Presentations," for more advice.

3. **Encourage client discussion.**

   Getting your client to talk about your recommendations is a critical part of this phase of the consulting process. You want the meeting attendees to ask questions, challenge your assumptions, consider the alternatives, request further information, or do whatever it takes to decide on an appropriate course of action. If your audience is silent after your presentation, encourage a healthy exchange of ideas by asking the participants whether they understand your recommendations and whether they have questions about anything you presented.

4. **Help your client decide on a course of action.**

   Your recommendations are exactly that — *recommendations*. Your job is not to make your clients' decisions for them — they have to absorb the data you present and make up their own minds. However, you should press your client to make a decision of some sort — preferably while you are around to help facilitate the process. After conducting your project, you are likely to be the person who is most knowledgeable about the problem and the fixes that have the best chance of working. You can offer your clients a great deal of help as they decide which course of action to take.

5. **Determine your role in future activities.**

In some cases, presenting your recommendations to your client may be the last step of the project. In other cases, your client may want you to stick around to help implement your recommendations. In any case, use the client feedback meeting to determine what, if any, role you will play in further activities related to your project.

If you need more help making a powerful presentation, keep reading. If you're confident in your presentation skills and are looking for ways to help your client implement your stellar recommendations, then flip ahead to the "Building Client Ownership of Your Recommendations" section.

Making Great Presentations

Making successful presentations, especially during a feedback meeting, is a key skill for every consultant. Some people seem to be natural-born presenters, but others grapple with making presentations before groups of any size or shape. If, like most of us, you think you fall in the second category, the good news is that you can dramatically improve your presentation skills with a little preparation and a little practice. And the better your skills, the more confident and credible you'll be when you make your presentations and the more likely your recommendations will be accepted.

Preparing to present

Preparation is the key to making an effective presentation in your feedback meeting. In fact, for knock-'em-dead presentations, you can figure on spending anywhere from one-half to one hour of preparation time for each minute of your presentation. In addition to the hints presented in the section that follows, be sure to check out *Presentations For Dummies* by Malcolm Kushner (Wiley), for a wealth of information on making great presentations.

The following tips can help you prepare for your feedback meeting or any presentation:

✔ **Describe what you're trying to accomplish.** What are the goals of your presentation and what are you going to have to do to achieve them? For example, the goals that you have in mind when you pitch a project to a prospective client (sell, sell, sell!) are substantially different from the goals you have in mind when you present an interim progress report on an ongoing project (to inform and to seek client buy-in). And because your goals are different, your presentations should be different, too. Be sure to tailor your presentation to achieve the goals you set and the outcomes you require.

✔ **Assess your audience.** You want your presentation to be as effective as possible, so you need to think carefully about your audience and write the presentation exactly for those people. Although an audience of scientific researchers is likely to expect and appreciate a jargon-laden, highly technical presentation, the same presentation would quickly put a group of corporate administrative managers to sleep. Before you make your presentation, be sure to assess your audience.

✔ **Develop the heart of your presentation.** Start writing your presentation by outlining the major points that you want to communicate to your clients. Then note any sub-points and visual aids you can use to support your presentation. Don't get overly ambitious; limit your major points to no more than three to five. If you have more information to communicate than you can "fit" into the actual presentation, convert the extra information into handouts that you give to your audience at the beginning of your presentation.

✔ **Write the introduction and conclusion.** The introduction of your presentation should

- Capture your audience's attention.

- Provide a brief overview of the presentation.

- Sell the members of your audience on the importance of the presentation.

The conclusion of your presentation is just as important as the introduction. Your conclusion should

- Briefly revisit your key points.

- Remind the members of your audience why your presentation is important to them.

- Leave your audience feeling energized and inspired.

✔ **Prepare your notes.** If you've given the same presentation many times before, you can probably get away without using notes. However, having notes in your hand is a real help if you momentarily lose your place, and they also ensure that you don't forget to cover any of your planned topics. Notes should be brief and specific — not a word-for-word script of your performance, but rather a reminder of your key points. Many people use computer PowerPoint slides for the same purpose. We address this in the next section.

✔ **Bring in reinforcements if necessary.** Depending on the nature of your project, its complexity, and the number of people you have working on it, you can consider bringing other project participants from your business into the presentation. This idea is particularly good when your project is highly technical. If you have experts on your staff who can add credibility to your recommendations and solutions, ask them to address specific aspects of the project as part of your presentation.

✔ **Practice makes perfect.** Depending on your personal comfort level or the complexity of the information you plan to present, you may find it advantageous to run through your presentation a few times before you present it. On one end of the spectrum, you may be comfortable simply running through your notes a few times the night before the big event. On the other end of the spectrum, you may prefer to rehearse your presentation in front of another person or even a video camera.

You can't be *too* prepared for a presentation — particularly when you're presenting your results and recommendations to clients. Make the most of the time that you have before your presentation because it pays off in a big way when the time comes to get up in front of your audience and start your performance. And believe us, every presentation you'll ever make is a performance, and, each time, you are the performer.

Using visual aids artfully

Did you know that scientists have proven that approximately 85 percent of all information received by the human brain is received *visually?* Think about that the next time you lead a client feedback meeting. Though your spoken remarks may convey a lot of valuable information, the people in your audience are likely to understand and retain far more information when you present it to them visually.

Here's an example of what we mean. Peter actually saw someone make an hour-long presentation to the executive team of a high-tech computer software development company using screen after screen full of tiny little words and numbers just like the ones in Figure 10-1. If you were sitting anywhere other than front-row center, the text and numbers became a blur of hieroglyphic-like gobbledygook. What really iced the cake was that the presenter read each and every figure directly from the screen. Ouch!

A much better alternative: Convert the mass of text and numbers into some simple graphs that convey the same information. Figure 10-2 illustrates exactly what we are talking about. Use a viewgraph like this one instead of the viewgraph in Figure 10-1, and your audience has an instantaneous, visual understanding of the numbers. As the presenter, you can concentrate on explaining the meaning *behind* the numbers instead of wasting time just reading them to your audience.

Calendar Year Product Sales						
	Washington	Boston	Atlanta	Los Angeles	San Diego	Dallas
January	1010	575	447	1819	554	150
February	2332	748	695	365	784	275
March	964	888	856	1635	254	365
April	2550	969	523	1450	699	184
May	3552	611	965	1788	955	432
June	2648	821	763	1193	419	231
July	1250	1352	712	1385	648	951
August	2451	1293	575	1230	499	785
September	3245	452	951	1721	744	626
October	2612	852	842	1521	654	441
November	1943	456	625	1352	951	239
December	3675	952	725	1420	842	855

Figure 10-1: A viewgraph that's painful on the eyes.

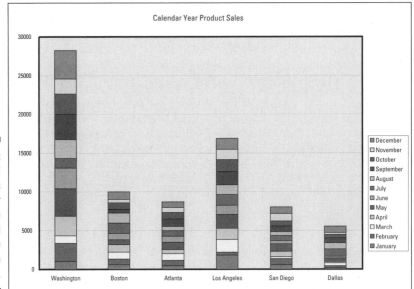

Figure 10-2: Good viewgraphs enable your audience to understand the information visually.

It took us many years of concentrated effort, but we eventually captured the essence of the visual element in presentations. Here for your consideration is the Nelson/Economy axiom of visual learning:

Information seen is remembered; information not seen is easily forgotten.

So how does this handy little axiom impact *your* presentations? It means that you should always consider your *visual* presentation as important as your *spoken* presentation. Whenever possible, think of ways to present your information *visually.* Maps, displays, product samples, prototypes, photographs, charts, and graphs are just a few of the many options available to you. Here are some of the most common kinds of visual aids used in presentations:

- ✔ **Handouts:** Providing your audience — no matter what size it is — with handouts of the information that you plan to cover — both text and graphics — can sometimes help your audience better follow your presentation. But heed this warning: Don't fall victim to the practice of providing handouts and then reading from them word for word; nothing is more boring to an audience than getting stuck in such a presentation.

- ✔ **White boards/chalkboards:** If you're working with a smaller group — say, up to about 30 people — using a white board or chalkboard is a very handy way of jotting down your main points as you proceed through your presentation. And if you make a mistake, you can simply erase it and write in the correct information.

- ✔ **Flip charts:** Like white boards and chalkboards, flip charts (those big pads of paper that mount on an easel) are good for making presentations to groups of up to about 30 people. However, the big advantage that flip charts offer over white boards and chalkboards is that you can prepare your entire presentation on the flip charts *before* the big event, in the privacy of your home or office.

- ✔ **PowerPoint:** Using Microsoft PowerPoint or similar presentation software, you can put together a complete multimedia presentation on your laptop computer and then take the resulting file anywhere you like (on your computer, a CD-ROM, or a flash drive) and project the presentation onto a full-size projection screen. However, be absolutely positive in advance that the equipment you'll need (for example, a computer, projector, and screen) are on hand for you to use. Or simply bring your own.

Before you get too crazy with your visual aids, keep a couple of things in mind. First, don't try to squeeze too much information into any one aid. Use a large typeface (font), keep the number of words and numbers to a minimum (16 words or less, please!), and use color to improve the professionalism and readability of your visual aids. Second, have your presentation ready *before* you show up to make your presentation! You definitely won't impress your clients if you start your presentation by spending five minutes fumbling with your computer or paging through a disorganized stack of handouts. Finally, don't forget that *you* are the heart and soul of your presentation — not your visual aids. Visual aids help to support your presentation, but they won't make up for a lack of preparation or for being an uninformed presenter.

Making your presentation on stage

Okay, the time to prepare has come and gone, and you're ready to make your presentation. All your hours of hard work and preparation are about to pay off. Heed this advice as you start your presentation and you're sure to do a great job:

- ✔ **Relax!** Breathe deeply and visualize making a successful presentation before your audience. There's no need to be nervous. Don't forget: Your client is paying you because you're an expert in your chosen field. And you are, *right?*

- ✔ **Greet the members of your audience.** Besides making sure that everything is in order for your presentation, the opportunity to meet your audience is one of the main reasons for arriving early. Before you start your presentation, try to greet as many members of the audience as you can. Not only does this practice help you break the ice with your audience — reducing any nervousness you may feel — but it also helps generate more interest in you and what you have to say.

- ✔ **Wait for your audience's attention.** When you make a presentation, try to capture the full attention of your audience right at the start. You can ask for your audience's attention, or you can seek it by standing in front of your audience and saying nothing until everyone's attention is focused on you.

- ✔ **Make your presentation.** Jump in with both feet and don't look back. One thing: When presenting, move about the stage a little and try to make eye contact with the critical decision-makers. Moving around makes your presentation much more interesting to your audience. Making eye contact enables you to pick up on critical cues from your key clients. (For example, a finger rapidly drawn across your client's neck means that you have a *big* problem!)

Getting your ideas across to your clients in an organized and effective fashion is a real art. Don't expect to be able to just wing it — it takes a great deal of work and preparation to prepare and execute killer reports and presentations. Fortunately, computers have done much to make preparation easier than ever before. But, don't forget: You're the one who determines whether a presentation will be just okay, or one that dazzles your client. So, what's it going to be?

Building Client Ownership of Your Recommendations

At some point in the consulting process, your clients have to take ownership of your recommendations and make them their own. Otherwise, your recommendations are doomed to be relegated to the recycling bin. You can directly influence the chances of your recommendations being implemented by working with your clients to build ownership of your recommendations. Although you've been setting the stage for this transition since the beginning of the project by creating partnerships with your clients and involving them in the consulting process, now is the time to drive your point home.

Your recommendations are only as good as their implementation by your clients. Even the best recommendations miss the mark if they remain unimplemented. Here are some ways you can help your clients take ownership of them:

- **Push for a consensus.** Don't allow issues to remain unaddressed or unresolved. For example, suppose that you recommend instituting a mandatory quality program for all the businesses that sell parts to your client's manufacturing operation. If one or more of the participants in your feedback meeting is opposed to your recommendation because such a program may lead to increases in vendor-supplied part prices, don't just drop the issue. Work with your client to mediate the differences between the two positions and come up with a consensus that can then be implemented. If you let the issue drop in your meeting, your recommendation may be ignored.

- **Push for decisions and commitments.** The client feedback meeting is the perfect time and place for you and your client to work out the details of an action plan for implementation. It's also the perfect time for you to push your client to make the commitments that ensure that the action plan is followed. After all, unless you have completely missed the boat, implementing your recommendations is the only step that helps your client.

- **Offer to continue your partnership through the implementation phase of the project.** Do you still have that selling cap we asked you to put on at the beginning of the chapter? That's okay; we'll give you a minute or two to dig it out of your closet. Your client may or may not want your help in implementing your recommendations. If implementation wasn't a part of your original client contract (and you almost always should try to make it a part), you can suggest it now.

  You have two good reasons for offering. First, you can help ensure that your recommendations are actually implemented and that the implementation is indeed what you recommended. Second, you can continue to reinforce and build the relationship that you've already developed with your client by continuing your work through the implementation phase. If the implementation goes well, your client will surely ask for your help when other problems arise in the future.

Congratulations! For some of you, this is the end of the consulting process. Your clients are now going to take your recommendations and implement them on their own. If this is the case, be sure to check in on your clients periodically to see how it's going and offer to help them in any way you can. You never know when your clients may want to take you up on your offer.

The rest of you — the consultants whose clients have engaged them to participate in the implementation phase of the consulting process — still have work to do. In Chapter 11, we discuss working with your clients to implement your recommendations.

Chapter 11

Implementation: Making Your Prescriptions Stick

· ·

In This Chapter

▶ Creating an implementation plan

▶ Helping to smooth the path to implementation

▶ Assessing the results of your implementation effort

· ·

*Y*our recommendations to your client represent the fruits of your labors. Much hard work — both on your part and on your client's part — goes into producing them. However, if your recommendations are filed away in a drawer or set aside on some manager's desk, then the fruits of your labor soon rot away to nothing. And although you are being paid to do the work anyway, no consultant alive can honestly say that it doesn't hurt just a little when the outcome of all that hard work is a recommendation that a client never acts upon.

As a consultant, you're in a difficult position. You may know *exactly* what needs to be done to solve your client's problem but, ultimately, you're not the one who decides whether or not to implement your recommendations — your client is. Indeed, your client may decide to pick apart your recommendations and use only the ones that he or she wants to at any given moment. That's the client's prerogative. All you can do is push hard for your point of view — that is, after all, what your client is paying for — and back off only after you're certain that your client has given your point of view due consideration.

You can (and should) participate in the process of getting your clients to adopt and implement your recommendations. This is, after all, the most satisfying payoff of all your hard work — seeing your recommendations implemented and watching your clients' problems disappear as a result. And, indeed, as an outsider, you may be the only one who can make the necessary changes without getting tangled up in nostalgia for the status quo or with office politics.

In this chapter, we show you how to work with your clients to put together implementation plans, and we give you some tips on making the implementation go easier for everyone involved. Finally, we consider why and how to assess the results of the implementation of your recommendations.

What Gets Planned Gets Done

To ensure the ultimate success of the implementation of your recommendations, you and your client need a plan that details the exact steps that have to be undertaken, who is responsible for carrying them out, and when they have to be done. Depending on the size of your project and the extent and complexity of your recommendations, your plan may be only a few paragraphs long, or it may go on for many pages. The best plan you can have is one you've worked out with the close participation of your client. Participation builds commitment, and commitment greatly increases the chances that your recommendations will be implemented successfully and completely.

As you work with your clients to put together project implementation plans, do the following things:

- ✔ **Define the implementation tasks.** Every good plan includes tasks that spell out each step in its completion. A plan for implementing your recommendations should also contain the tasks that ensure that the implementation phase of the consulting process is completed successfully and with a minimum of confusion and client resistance. Because your client plays such a critical role in bringing your recommendations to fruition, be sure that he or she plays a big part in defining the specifics of implementation.

    A word of caution: Defining the task correctly is very important, but sometimes the wrong tasks sneak into the plan. Before moving on to the next steps in this process, be sure that the tasks do, in fact, support the objectives and goals of the plan. Some tasks that look like they're working in support of the objectives and goals actually may not be. For example, say your recommendation is to document your client's employee hiring procedure. You've determined the procedure is fine as it is, but that it just needs to be documented. However, a task mysteriously sneaks onto the list to review the entire hiring process. While this may be a good idea, it may also be a stalling tactic on the part of your client. You need to be vigilant.

- ✔ **Define implementation task schedules.** For a plan to be effective, it must have schedules for completion. Otherwise, the people who are assigned implementation tasks don't have a sense for their priority, and they tend to let other priorities — ones with specific deadlines — take the front seat. In other instances, there may be a required sequence to the order of tasks — if the first one isn't completed the second one can't start. For every task in your implementation plan, make sure to establish a start date and an end date.

✔ **Assign roles and responsibilities.** Every task in your plan needs someone who takes responsibility for its successful and timely completion. The best way to avoid confusion in the implementation process is to assign the responsibility for each task to one and only one person. When you assign responsibility for a task to more than one person (or, heaven forbid, to a committee), no one is truly responsible for the task. Given the way that human nature often works, this can lead to confusion, dropped tasks, missed deadlines, and project failure. And that's one result that you won't want to be blamed for as a consultant who is supposed to be solving existing problems and not creating new ones.

For employees to carry out their assignments effectively, they must also have the authority and resources necessary to do so. Ensure that your client gives his or her employees the authority and resources to do the tasks they are assigned.

✔ **Consider pilot projects.** If you're working on a fairly minor set of recommendations for a fairly small organization, you probably can implement your recommendations in a straightforward manner with little or no need to do extensive testing along the way. However, as the size of the implementation phase grows, along with the possible impact on your client's employees and customers, creating a pilot project to test the implementation of your recommendations before they are actually put into service often makes sense. For example, a Web design consultant may want to set up a test Web page for a client before actually posting the real Web page to the Internet. The test page lets you check all text and graphics so that they look the way you (and your client!) want them to look and gives you a chance to ensure that the site looks good and functions well, and that the links and other features function appropriately. Pilot projects are a virtual necessity if the changes you recommend impact particularly important client business systems, such as computer-based accounting systems and inventory systems.

✔ **Define how you will assess the success of the implementation.** The final part of your implementation plan is a description of the baselines, measures, and outcomes that you will use to decide whether your implementation was successful. These link back to the original baselines, measures, expectations, and goals that you worked out and agreed to with your client at the beginning of the project. What are your client's expectations for success? What are *your* expectations? If there are differences in your client's perspective and your own, make sure that both points of view are incorporated in the overall plan. If your implementation isn't successful, you need the information from this assessment to determine why. There are two levels of assessment and measurement to consider. The first is the measurement of the individual tasks. Did they do what they were intended to do? The second is the measurement of the overall plan. By separating the two, you and your client will be able to make corrections during the process and more easily measure the overall plan.

Although you can follow any variety of formats to present your implementation plan, the plan should at least address each one of the points discussed in this section. Figure 11-1 is a sample implementation plan, based on the recommendations of an audiovisual consultant, for the installation of a new public address system in an auditorium. Note how the plan specifically incorporates the activities that should be part of an implementation plan, as described in this section.

**Kennesaw Auditorium Public Address System Upgrade
Implementation Plan**

After a thorough study of the acoustics of the Kennesaw Auditorium and a review of the adequacy of the current public address system, the project consultant — Superb Audio Associates — recommended that the current system be upgraded with the Friztek Model 1000 public address system. Implementation of this recommendation involves accomplishing the following tasks:

Task 1: Purchase new Friztek Model 1000 public address system. Superb Audio Associates will seek competition to obtain the lowest price on the Friztek equipment, purchase, and take possession of it not later than May 25.

Task 2: Remove the current public address system from the Kennesaw Auditorium. Employees of the Kennesaw Auditorium Trust will remove the current equipment and repair any resulting damage to the facility not later than June 1.

Task 3: Install new Friztek Model 1000. Superb Audio Associates will install, mount, and wire all components of the new public address system not later than June 5.

Task 4: Perform system testing. Superb Audio Associates will completely test the installed new public address system, ensuring that it meets all published specifications for power output, signal-to-noise ratio, and distortion, not later than June 7. Superb Audio Associates will be responsible for making any required adjustments to bring the equipment within specified performance limits.

Task 5: Train Kennesaw Auditorium employees in the operation of the new public address system. Superb Audio Associates will train all Kennesaw Auditorium employees in how to operate the Friztek Model 1000 public address system not later than June 10. Consultant will also be available for retraining of employees as required.

Success Measures:

Superb Audio Associates will be considered to have successfully completed the project when all of the following events occur:

- New Friztek Model 1000 public address system is installed, mounted, and wired not later than June 5.
- New Friztek Model 1000 is tested to meet all published specifications for power output, signal-to-noise ratio, and maximum distortion not later than June 7.
- All Kennesaw Auditorium employees are trained in the operation of the new Friztek Model 1000 public address system not later than June 10.

Figure 11-1:
A sample implement-
ation plan.

Regardless of how extensive the implementation is or how long it may take, a plan helps to ensure that no confusion arises over who is supposed to do what when. Of course, every implementation program can have its ups and downs. We give you some advice on avoiding the downs and maximizing the ups of your implementation in the next section.

Just Do It! Implementation Tips

Wouldn't it be nice if you could snap your fingers and have all your recommendations implemented, just like that? Unfortunately, the implementation phase of the consulting process can be difficult — for both you and your client. If you aren't careful to attend to the details, the entire thing can unravel very quickly, and your client's organization quickly moves back to where it is most comfortable: the status quo.

You can actively do several things to help ensure that your implementation comes off without a hitch (well, at least with only a few hitches here and there). To facilitate the implementation of your recommendations, you need to do the following as you work through the implementation process:

- **Deal with resistance.** If you thought that your client's employees were resistant during the data-collection phase of your project, you haven't seen anything yet. Now that your recommendations are soon to become reality within your client's organization, the people who have the most to lose with coming changes will be sure to rally their forces against you and your supporters or sponsors in a last-ditch effort to preserve the status quo. Resistance is best dealt with before it becomes entrenched in your client's organization. Whenever possible, bring the naysayers, doubters, sticks-in-the-mud, and their friends into the process as early and often as possible. Also, regularly testing as described in Chapter 9 can help you avoid big pockets of resistance. If you hope to make your recommendations last, you have to identify all the possible sources of organizational resistance and then neutralize them one by one.

- **Be realistic in your expectations.** Organizations don't change overnight. Even after a massive reorganization, line workers still do their jobs in pretty much the same way they always have. Lasting change takes time to bring about, and you must have patience as the organization slowly moves in the right direction. Be realistic in your expectations for the implementation of your recommendations. As you develop your implementation schedule, allow plenty of time for employees to soak up the changes and work them into their day-to-day work routines.

✔ **Watch out for dropped responsibilities.** The successful implementation of your recommendations requires close attention to the performance of tasks — ensuring that they are completed when they are supposed to be — and to the continued participation of all personnel assigned to carry them out. Employees resisting change commonly do so by conveniently "forgetting" to carry out their assigned duties, by simply ignoring them, or by allowing other tasks to take priority. The best way to prevent this type of behavior is to establish clear tasks, assign definite responsibilities to specific individuals, track task completion closely against the established schedule, and hold individuals accountable. Also, regularly scheduled progress review meetings can help keep everyone on track and on board.

✔ **Nourish your client partnership.** You need the complete and committed participation of your client to make the implementation of your recommendations work and ensure that it lasts. The ongoing care and feeding of your client relationship is an important factor in getting your recommendations implemented. You can demonstrate this care by keeping in touch with your clients, inviting their input and suggestions, and maintaining a good working relationship. If you find yourself on the outs with your client, your recommendations probably will soon find themselves there, too.

✔ **Beware of the perpetual implementation syndrome.** Some implementations drag on. And on. And on. Before you know it, the entire project — recommendations and all — falls off the radar screen and everyone forgets that it ever happened. By allowing implementations to drag on without end, you risk letting all your work go to waste. Be sure to work closely with your clients to establish a firm implementation schedule that has a clear beginning and a clear end — one that is written in terms of weeks or, at most, months, not years. Exact timetables depend on the nature of the project — its complexity and the desired speed of implementation — along with the availability of required client resources and support.

By following this advice, you're doing just about everything you can to do your part in the implementation process. Don't forget that your clients must do their part, too. As the old saying goes, you can lead a horse to water, but you can't make him drink. You can't force your clients to implement your recommendations. All you can do is to point out the many benefits to their organizations by following your prescription for change. If they decide to ignore your advice, the decision is theirs to make, and you have to accept it and move on. As we mentioned earlier, however, don't give up until you're convinced that your point of view has been given serious consideration by your client.

The final step in the implementation phase of the consulting process is to assess the results of the project. We just happen to cover this topic in the next section.

Assessing the Results

So, you've reached the end of your consulting project. It was a long haul, but you managed to develop a great set of recommendations with your client. In addition, those recommendations were implemented just as you planned. How do you determine whether they had the effect you intended? You do so by assessing the results of your project implementation and then comparing the results to your original plan.

Fortunately, assessing the results of your recommendations is fairly simple because you took the time at the beginning to develop a detailed implementation plan that you can now use to measure the results. (You did create an implementation plan, didn't you?) Here's how to assess the results of your project implementation:

1. **Gather data.**

   Just as you gathered information in the data-collection phase of the consulting process, you need to gather data that tells you whether your recommendations are working. Some results of your recommendations may be readily apparent; others may take months or even years to come about. If, for example, you are implementing changes that impact employee morale, surveys may tell you within a few weeks whether morale is improved. However, changes to large and complex manufacturing systems to improve product quality may require many months of gathering product quality data to show whether the recommendations are working. Whatever the case, you don't know which way your project went until you collect the data that tells you whether it was a success.

2. **Assess progress against plan.**

   Keep close tabs on the progress of all implementation tasks against the plan you created. Depending on the nature of the project — its complexity and speed of implementation — daily or weekly checks wouldn't be too often. Assess whether some tasks should be accelerated or whether the schedules for other tasks should be lengthened.

3. **Assess your client's satisfaction and view of your effectiveness.**

   One of the most important measures of success (some may say the only measure worth worrying about) is how satisfied your client is with the implementation of your recommendations and his or her view of your effectiveness as a consultant. Ask questions; send surveys; call your client. How you choose to solicit and measure your client's satisfaction is up to you. The important thing is that you ask.

4. **Assess your own satisfaction and view of your effectiveness.**

   Project satisfaction is a two-way street. Consider whether you were satisfied with the project. Did you handle your client in the right way? Did you approach the project in the most effective way possible? Would you change anything about what you did and how you did it? Do you want to do future work with this client? Did you make any money on the project, or did your work turn out to be pro bono? Ask yourself these questions and others like them to gauge your own level of satisfaction.

5. **Write an impact study.**

   This is a definite discipline of top-quality consulting firms. Writing an impact study forces you to document lessons, both positive and negative, that ensure that your process improves consistently and that provide valuable marketing data for future clients.

6. **Use feedback to adjust future projects.**

   As you obtain feedback on the way you conducted the project and implementation, note the information that you should keep in mind for future projects. Use this feedback to adjust the way you approach the different steps of the consulting process — defining the problem, collecting data, diagnosing, presenting your recommendations, and implementing them. No one knows everything there is to know about consulting, and you can always discover something new that helps you do an even better job the next time.

As you can see, assessing your project — whether it's the most successful project you've ever pulled off or the least so — is the way that you and your client's organization learn. By obtaining feedback and using it to figure out what you did right and wrong, you can improve your services to clients and become a better consultant. You can gain new insights from every project you participate in and every client you work with, and doing so is always in your best interest.

Part IV
Selling Your Consulting Services

The 5th Wave   By Rich Tennant

Gesundheit.

In this part . . .

It's one thing to have a great idea, but it's another thing altogether to attract the attention (and money!) of the clients you need to make your consulting business take off and grow over a sustained period of time. In this part, we explore the sales process and present strategies for publicizing your business and building business through referrals and with new clients.

Chapter 12

The ABCs of Selling

So, you've got a great consulting thing going. Either you're working for a consulting firm, or you own and operate one yourself. Either way, you'll quickly notice something: If you want to stay in business, you have to keep a steady flow of new business coming into your firm. To accomplish this often means becoming a pretty competent salesperson. This is especially the case if you have your own consulting business — you may be the one and only person who sells projects to clients, signs the agreements, and delivers your company's services. As long as you sell new work — whether to current or new clients — the cash you need to run your business and pay your bills will keep making its way into your bank account. Fail to sell new work, however, and that bank account will soon be a very dusty and lonely place.

Even if you work for someone else you may be called upon to participate in the selling process. You may call on prospective clients to pitch the merits of your firm or your approach to doing business, or you may sell current clients by way of your great project performance and excellent service. Indeed, many consulting firms expect their consultants to take an active role in the selling process.

Whatever your situation may be, your future success — and the future success of your consulting firm — may very well depend on your own ability to sell. This is why we devote an entire (very large) chapter to this important topic.

The Classic Selling Process

So, what exactly is this selling process we keep talking about? The classic selling process comprises seven parts, which we consider in detail in this section. This generic process is good enough to get you through selling your consulting services at almost any level, but some alternatives are gaining popularity. We cover two such alternative approaches — relationship selling and the SPIN selling model — at the end of this chapter.

Prospecting for leads

Before you can sell your services, you've got to find prospective clients. Prospecting for leads is all about finding those prospective clients. Many salespeople dedicate a significant portion of their day-to-day schedules to prospecting. Generally, the more leads you can gather — especially *qualified* leads — the greater your chances of making a sale. This first step in the sales process is so important that some companies have dedicated staff whose sole job is to generate leads.

Leads can come from a number of different places — some expected, and some not — including

- **Networking:** Selling is a very social process, built on relationships. Who do you know who may be interested in buying what you have to sell? Who do *they* know who may be interested in what you have to sell? Are there professional groups, clubs, or associations you can join that will increase your exposure to prospective clients? Many people join chambers of commerce, industry associations, and the boards of local non-profits for this very reason.

- **Referrals:** Are you taking care of your current clients? If so, they're highly likely to become an excellent source of referrals — prospective clients who come to you already sold to some extent. Because your clients have recommended you to them, much of your selling work has been done for you.

- **Cold calls:** Making cold calls to prospective clients — that is, contacting prospects you don't already know to see whether they may be interested in your services — is a time-honored and sometimes effective tradition in selling. Truth be told, your chances of landing a client as a result of cold calling increase dramatically when you've done your homework and limit such calls to prospects you've determined are most likely to need your services. Shot-gunning hundreds or even thousands of prospects who are unlikely to buy from you is a waste of your time and money.

✔ **Promotions:** Promotions cover a wide variety of different approaches to enticing prospects into giving you the information you need to contact them, including contests, coupons, and freebies. For example, you might offer prospects free admission to your investment seminar as a way of attracting prospects and then gathering their contact information, or you might offer visitors to your Web site a free subscription to your online newsletter in exchange for their e-mail address. Not only will you get contact information for people who are interested in your offers (which you can then use to make follow-up sales calls), but anyone who follows through can also be considered a solid sales lead.

✔ **Mailing lists:** A number of companies sell mailing lists of individuals and companies that may find your consulting services of interest. You can buy or rent these lists and use them for client prospecting. Be sure you narrowly define your selection criteria to improve your chances of prospecting success, and design your mailing piece in such a way that you can track the results of that effort.

✔ **Walk-ins:** Believe it or not, every once in a while a prospect will contact you out of the blue — perhaps as a result of seeing your name in the newspaper, or running across your Web site (you've got a Web site, right?), or reading the comment left on a blog by a happy client. Be ready for walk-ins, and treat them well.

Before you go running off to look for prospects, however, first take a few moments to focus your efforts by considering who your ideal client really is. You can do this by asking questions like these:

✔ What kinds of problems can your consulting firm solve?

✔ Who needs these problems solved?

✔ Where are these prospects located — across town, across the country, around the world?

✔ Are they individuals or businesses?

✔ What are their exact needs?

✔ What is most important to your prospects?

✔ What is least important to your prospects?

✔ What advantages does your firm offer over your competitors?

✔ Can you communicate these advantages effectively to your prospects?

Use the answers to these questions and others like them to build a model of your most likely prospects. Determine who they are, where they are, what their needs are, and how you will address them. While you don't want to be too narrow in your focus, which may cause you to overlook many likely future clients, you also don't want to cast your net too widely. Doing so may overwhelm you with prospects who aren't really right for you or your business — wasting your time and theirs.

Sage advice from Peter Psichogios, an expert at selling consulting services (Part I)

When it comes to selling consulting services, some people are good at it, and some not so good. Peter Psichogios (San Diego, California) is an expert in this department. Peter brings over 20 years of experience, delivering stellar results and celebrity service to client projects. Before founding the Celebrity Service Institute, Peter served as CEO of one of the most successful e-learning companies in the sales and service space. Prior to that, Peter served as an executive member of one of the largest Instructional System Association companies in the world. In this role Peter managed the sales organization, trainers, facilitators, and consultants. We spoke with Peter to get his unique perspective on the process of selling consulting services.

Consulting For Dummies: Do you follow a defined selling process?

Peter Psichogios: I don't follow a prescribed sales process; I use an amalgamated approach. I believe you first have to clearly identify the situation and the potential opportunities for improvement. Consulting is selling the invisible, as it is an intangible. What I mean by that is the results manifest at some point in the future. I believe it is critical to help your client monetize the potential gap or opportunity for improvement. When your current or potential client understands both the direct and indirect cost of the issue you are addressing, then it makes the selling process much easier. As an example, if you can educate the client and mutually agree that there is a $20 million opportunity for improvement and the solution or implementation that you're proposing is going to require an investment of $800,000, while that is a significant investment, given that you've just agreed that the potential ROI is $20 million, it makes it a much different discussion.

I believe you really have to take the future benefits and the payoffs of your solution or process out of the ether and turn them into a tangible monetary number that is compelling. Once you have the opportunities for improvement identified, then it's best to move into the implications to the organization if the opportunities or problems aren't addressed. In the case of employee turnover, for example, many people look only at the cost of replacing that person. But the true implications of the cost are actually significantly higher when you consider the stresses upon the organization, the intelligence that is lost when the employee leaves, the cost of retraining, the cost of not having continuity in who is serving the client, the disruptions for the customers who might see a different face, and more.

So, the selling process really needs to be more of a discussion about the desired future state, prioritizing the most important or critical steps to start closing the gaps, then building action plans and timelines. Selling then really becomes planning as we've already agreed that we have a significant opportunity for improvement, whether it be gains at the top line or providing cost reductions by reducing scrap or waste. However, this can only be possible once you have monetized the gap in between the current and future desired state.

What I have found in my various consulting businesses is that the ideal relationship becomes more of a partnership where the consulting staff and the client staff actually come together and develop a joint value proposition. My goal is to make it as hard as possible for the employees of our clients to tell whether we worked for them or with them. I truly believe it's about getting to a partnering orientation and moving away from a sales orientation.

CFD: Tell us how you go about closing a deal.

Psichogios: Many times the person you're selling to isn't the person who can write the check. So one of the key metrics or variables in closing business is you have to be in front of the person who can say yes. I rarely talk money until I know that I'm in front of the person who can say yes, so I insist on getting with the people who can say yes and informing them about what the costs are going to be. We want to make sure that the decision-maker is in the game, that we have access, and that he or she is committed to doing something. Then and only then do I think it makes sense to talk about the cost of doing something — the investment. My success rate following this approach is over 85 percent. But you'll notice I did not talk about close rate, because my whole mindset is about opening up business and building relationships, not closing anything. Some people reading this might think 85 percent is high, and I'm proud to say it is. However, there is a caveat. I do very good client selection. You have to pick clients that are the right size, scale, and scope for your consulting firm. It's also important to get line or operational management people to endorse and embrace your solution. Even if somebody else is going to fund it, it's the operations people — the line management — who will either kill it or embrace it. Getting them on your side takes one of the biggest obstacles off the plate.

CFD: It seems like many clients get hung up on hourly fees and don't look at the big picture of the value that consultants provide. How do you deal with this?

Psichogios: My experience has shown that when you're selling to someone, and he or she becomes focused on the fee, one of two things has happened. One, you haven't done the job to link your solution to a strategic value proposition of the overall business case of the organization. Second, you're probably dealing with somebody who's not responsible for the macro or aggregated goal of the organization. That usually means you're talking to the wrong person. At the end of the day, everybody wants to know what they're going to pay for your services. I strongly dissuade anybody who's in the consulting game from getting into an hourly billing situation. When I was running a pure performance consulting company, we charged flat fees and we would not unbundle our solutions. Obviously at some point we need to incorporate time into our overall solution, but we're really selling results or outcomes to our clients. I see selling a bundled solution as the way to do it. Some clients may insist that you unbundle, and you may choose to break it down sometimes, but I just don't think it ever makes sense to engage in discussions of hourly or billable rates. If you've done your front-end work right, you've provided value, and you're with the right person, I think it makes much more sense to focus on the value your firm is going to bring, and work on the long-term partnership that you're forging.

(See "Sage advice from Peter Psichogios, an expert at selling consulting services (Part II)" later in this chapter for more words of wisdom.)

Qualifying your leads

All leads are not created equal. Some prospects may want to buy your products and services but not be able to afford them, while others may be able to afford them, but not see a compelling reason to buy them. Qualifying your leads will help you figure out who is ready, willing, and able to buy from you, so you can focus your efforts on those leads that are most likely to pay off.

When Peter used to work in the wonderful world of software development, his marketing folks used to prioritize sales leads in the following way:

- ✔ **First priority:** Sell existing products/services to current customers.

- ✔ **Second priority:** Sell new products/services to current customers.

- ✔ **Third priority:** Sell existing products/services to new customers.

- ✔ **Fourth priority:** Sell new products/services to new customers.

The point here is that your strongest and most highly qualified sales leads are almost always going to be your current clients. This makes sense because they already know and trust you. And, chances are, you'll have much better luck selling them what they're familiar with than trying to introduce them to something new. So, keep your primary focus on your current clients. Make sure they're happy with your services, and give them good reasons to want to purchase even more of what you've got to sell (and to refer their own colleagues and associates to you).

Of course, you'll always need to keep a constant inflow of new clients — not just to grow your business, but also to keep up as some current clients inevitably fade away. For that reason, you need to qualify your leads. Here are some questions to ask for doing just that:

- ✔ **Do they need what you've got to sell?** Be honest now — does your lead really need what you're selling? Say you're a management consultant for fast-growing technology businesses. Trying to sell your services to a slow-growing government agency wouldn't make much sense for you, would it? (*Hint:* No.) Be sure your prospects really need you and your consulting firm.

- ✔ **Do they have the necessary funds?** You may find that a lot of prospects need your excellent consulting services, but really can't afford the price. When you run into a prospect like that, you have essentially two choices: Move on to a different prospect, or lower your prices. Unless your prices are entirely out of whack, moving on is probably better in most cases.

- ✔ **Can you get to the decision-maker?** Generally, if you hope to gain success in your consulting sales efforts, you need to get your proposal in front of someone within your client's organization who can make a decision in favor of contracting with your firm. Countless salespeople have wasted billions — perhaps even trillions — of their precious hours barking up the wrong tree and trying to sell something to someone who doesn't have the authority, budget, or responsibility to buy it. If you can't get to a decision-maker, you should probably write off that particular lead.

- ✔ **Will you be able to convince them of the value you bring?** Some prospects will be easier to convince than others — and some will never be convinced, no matter how much value you bring to the table.

Unfortunately, some clients-to-be will focus on your hourly rate — even when you can potentially save them millions of dollars. If they can't see the value, then these leads may ultimately be a waste of your time.

✔ **Are they in a position to buy from you?** In some cases, a client will need to have already purchased and used certain products or services before whatever it is you sell will be appropriate for them. For example, it would be hard for you to optimize a prospect's computerized customer relationship management (CRM) program if they're still using Rolodex cards to track all their sales contacts.

Consider an old sales maxim — the *8-4-2-1 rule*. According to this rule, out of every eight qualified leads you bring into your business, you'll get four sales presentations, which will result in two sales quotes, which will ultimately lead to just one sale. While we don't know if this particular rule is precisely accurate, we do know that it's true in a general sense. Out of any group of qualified leads, only a fraction will actually turn into clients. The higher the quality of your leads, the higher that fraction will be.

When it comes to qualifying your leads, be smart, and be sure to take off your rose-colored glasses. Not everyone is qualified to be your client. Some prospects don't need your consulting services, some can't afford them, and some will never understand just how much they really need them. In any case, your job is to focus on your very *best* prospects, and to ignore the rest. Ultimately, you're the one who has to decide which are which.

Preparing to make your pitch

Before you present a proposal or quote — or make your pitch — to a prospective client, you need to consider and take care of a number of things. Calling on a prospect without knowing what their needs are and how you can best respond is a sure way to get your proposal rejected. As the old Boy Scout saying goes, *Be prepared!* Here are some things to consider as you prepare to make your pitch:

✔ **Figure out who the decision-maker is, and how best to get to him.** You're wasting your time if you make your pitch to someone who can't approve working with your firm. Take time to find out who the decision-makers are in your targeted organization, and then chart out a strategy for getting in touch with them. Many managers and executives have assistants (also known as *gatekeepers*) who specialize in keeping sales people away from their bosses. There are many ways to deal with this obstacle — from schmoozing the gatekeepers to making a direct approach to the decision-maker via phone call or e-mail to simply making an appointment. The best approach is the one that works best for you and your clients-to-be.

✔ **Research, research, research.** Using Internet search engines such as Google and Yahoo!, you can find a lot of information about prospective clients — information that can provide you with insights into their challenges and opportunities, and help guide the development of your proposal. This research can turn up information about the products and services they buy; their organizational structure and leadership hierarchy; key contacts, phone numbers, and e-mail addresses; news; and much more. Not only can this information help you better understand your prospect's problems, but it can also provide you with ideas for structuring solutions.

✔ **Make initial contact.** When it's appropriate, you can make initial contact before your sales call to discuss your client's issues and then scope out a solution. This will enable you to make an actual pitch in your first client meeting rather than using the meeting to scope a problem and then delivering a proposal later. If your solution and pricing are fairly straightforward, you should be able to do this relatively easily. However, if your solution is complex and the pricing is not standardized, you'll most likely need to actually meet with your client — in person or on the phone — before you can make an effective pitch.

✔ **Create your proposal or quote.** If you've already spent some time talking with your prospective client about their problems, challenges, and opportunities — and you've had time to define and price possible solutions — then by all means create a proposal to take with you when you make your pitch. If you need to spend time with your client before you develop your proposal, then wait until you've finished doing your homework. For details on creating a winning proposal, see Chapter 7.

The better prepared you are to make your pitch, the better your chances of finding success with your prospective clients. Take time to work your way through the above list before your next client sales call.

Making your pitch

After you've outlined your clients' issues and problems and you've developed solutions and prices to implement them, it's time to make your pitch. The better prepared you are for this moment, the better your chances of success (see the preceding section for more details on getting prepared). Every step in the selling process has led you to this point. Now go get 'em, tiger!

The U.S. Small Business Administration offers the following advice for making effective sales pitches:

✔ **Know what to say, even if you don't say it.** Understand your approach and solutions fully — from the most basic parts all the way up to those detailed specifics that clients love to ask about when you least expect it.

Rather than foundering for an answer that you just can't seem to pull out of the depths of your mental archives, be ready for whatever questions come your way.

✔ **Organize around your key selling points.** You don't have much time to get your prospect's attention. According to research, the first 30 seconds are pretty much the limit. Lose your prospect's attention, and you'll have one heck of a time getting it back. Be sure your sales pitch is organized, with a natural flow that takes your client from problems to solutions in a logical manner. And be sure to limit your key selling points to just three or four at the most. Offer any more than that and you'll lose the impact you need to sell your client.

✔ **Be flexible.** If there's one thing to expect during the course of almost any sales pitch, it's to expect the unexpected. Be ready at any time to take your carefully prepared proposal and throw it out the window when a prospective client wants to move in a different direction. This is a common occurrence, and you should be prepared to deal with it. Be light, be nimble, and always be ready to change your approach to adapt to your client's needs.

✔ **Be honest.** To make a sale, some salespeople end up telling their prospective clients what they want to hear, even if it isn't true. Don't fall victim to this temptation. It's always better to be honest about what your consulting firm can and can't do, and what your client can reasonably expect as a result of hiring you. It's better to lose a prospect or two when you both realize that your firm isn't the best fit for them, than to lose a contract when you prove it later.

Making your pitch is perhaps the most important step in the sales process, and your ability to do it well goes a long way in determining your success as a consultant. Believe us, practice makes perfect. The more sales pitches you make to prospective clients, the better you'll get at it. Always be on the lookout for ways to make your pitches better and become alert to the approaches that work — and the ones that don't. Then do more of the former and less of the latter.

Addressing client concerns

While some sales pitches will go smoothly, with your client-to-be perhaps asking only a couple of minor questions here or there, other sales pitches may have you feeling like you've just gone through the Inquisition. Some clients are bound to feel that your proposal doesn't address their needs, that you've missed the mark on describing the problem, that your solution is the wrong one, that your price is too high, or that your schedule is inadequate. Now what?

First, understand that when a client expresses doubts or concerns, that shows that he or she is listening to what you have to say and isn't just tuning you out. This is a good thing. Next, here are some tips for addressing client concerns:

- ✔ **Deal with misunderstandings.** Some client concerns are simply the result of misunderstandings — of your approach, of your pricing, or of some other aspect of your proposal. Dig deep to identify any misunderstandings that may have crept into your client's mind, and defuse them immediately — before they can become permanent obstacles to your deal.

- ✔ **Deal with lack of urgency.** Some clients may not fully appreciate the importance of dealing with a problem before it grows larger or capitalizing on an opportunity while it is still available. Or they may simply be too busy dealing with other matters to focus on the matters that you bring up in your proposal. Clearly explain the issues or opportunities that you have unearthed, and explain how ignoring them will cause the problems to grow and the opportunities to disappear. Build a sense of urgency in your clients-to-be.

- ✔ **Deal with lack of perceived need.** Prospects may not make the connection between the problems or opportunities that they have and your proposed approach. If this is the case, then you haven't done an adequate job of presenting the issues or opportunities, nor the value that you bring to the table. Pay close attention to your client's objections in this area and use objective data and responses to help tip the balance in your favor.

- ✔ **Deal with funding issues.** Sometimes a client has a real lack of funding and nothing you do will solve it, and sometimes a client has a *perceived* lack of funding. In the latter situation, you can do a lot to help your prospective client realize that he or she *does* have the resources available to pay for your consulting services. Show your client how much money the organization will save when they bring you on — perhaps far more than the fee that you will charge. Offer to allow monthly progress payments or other payment arrangements that make it easier for your client to say *yes*.

- ✔ **Deal with lack of trust.** What if your prospective client doesn't think she is dealing with the right person (you!) or the right consulting firm (yours!)? Perhaps you haven't spent enough time with your prospect to establish the firm foundation of trust that you need to sell effectively, or maybe other concerns need to be addressed before you can build trust. Ferret these out and deal with them so that trust is built and this source of objections is no longer an obstacle to your sales efforts.

Once you have successfully addressed your client's concerns, you can move on to the next step in the selling process: closing the sale. Many sales are lost in this transition — much as a fish will often jump off the hook and escape as he is being reeled in. It's your job to reel those prospects in and close the deal.

Closing the sale

Reaching agreement with a client — that is, closing the sale — is a powerful, and sometimes mysterious, part of the selling process. This is where all your powers of persuasion and understanding of human nature are put to the test. As the moment approaches, you've got to be ready for it by saying the right thing at the right time — making a very specific offer to your prospect while gauging his response closely.

The best closings are ones where your client is the one who initiates the closing process of her own volition — for example, "You're right — we can't wait any longer to get you on the job. I'll send out a contract to you tomorrow with the terms you set forth in your proposal." This is music to any consultant's ears.

The worst closings are the ones that require you to push your clients into an agreement that they seem not to actually want to enter into. In this situation, you have to decide whether simply dealing with the client sales resistance (as outlined in the previous section) will get you to your goal, or whether you should back off, fold up your tent, and move on — before your client-to-be throws you out.

If you decide to move to closing — the normal situation in most cases — consider the following:

- ✔ **Look for signals that the client is ready to buy.** If your prospect is interested in your pitch, asks good questions, and indicates that he wants to move forward, then you know it's time to close the deal.

- ✔ **Overcome any final client concerns.** If there are any lingering client concerns, now is the time to deal with them.

- ✔ **Reassure your client.** Let your client know that she is making the right choice in hiring your consulting firm to do the work you've proposed, and hold her hand throughout the process.

- ✔ **Don't be too pushy.** Again, if you've moved your client through the preceding steps in the selling process and the client is still interested, you don't need to push him to get the deal you seek. Pushing clients too hard will either anger them or convince them that what they need to do is find a less obnoxious consultant.

- ✔ **Shake on it.** When you reach agreement, seal the deal by shaking hands with your client and expressing your thanks. These simple actions will help encourage your client to follow through with your agreement and set the stage for building a strong, long-term relationship.

If you don't close your deal and reach agreement on a contract for your consulting services, then you've potentially spent a lot of time with nothing to show for it. If this happens with a number of prospects, it can be devastating for your business. However, if you've followed the selling process to this point and have willingly brought your prospective client along with you, chances are that the closing will happen quickly and with little prodding from you. And that's really a dream come true.

Following up

There may be much celebrating and back-patting when at long last a sale is made and a new client is signed on (or an old client signs up for more work) but the sales process hasn't ended yet. In fact, in many ways, it has just begun.

Following up with clients after you sell them your consulting services is a key ingredient in the recipe of developing long-term client relationships — the kind that every consultant worth his or her salt dreams of — and it's the never-ending part of the sales process. You see, if all you care about is landing a client — at the expense of following through to make sure the client is satisfied with the results you provide — then your client will eventually figure that out and act accordingly. In most cases, acting accordingly means either cancelling your contract or rejecting any future contracts with your firm.

However, when you treat clients like partners and keep up with their projects and the state of their satisfaction — or lack thereof — you're building clients for life.

There's a right way and a wrong way to follow up with your clients. Here's a list of the right ways:

- ✔ **Get a signed contract.** The very first follow-up item after shaking on the deal should be to get the contract signed and collect your initial payment if it's a part of the deal.

- ✔ **Work on that relationship.** Now that you've got that client you've been chasing, you can (and should) work on building a solid, long-term relationship. You can do this by first doing good work — on time and within budget — and by building an ongoing dialog with your client. Ideally, you will establish a mutually beneficial partnership, where you look out for your client's interests and your client looks out for yours.

- ✔ **Drop in for a visit (or two or three).** Sure, you can give your client a call or you can send out an e-mail, letter, or fax, but nothing tells a client that you really care more than taking time out of your schedule to visit their offices. You can do this on a regular basis, whether or not you've got a presentation to make or business to do. While you're there, it doesn't hurt to take your client out for lunch or dinner, either.

- ✔ **It's called a telephone (use it!).** When you're miles away from your clients, jumping on an airplane every time you want to say hello isn't always going to be your best option. A good substitute is a simple phone call. With the proliferation of e-mail, blogs, and other online forms of communication, telephones have taken a bit of a back seat. Don't neglect your phone. Call your clients on a regular basis to check in on projects, gauge satisfaction, suggest additional solutions, or simply to say hello. Your clients will appreciate the personal touch, and you'll appreciate their business.

✔ **Send letters and e-mail messages.** While letters and handwritten notes are increasingly finding themselves on the endangered species list, e-mail messages have become endemic in most organizations. While it's fine to use e-mail to communicate with clients and follow up after the sale, mix it up with letters and handwritten notes and cards. When you do something special for a client, like sending a handwritten note, he or she will notice, and that's a good thing.

The sales process doesn't end when you sign a contract with a client. It continues as you deliver your consulting services, and often beyond. Make following up with clients a regular part of the way you do business. The relationships you build will make the time you spend doing this very well worth your while.

Considering New-and-Improved Selling Methods

Selling experts have devised a number of new-and-improved, alternative approaches that can be successfully used to achieve even better results. In the sections that follow, we focus on two such alternative approaches: relationship selling and the SPIN selling model.

Relationship selling

While the classic selling process described in the previous section will take you a long way towards achieving your goals of sales success, the emphasis recently has been on the importance of doing one more thing: building long-term relationships with clients. This move from *transaction* selling (which focuses on maximizing the number of sales) to *relationship* selling (which focuses on building ongoing, long-term relationships with clients) has resulted in increased sales and decreased selling costs for those who have practiced it.

Consider the example of a pushy, used-car dealer who will seemingly stop at nothing to get you to buy a car — *any* car — right now! Your credit's bad? No problem — we do our own auto financing. Don't like the color? No sweat — we've got every color of the rainbow out on the lot. You want a two-door and not a four-door? Nothing to it — we'll have our body shop weld two of the doors shut for you. And, of course, the ultimate weapon of the transaction salesperson: This offer is good for today only.

Sage advice from Peter Psichogios, an expert at selling consulting services (Part II)

See "Sage advice from Peter Psichogios, an expert at selling consulting services (Part I)" earlier in this chapter for the beginning of our conversation with consultant selling expert Peter Psichogios (San Diego, California).

Consulting For Dummies: Is it true that you sometimes offer clients guaranteed results, whereby they don't have to pay unless your results stick?

Peter Psichogios: If it's the right environment, absolutely. However, I have to have access to senior leaders, and they have to be committed to changing policies and procedures if they're getting in the way. There has to be some type of ongoing access to decision-makers, along with coaching and feedback.

CFD: How do you engage your prospective clients?

Psichogios: On the front end, I let them know very clearly from the beginning that we view this as a mutual selection process. In the case of the firms that I have run, I explain that we didn't have 40,000 consultants marching around the planet billing hours. I explain we were a firm that sustained itself to ensure we had intimate relationships with our clients and that we had to have a strong conviction that we could produce sustainable results. We know that we can't do that without an engaged senior leadership team — they have to do the right thing. I'm real clear when I say, "We're selecting you as much as you're selecting us." They will often ask, "How do you make your selection?" It creates an entirely different dynamic — especially when we say, "We picked you because we think you're an organization that we can help. But we have to make sure that you're really committed." I put requirements on them because it's a mutual partnership. They can't

just write a check and expect the results to follow. There are things they're going to have to do and I make it real clear what their role is and what our role is. I once gave millions back to a client because they weren't taking the required actions to produce the results that we both wanted. My experience has proven that it's much better to unwind from a client, even if there are multimillions of dollars at stake, than to continue to perform services or offer advice if they aren't taking the required actions or steps to close the performance gaps. To some degree, it's the best advertising you could do if you're really focused on creating long-term partnerships, and if you're really focused on results. I'd rather do this than end up with a bad situation that negatively affects your reputation and your firm's reputation, and typically a bad client will cause stress in your organization that negatively affects other clients as well.

CFD: Do those requirements actually end up in your written consulting agreements?

Psichogios: If we're doing a performance guarantee, those mutual commitments are dialed into the agreement. They've got to do their part, too. It'd be like you going to the doctor and the doctor saying, "You're going to have a heart attack if you don't stop smoking, and you'd better start exercising — and take your drinking down from two bottles of wine to maybe one glass a day. If you follow the recommendations, we can help you, but if you don't, then we're not responsible." We can give our clients the right answers, but if they don't care to implement them, then we're not responsible for the lack of results. But if they do their part, then we guarantee the results. We are basically accountability people. We help people follow through because anything that they follow through on will make a difference.

CFD: What is the one piece of advice you would give to a consultant who's really trying to grow his business?

Psichogios: It's hard to give you just one answer, but if I would give advice to anyone who is consulting and trying to grow their practice it would be to become a valuable resource for the client first, and figure out how to help your client help their customers. If you can focus on your customers' customers — and help them solve their problems and serve their customers better — you become an invaluable resource. If you come in there talking about your product, your solution, and your billable days, you may help them, but you're not going to be seen as a long-term partner. The other piece of advice I would offer is when things go bad, *that's* the time to over-communicate. Clients expect you to run away when things go wrong. When you dig in and say, "Hey, it's not working like either of us want, but we're not going away and we're going to dig in and make it right," you earn their respect forever. When things aren't perfect, most consultants become unavailable or make excuses. When you just say, "I don't care whose fault it is, we're going to dig in and make it right, and not worry about getting paid for that day," you're going to get paid for *many* days.

When you're engaged in relationship-based selling, you're focused on

- Building long-term relationships with clients
- Being totally committed to clients
- Talking to your clients continuously
- Selling the benefits of your services to clients
- Consistently providing the highest levels of customer service

If you're ready to make the move to relationship selling, then your most expeditious route there will be to work on building trust and creating bonds with your clients while being empathetic to their needs and challenges. The idea is to focus on your client — and your client's needs — first and foremost. Once you build a strong, long-term relationship, the selling will come naturally.

Extra credit: The SPIN model

As a result of his 12-year research study on sales excellence, Neil Rackham, a behavioral psychologist and author of *SPIN Selling* (McGraw-Hill), developed a selling process that is particularly effective for consultants. This process, known by its acronym, SPIN, suggests that salespeople can ask a sequence of four specific kinds of questions to encourage prospects to both help define their problems or challenges and express their desire to find solutions.

The four kinds of SPIN questions — asked by salespeople, in this particular order — are

- ✔ **Situation questions:** These questions are used to gather general information about the prospect's business, market environment, customers, and related areas. For example, "Exactly what business are you in?" Situation questions create a context for the next type of question — problem questions. Rackham cautions salespeople against overusing these basic questions because prospects often find them boring. Do your research first.

- ✔ **Problem questions:** These questions are used to identify and zero in on areas of prospect dissatisfaction — what Rackham calls *implied needs*. For example, "Are you finding it a challenge to recruit and retain talented employees?" Asking these questions enables you to discover problems that provide you with opportunities to offer solutions. According to Rackham's research, these questions are particularly important in smaller transactions.

- ✔ **Implication questions:** These questions take the answers to problem questions to the next level, by helping the prospect understand the negative consequences of problems to the organization. For example, "How much does it cost your organization to recruit a replacement when one of your employees decides to leave?" According to Rackham's research, these questions are particularly important — perhaps essential — in larger transactions.

- ✔ **Need-payoff questions:** These questions are used to show your prospect the value (in terms of money saved, time saved, additional problems averted, opportunities capitalized on, and so forth) that your solution will bring to his or her organization. For example, "If I can solve your employee retention problem, how much money would your company save in a year's time?" According to Rackham, asking need-payoff questions will compel prospects to state their explicit needs, allowing the salesperson (you!) to present the benefits of his unique solution.

By walking through these questions, a salesperson can help prospective clients focus on potential solutions while defusing objections and increasing buy-in. Long story short, SPIN selling is an approach that any consultant should consider taking out for a spin. Who knows where it may take you?

Chapter 13

Getting the Word Out: Promoting Your Business

In This Chapter

▶ Lending a human touch to your promotions with personal selling

▶ Seeking the spotlight through public relations and publicity

▶ Exploring advertising channels to reach the masses

▶ Keeping your name in the forefront through freebies and sales promotions

▶ Creating a marketing plan and evaluating how well it works

*P*romotion is informing your potential clients that you have a product or service that they need. Unfortunately, very few products (with the possible exception of whatever product Apple happens to have on its drawing board for next year) sell themselves. Most products — including consulting services — need to be promoted in order to sell in quantities sufficient to maintain a business. If you're lucky, word-of-mouth advertising and referrals may be enough to sustain your business, but even then an element of promotion is involved when the client-to-be contacts you, the consultant, and you must *sell* the client on the wisdom of having you do the proposed work. You promote yourself by using various channels of communication to inform and to persuade prospective clients.

You can promote your firm and its products and services in four main ways: personal selling, public relations and publicity, advertising, and sales promotions (we define each category later in this chapter). Some consultants use a mix of all four categories of promotional techniques, while others pick and choose from the list. We suggest that you develop a mix of techniques from each key promotional category. Although these listings are quite comprehensive, you can promote your business in other ways as well. Don't hesitate to be creative and try something new!

After you review the many different ways to promote your business, you need to develop a marketing plan that incorporates your selected mix of the approaches and techniques. You'll find information on developing a marketing plan later in this chapter. All these approaches must be integrated to present and reinforce the professional image you are trying to project. Don't forget to closely monitor the results of your promotional efforts and to fine-tune your approach based on your market feedback.

Getting Up Close and Personal with Personal Selling

Personal selling is promotion by person-to-person communications directly between you — or representatives of your business — and your prospective clients. Consulting is built on relationships, and personal selling is the cornerstone of many consultants' promotional efforts. *Networking* — or building contacts with new clients through personal selling and referrals from current clients or associates — is a very effective way for you to promote your consulting business. Some kinds of consultants — legal, financial, and medical consultants, for example — primarily use personal selling to find qualified prospects.

Here are some of the ways that consultants promote their services through personal selling:

- ✔ **Face-to-face meetings:** Nothing promotes your business and its products or services like a good old-fashioned, one-on-one meeting with a client. The advantages are endless: You can tailor your message to the individual client with whom you are meeting, gauge his or her reaction in real time, and then adapt your message to address any concerns that your client may express. In these days of "technology this" and "technology that," people seem to find the human touch very comforting.

- ✔ **Telephone calls:** If you can't meet with someone in person, you can use the telephone to promote your business. If you have new information of interest to your clients or just want to keep in touch, most clients will welcome your call. Although you miss the nonverbal cues that you pick up in a personal meeting, you can call far more clients in a day than you can meet with in person.

- ✔ **Letters and e-mail messages:** Keep in touch with your clients and your highest-potential prospective clients by occasionally writing them a personal letter or e-mail message. Your clients will appreciate that you took the time to keep in touch, and they're much more likely to remember you when they need to hire a consultant. If you can include a newspaper or magazine clipping, brochure, or link to your Web site highlighting your business or products or something they may be interested in professionally or personally, then by all means do so. It's a small investment to make for a potentially high payoff.

✔ **Blogs and Internet forums:** Today, you can find blogs and Internet forums on just about any topic you can imagine. There are blogs and forums for small-business owners, scriptwriters, engineers, doctors, and just about every other profession. Savvy clients search these boards for talented consultants to do work for them. For example, more than a few consultants receive unsolicited requests to perform consulting work because of their posts on blogs and Internet forums dedicated to their particular line of work.

✔ **Association memberships:** Most industries have trade groups and other associations that you can join for a nominal annual fee. These associations offer opportunities to promote your business by networking with other members and potential clients at events including regular meetings, conferences, trade shows, and more. Locally based groups, such as the chamber of commerce or chapters of The Entrepreneurs' Organization or Vistage International, offer the same kinds of opportunities, but with a much broader membership base — including an international focus.

✔ **Speeches:** Giving speeches — before community groups, clients, or groups of your peers — is a great way to network with potential clients or with firms that may offer you subcontracting possibilities. You may even pick up the attention of the print or broadcast media. In fact, hiring a public relations specialist can help you ensure that your appearances get the attention they deserve. Not only do you enhance your personal credibility and image by making speeches, but you also may generate numerous qualified leads.

✔ **Seminars and workshops:** Many consultants find great success in promoting their businesses by offering seminars and workshops — often for free — to prospective clients. For example, stockbrokers and financial planners love to drum up business by offering personal finance seminars to people who are interested in learning how to better handle their finances. A certain number of attendees then naturally turn to the broker for help in executing and managing their personal stock transactions.

✔ **Social events:** A heck of a lot of business is done informally at cocktail parties, golf tournaments, and other social events. Picture this conversation: "What do you do for a living?" "I'm a chiropractor." "Oh, you are? I've had this kink in my neck for weeks. Is there anything you can do for it?" Although you should usually avoid making a sales pitch at the event or asking your client-to-be to lie down on the dining room table for an impromptu adjustment — hand out your business card instead and approach your prospect during normal business hours — you can certainly be ready to respond if you're asked to share your opinions. Many consultants seek invitations to social events simply for the opportunity to meet prospective clients.

✔ **Telemarketing:** Although many people cringe when the phone rings at dinner time, if telemarketing didn't work, the telemarketers would stop doing it. (Big hint: Telemarketing *does* work!) Telemarketing can be an effective way to drum up business if you can reach your intended market. Just be sure to use a targeted list of people who are most likely to want your product — random phone calls do little to bring you qualified prospects — and hire a qualified and properly licensed firm to do the calling for you.

✔ **Community events:** Community events — everything from block parties to park dedications to museum openings — are great ways to network with members of the community who may need your services. Be sure to bring plenty of business cards to hand out to your new friends and acquaintances!

Personal selling adds a human touch to your promotional efforts. Because consulting is so dependent on the care and maintenance of personal relationships, most consultants discover that personal selling techniques are the most effective way to promote their products and services. Not only that, but they can be a lot of fun! Make sure you make them a big part of *your* marketing mix.

Using Fame to Build Your Fortune: Public Relations and Publicity

Public relations and publicity are the fine art of building and enhancing your public image through a variety of carefully crafted techniques, all aimed at getting a positive message about your business and its products and services into a variety of media outlets. Whether you just won the Nobel Prize or you're simply volunteering your time to help a good cause in your community, public relations and publicity make sure you're not the only one who knows what you have done.

Here are some proven ways to ensure that you get your 15 minutes of fame:

✔ **Press releases and media kits:** If you're serious about getting a publicity campaign off the ground, you need to send out press releases and media kits to a list of media outlets that have the greatest probability of reaching your prospects. *Media kits* — folders that include a photo, biography, and information of interest to readers, listeners, or viewers — are a definite must if you want to line up print, radio, and television interviews.

✔ **Articles and books:** Writing articles or books on your field of expertise is a great way to both build your credibility and get your name in front of a wide range of potential clients. Writing a book can make you an instant expert in the eyes of the media and gain you entry for interviews and other opportunities to get your word out.

Many trade journals and association magazines are particularly hungry for articles written from an insider's perspective. They usually don't pay you for your efforts, but you reap some free publicity. Just make sure that the publications you write for have a large readership of your target prospects. A public relations professional can help you place articles in the best print media to obtain maximum exposure.

✔ **Web pages and blogs:** The Internet has exploded as an opportunity for promoting your services and products. A Web page can be a showcase of your business and the unique skills and expertise that you offer your clients. (See *Building a Web Site For Dummies,* 3rd Edition, by David A. Crowder [Wiley] for more information about creating your own Web site.) In addition, putting together a blog — and posting to it regularly — can create a dynamic and interactive experience for your clients and clients-to-be. (See *Buzz Marketing with Blogs For Dummies* by Susannah Gardner [Wiley] for more details.)

Jana Matthews, a management consultant specializing in high-growth businesses, started her business, originally named Boulder Quantum Ventures, a number of years ago. In a recent revamp of her brand, which included giving her company a new name — The Jana Matthews Group — to leverage her good reputation with clients, Jana also took her business to a much higher level by investing in a highly professional-looking Web site: www.janamatthewsgroup.com. Now, her Web site reinforces the high-level services provided by Jana and her team.

✔ **Newsletters:** Newsletters are a particularly effective way to generate favorable publicity for your business *and* keep your clients informed about the latest happenings and innovations in your field and in your consulting practice. Not only can you keep in touch with your current clients, but you also can reach out to new ones. The good news is that instead of spending a lot of money to print and mail hard-copy newsletters, nowadays you can simply e-mail an electronic version to your clients for little or no money.

Bob reaches out to a very focused group of clients, potential clients, and media outlets with his tip-of-the-week newsletter. Once, as a special thanks to his loyal subscribers, he sent each one a personally autographed copy of one of his books.

✔ **Media interviews, talk shows, and podcasts:** The various media — newspapers, magazines, radio, television, and now the Internet — have an insatiable appetite for interviewing interesting, informative, and entertaining people. You can either approach the media directly with story ideas or hire a publicist to take care of the heavy lifting for you. Every media outlet that you may want to target is looking for one thing: a personality who can entertain an established audience. If you are entertaining, informative, and engaging, you should have no problem getting the attention you desire. And even if the media doesn't come knocking on your door, you can easily create your own podcasts and place them on your Web site or blog for visitors to download and listen to. Be sure to pick up a copy of *Expert Podcasting Practices For Dummies* by Tee Morris, Evo Terra, and Ryan Williams (Wiley) for lots more information on this topic.

✔ **Community service:** By offering your services to nonprofit community organizations for free, you are helping them obtain the kinds of services that they might not otherwise be able to afford. You also have the opportunity to network with other businesspeople who often comprise the boards and leadership of these types of organizations.

✔ **Independent surveys:** Some consultants are very successful in garnering tons of publicity by conducting surveys and then publishing the results in a press release. If the results are newsworthy, the media may pick up your study (and the name of your business) and distribute it nationwide.

✔ **Sponsorships:** By sponsoring an event in your community — perhaps a charity fundraiser or a job fair — you help create a positive public image for your business in the community and have the opportunity to draw media focus to your efforts. Imagine the value of explaining on camera to your local television news shows why your event is so important to the community and why you feel so strongly that you should sponsor it.

✔ **Awards and honors:** Many consultants seek professional awards and honors, not only for the prestige that they bestow upon the recipients but also for the value of the publicity that they generate.

Successful consultants (and other businesspeople, for that matter) pay close attention to their public image and are always on the alert for new ways to get their message out to the public through the media. Don't forget: If *you* don't create your public image, you may not end up with the one you want.

Paying to Put the Word Out: Advertising

Advertising is promotion through paid, impersonal channels of mass communication, such as newspapers, direct mail, radio, Web sites, and television. For many businesses, advertising is necessary for survival. For other businesses — including many different types of consultants — advertising is an effective adjunct to their primary sources of qualified prospects. For example, although stockbrokers and real estate agents depend on referrals from satisfied clients as their primary source of new client leads, advertising is an important supplement to this source, and it helps build their image in the community at the same time.

The best thing about advertising is that you can exercise a large degree of control over the message that your clients-to-be receive and when and where they receive it. You can send your message to the public in a shotgun fashion — gaining exposure to a huge number of people, some of whom may be interested in what you have to sell — or you can direct it with rifle-sharp accuracy to only those potential clients who are your best prospects. And you can repeat the message often for maximum impact.

Advertising may or may not be for you — not every consultant will benefit from it. However, it can be a powerful part of your overall marketing mix, and you shouldn't write it off too quickly. Here are some of the most common forms of advertising available to you:

- **Newspaper and magazine advertisements:** Newspaper and magazine advertising can be an effective way for certain kinds of consultants to promote their services. One thing is for sure: You get your message out to a lot of potential readers. But even though a large audience is reached, your message may be of little interest to most of them. For example, a newspaper may not be the best place for an aerospace consultant to advertise. But it may be a great place for a home audio and video consultant to advertise, especially in the weekly television guide. The wide variety of narrowly focused special-interest magazines on the market today — as well as trade journals and association magazines — can make magazine advertising a particularly effective way to reach your targeted audience.

  Note: Newspapers have a very short shelf life — one day — whereas magazines tend to hang around for weeks and even months. Your message, therefore, may have a greater chance of being noticed in a magazine, unless you run newspaper ads on a daily basis.

- **Direct mail:** Direct mail is the mailing of advertisements in the form of letters, flyers, brochures, coupon books, or other offers to your prospective clients. This is one of the best ways for consultants of all sorts to reach a large audience of qualified prospects. The real beauty of direct mail is that you can target your mailing with extraordinary precision. If, for example, you make your living as an advertising consultant, you can buy mailing lists from magazines and associations whose subscribers and members contain a high percentage of individuals who likely would be interested in receiving your message. The mailing lists — complete with names and addresses — are available for direct download over the Internet, via CD-ROM or DVD, or even as preprinted mailing labels.

  If you can profile your clients, a mail list house, for a modest fee, can produce a list of other clients whose characteristics match those of your clients. For consultants, customized mailing lists are both effective and efficient. And besides attracting *new* clients, direct mail can also help you keep in touch with *existing* clients.

- **Yellow Pages and other directories:** The Yellow Pages and industry-specific directories, such as those published by the American Institute of Architects (AIA), are a fantastic way to reach qualified prospects. Most professional and industry associations list member firms in their directories for free. If you have a business phone line, you earn a simple telephone listing in your local Yellow Pages telephone directory. However, if you want to buy a display advertisement, be prepared to pay a *lot* of money for this particularly effective form of advertising. Not only do readers of these publications have a need when they pick up a directory, but they also are usually ready to buy in the very near future. One possible downside with Yellow Page advertisements is that an increasing number of people are turning to the Internet for their information instead of the old paper-based directories. For example, Peter makes a habit of tossing each new copy of the local Yellow Pages in the recycle bin as soon as it arrives.

✔ **E-mail:** Those of you who are already online have probably noticed the proliferation of advertising on the Internet — on Web sites and blogs, and via e-mail messages, both solicited and unsolicited.

As you may already know from reading your own Internet e-mail in-box, unsolicited, mass-mailed advertisements can be *very* annoying to recipients. How many get-rich-quick schemes and lowest-rate-in-the-world long-distance phone ads can you tolerate before you're ready to unplug your computer once and for all? Mass mail at your own risk! If you do decide to use e-mail to advertise your consulting business, choose your recipients very carefully, be sure they want to receive your message, and provide them with an easy and reliable way to permanently opt out if they so desire.

✔ **Pay-per-click ads:** If you've ever done a search on Google, you've probably noticed all the advertisements that pop up along the side of the search results page. Businesses and individuals pay Google to be presented along with the search results of a relevant keyword. For example, do a search on the word "television," and your result will be surrounded by advertisements for companies that sell and service televisions. Advertisers bid to have their ads presented higher up the list, but they pay only when someone actually clicks on the ad. As of 2007, the largest pay-per-click operators were Google AdWords, Yahoo SearchMarketing, and Microsoft adCenter.

✔ **Radio and television advertisements:** As with newspaper and magazine advertisements, radio and television advertisements can reach a large audience; everybody has at least one radio or television at home or at work. Your message, however, may be of interest to only a very narrow market. Cable television — with boutique channels such as The Weather Channel, MTV, The Cable News Network, Nickelodeon, Bravo!, and more — and radio stations that specialize in news, talk shows, and different music formats offer you the opportunity to aim your message at specific demographic groups. However, the relatively high cost of running ads in these media outlets and the complexity and expense of putting together a quality advertisement make running radio and television advertisements a daunting task for most consultants.

✔ **Outdoor advertising:** Unless your last name is Goodyear and you're in the tire consulting business, sticking an advertisement on the side of a blimp or on a billboard is probably not the best way to drum up business. However, if you're an immigration consultant who advises people on their legal rights when they are threatened with deportation, advertising in buses and subways and on street benches may work. For the rest of you, at least you know that outdoor advertising is always an option should you choose to pursue it.

Make sure that you consider advertising when you develop your marketing plan. It's one of the best ways to get the exact message you want to send to your most likely prospective clients.

Factoring In a Little Fun: Sales Promotion

What do you do if you want to try to get a potential client to buy your product or service *right now* or at least keep your name and phone number handy for the time when she needs you? Independent consultants use sales promotions — coupons, imprinted coffee mugs, free samples, and the like — to fulfill this task. Many sales promotions are fun and exciting for your clients, and they help to generate excitement about your business and its products.

Sales promotions come in all kinds and all flavors, so you surely can find something that fits your business and its clients. Consider some of these options:

✔ **Business cards:** Business cards are probably the ultimate low-cost way to promote your business. For less than $50 (even less if you print your own), you can have a box of 500 cards printed to your exact specifications. Once you have them, use them. Hand them out at parties, give them to your clients, staple them to proposals and reports, and always carry extras when you're out in the field. Some consultants print messages on the backs of their business cards, such as The Rules of Negotiating or other tips that may be valuable to prospective clients. If you have employees, give them business cards, too.

✔ **Brochures and sales materials:** If you are actively selling your product or service to others, then you've probably already developed your own promotional brochures and sales materials. They're easy to design and inexpensive to have professionally printed. If you haven't gotten on board yet, you're missing out on a great opportunity to promote your business. Few clients are ready to hire you immediately; most would prefer to look over your promotional literature first. Of course, your brochures and sales materials should be as attractive and inviting as possible, and they should be easily accessible via your Web site as well as by request via mail.

✔ **Discount coupons:** Discount coupons are a time-honored tradition for promoting consumer goods and certain kinds of services, such as automobile maintenance and carpet cleaning. You can distribute them to your targeted clients through newspaper or magazine advertisements, through direct mail, or via the Internet. Depending on what kind of consulting you do, discount coupons may be worth a try.

✔ **Advertising specialties:** How could we live without coffee mugs, pens, pencils, refrigerator magnets, calendars, and more — all bearing the name of your business and your phone number or Internet address? Handing out inexpensive and useful imprinted specialties can help you keep your name in front of your clients year-round.

✔ **Contests and prizes:** There's nothing like a good contest with some fun prizes to get everyone excited about what you have to say. A real estate agent in our area gathers lists of potential clients and promotes his business at the same time by running periodic contests in a local newspaper. The contests are keyed to Valentine's Day, the Fourth of July, and other important dates. To enter, people fill out a brief entry form (that just happens to include questions about whether they are planning to sell or buy a home in the near future) and submit it by a certain date. Winners receive a free dinner for two at a local restaurant.

✔ **Free samples:** Everyone loves to get something for free. Offer free samples — a free home inspection, a free newsletter, a free Web page — in exchange for trying your product or listening to your sales pitch.

Creating a Simple Marketing Plan that Really Works

Throughout this book, we mention the importance of creating a marketing plan. A *marketing plan* is a document that contains your marketing goals, along with the strategies and tactics you'll use to achieve them — the mix of personal selling, public relations and publicity, advertising, and sales promotions that you plan to use to market your consulting services or products. As you'll soon see, a simple marketing plan can also be an effective marketing plan — there's no need to kill a forest of trees to create your plan and make it work.

Because your consulting business is always changing, so should your marketing plan. If your consulting firm is brand new, your focus should be on strategies that introduce your company and its products and services to your primary customers. As your business matures over time, you should revise the plan to capitalize on your brand equity and brand recognition in the market. In this section, we explore how to build the right marketing plan for you and your consulting firm.

Be prepared: Getting ready to plan

Before you create your marketing plan, it's a good idea to do some preparation first. A marketing plan is only as good as the information that you use to build it, so make sure you've got the best information possible. Here are some ways to get prepared to plan:

- **Brainstorm marketing strategies and tactics.** Before you focus on just a few specific marketing strategies or tactics, brainstorm a list of ones that might work for you. Make the list as long as you can — now is not the time to edit them down to just those that might be feasible. You'll have plenty of time to do that in the coming steps.

- **Think like a customer.** Step into your potential clients' shoes for a moment and look at your firm's services and products from their perspective. What do you offer that clients will find particularly attractive and make them want to do business with you?

- **Know your competition.** Why reinvent the wheel when your competitors may have already figured out the best ways to market their own consulting services? What are they doing that you're not? What approaches should you adopt? And which of your current approaches should you improve on — or discard?

- **Rank your options.** Now is the time to decide which marketing strategies and tactics you should incorporate into your marketing plan, and which should be discarded. Take a look at your list, and immediately eliminate the ones that just don't make sense for your firm right now. For example, running television ads may be out of the question because of their high cost. Next, consider the remaining strategies and tactics from your clients' perspective, and zero in on the ones that meet your clients' needs while finding them where they're most likely to be.

Okay, if you've worked through the process of getting prepared to create your marketing plan, there's just one thing left to do: create your marketing plan. Believe it or not, that's exactly the topic we cover in the next section.

Create a one-paragraph marketing plan

While you can create a huge marketing plan that numbers in the hundreds of pages, we're here to tell you that that is not necessary. In fact, all you really need for most purposes is a paragraph. Of course, that one paragraph needs to contain some specific information to guide your marketing efforts — information detailed by these bullet points:

- **Purpose:** What will the marketing plan accomplish?
- **Benefits:** How will your consulting services and products satisfy the needs of your clients?

✔ **Customer:** Who is your primary customer and what strategy will you employ to build long-term relationships with that customer?

✔ **Company:** How will the customer see your company?

✔ **Niche:** What unique market niche does your firm serve?

✔ **Tactics:** What specific marketing tools will you use to reach customers?

✔ **Budget:** How much of your budget will you allocate to put your marketing plan into action?

We know that this seems like a lot of information to get into one paragraph, but it can be done. Consider this sample one-paragraph marketing plan for a management consulting firm:

> *This marketing plan will create awareness of Kluson Consulting Group, which will provide state-of-the-art management consulting services to fast-growing consumer products companies through direct contact and via the Internet. The niche that Kluson Consulting Group will serve is the small, but growing, consumer products company. The client will see Kluson Consulting Group as a high-quality management consulting firm that provides the latest proven strategies and tactics for managing in a time of rapid change. Initial marketing tactics will include pay-per-click advertising on Google AdWords and advertisements in consumer product industry trade publications. Twelve percent of Kluson Consulting Group's top-line revenues will be used for this marketing strategy.*

Measuring Your Results

Once you've started putting your marketing plan into effect, there's just one more thing to keep in mind: You have to weigh the cost of your chosen marketing strategies and tactics against the benefits. Buying a big display ad in the Yellow Pages or building a professional-looking Web site may be an expensive proposition, but if it brings in far more business than it costs, it's worth it. The key is to discover what works for your particular consulting business and then use it to your best advantage. The best way is to experiment and then measure your results.

One challenge in determining whether or not your strategies and tactics are having the desired impact is figuring out exactly where your prospects are coming from. There are two possibilities:

✔ **Direct source:** Such as when you make an unsolicited ("cold") telephone call to a prospective client, and he or she returns your call to discuss your offer.

✔ **Indirect source:** Such as when a current or past client refers a colleague to you — without your knowledge, and through no direct effort on your part.

As you can imagine, tracking and measuring the results of your marketing efforts is much easier when new prospects arrive through direct, rather than indirect, sources. In either case, one of the most effective ways to figure out how a prospect or new client found out about you is to simply ask. For example, if you're running an expensive Yellow Pages ad but a survey of your clients tells you that none of them came to you as a result of the ad, that's an indication that your valuable promotional budget could be better spent elsewhere.

You can also "tag" your promotional efforts with unique identifiers, offerings, or calls to action to identify which are the most effective. For example, you might offer a special limited-time 20-percent discount via a pay-per-click ad service such as Google AdWords, but offer a free newsletter subscription in a direct mailing. When a prospective client calls and asks for the free newsletter, you'll know which promotion they're responding to. This is helpful because with the millions of advertising messages hitting us almost daily, we often don't remember where we heard it; we just remember the freebie.

Whatever approaches you choose to collect your data, be sure to record and track it. Some customer relationship management (CRM) software programs allow you to input such data — generating up-to-the-minute reports that will help you guide your marketing efforts. But even if you don't have a CRM program that allows you to track your results, you can use a program like Microsoft Excel to record your data and manipulate it in a variety of ways. You can even create graphs and charts to see which marketing strategies and tactics are giving you the best results.

Chapter 14

Building Business and Referrals through Current Clients

. . . .

In This Chapter

▶ Approaching different sources of referrals

▶ Greasing the skids

▶ Obtaining quality referrals

▶ Following through with your referrals and your clients

. . . .

*E*very consulting business needs new clients to thrive and to grow. First, as you lose clients — and every business is bound to lose some each month and each year for a variety of different reasons — you need new clients to replace the revenues that are lost. Second, new clients can play a crucial role in helping you grow your business in the future. While you may be able to grow your business to some degree by expanding the projects you do for current clients, you shouldn't rely on them for 100 percent of your future growth prospects. Your future success depends on maintaining a balance between keeping your current clients happy and devoting time and resources to finding new ones.

Building your business is an activity that should never stop. Sure, you have to attend to your current clients and your current projects (after all, the very first place you should look for new business is with your current clients), but you always should be looking down the road — a month, six months, a year into the future — for new clients.

Just as there are many different ways to drive a car from Vancouver to New York City, there are many different ways to bring new clients into your business. You can place advertisements on television, in newspapers, or via the Internet and hope that your clients-to-be see them and decide to contact you; you can go door-to-door and sell your services personally; you can conduct public presentations and workshops that create interest in your services; you can run a contest or give away free samples and gather leads that way; or you can choose any one of an almost unlimited number of different approaches for attracting new clients.

However, there is another way to get new clients — a way by which some consultants derive almost all their new business but that others overlook entirely. This way of building your business is through referrals. *Referrals* are prospects sent to you by someone outside your own business. For example, say you're a successful nutrition consultant. If your clients are happy with the work you do for them (they *are* happy, right?), then your clients are bound to want to tell their friends about their positive experiences. In fact, they may think they're doing their friends a favor by telling them about that great consultant they found (you!). When your clients' friends call you as a result, *those* are considered referrals. Referrals are a fantastic way to obtain new clients, and you should not overlook this method.

In this chapter, we help you determine who the best sources of referrals are for your business, and we consider the importance of keeping your current clients happy with the work that you're doing for them and the way that you do it. We look into the very best ways to get referrals and then tell you what to do with them once you have them.

Considering the Benefits of Referrals

The benefits of referrals to your business are many. Here are some specific reasons why referrals are worth pursuing:

- ✔ **Referrals are a major source of new business for many consultants.** Although some consultants depend on referrals to identify almost all their new business leads, others may not have tapped very deep into this vast resource. If you have not taken advantage of this important source of new business to the full extent that you are able, you can increase the number and quality of your referrals easily by following the advice in this chapter.

- ✔ **Referrals are easier to close than other kinds of prospects.** Because the people who send you referrals have most likely already told the referrals who you are, what you do, and — hopefully — what a great job you do, your referrals come to you to some extent presold. The hard part of attracting their attention and getting them to listen to what you have to say has already been accomplished, so you can focus on identifying the solutions they need.

- ✔ **Referrals cost fewer marketing dollars than other kinds of prospects.** Because referrals are sent to you by other people, you don't have to spend much of your promotional budget to get their attention. This is marketing of the very best kind — targeted and, in many cases, costing you little or no money. And because these prospects are, to a large degree, presold on you and your business, convincing them to buy your product or services doesn't take you as much time as convincing a prospect who was not referred to you.

Deciding Who to Approach for Referrals

Referrals can come from anyone at any time. Your best and most obvious source of referrals is likely your many current, happy clients. Assuming you've been doing good work for your clients — and you've delivered your services or products on time and within budget — then they will generally be the ones most loudly singing your praises. However, referrals can pop into your life from the least expected places at the least expected times. Every consultant has gotten a call from a friend of a friend of a friend. A positive mention by the press or on a blog or Web site can also generate referrals. Of course, like anything else in business (and in life, for that matter), you can greatly improve your chances of getting referrals by making a conscious effort to seek them.

You have two choices: You can either choose to wait for people to make referrals to you or your business, or you can actively work for them. Which of these choices do you think improves your chances of getting the referrals your consulting business needs? (Hint: If you're sitting around waiting for people to make referrals, then you'd better be ready to do a lot of sitting around.)

Assuming that you've made the decision to seek referrals (good choice!), whom should you approach for them? Although you can approach almost anyone, the following sources of referrals are likely your best bets and, therefore, the best use of your time:

- **Current clients:** Your current clients are, without a doubt, your best source of referrals. Not only do they know the quality of your work on a firsthand basis, but they are often your biggest fans and boosters. And when your clients are out looking for new clients for you, your own marketing and promotion efforts are multiplied many times. The best approach with your clients is a direct one. Simply tell them that you would be happy to work with any associates of theirs who may also need your services. The best time to make the approach is after you complete a project successfully for your client — when the glow of the great work you did is still fresh in their mind. Be sure to take care of your current clients first, and they'll be sure to take care of you.

- **Other consultants:** Consulting can be a very cyclical business. One week you have hardly anything to do; the next week you're so busy you don't know how you're going to get all your work done. The fact is, other consultants are in much the same situation, and juggling projects is a skill that almost every consultant finds essential. Many consultants, when temporarily overwhelmed with business, contract out some of their work to individuals and firms they know and trust. Doing so enables them to get the work done on time without having to hire permanent employees. Some consultants actually refer their clients to other consultants when they're already booked up. By getting to know other consultants — and helping them get to know you — you can pick up referrals that help you get through your slow times.

- **Business associates:** During the course of a typical business day, you probably interact with a number of business associates — perhaps your accountant, a clerk at your favorite office supply store, or even your mail carrier. Do *they* know about the products and services you offer? If not, you have another opportunity to bring an entirely new group of referral opportunities to your business. Your attorney and accountant can be terrific sources of referrals because they're likely plugged in to your local business community. You just need to get them the information about your business and what you can do for them (and for *their* clients) so that they know. Here's where having a good Web site for your business can be a real asset. Simply send them a link to the site and your work is done.

- **Business-oriented online social networking sites:** It's the rare person who hasn't heard of the popular online social networking Web sites MySpace and Facebook. Well, guess what? There are now a number of business-oriented social networking Web sites, too, including LinkedIn (www.linkedin.com), Ziggs (www.ziggs.com), Doostang (www.doostang.com), Plaxo (www.plaxo.com), and others. By the end of 2007, LinkedIn reportedly had more than 16 million registered users in more than 150 different industries and more than 400 economic regions.

- **Family and friends:** Unless you just recently arrived from another planet or galaxy, you have lots of family and friends who can be a great source of referrals. Be sure to remind them periodically of what you do for a living and invite them to tell *their* families and friends. Keep them up-to-date by mailing them copies of newspaper or magazine articles about your business and by sending them copies of your brochures or other sales materials. And be sure they know how to find your Web site.

How you find referrals is really up to you. If you're more comfortable waiting for your contacts to make referrals to you and would really rather not push them in that direction yourself, then that's what you should do. However, if you want to enjoy the benefits of a greatly enhanced quantity and quality of business referrals, take a close look at the people with whom you are acquainted and do business, and ask yourself whether they would be good sources of referrals. You may be surprised by how many of your clients, friends, and other associates are more than happy to refer new clients to you, if only you ask them to do so.

Setting the Stage with Current Clients

Because your current clients are your most likely source for referral business, you want to focus your efforts on them before you explore the other possibilities, such as the guy who drives your local ice cream truck or the gal who walks by your home office every morning at 8 a.m. walking her dog. You can (and should) do a number of things to keep your clients happy and set the stage for the referrals your business needs to grow. Here are some ways to motivate your clients to send those referrals your way — and keep them coming:

- ✔ **Do great work.** We've said it before, and we'll say it again. One of the best ways to keep your clients happy is to do great work for them. If you do, they'll probably be so happy that they'll want to tell all their associates about the great job you did. Similarly, if you *don't* do great work, why would anyone bother to tell their friends and associates about you? Believe us, they won't.

  Years ago, a house painter did a job for Peter's next-door neighbor. The painter did such a great job for such a great price that Peter immediately hired him to paint some rooms in his house. When Peter recommended him to another neighbor, *she* hired the painter to do some work for her. This went on and on until the painter — who was completely unknown to anyone in the neighborhood only a few weeks before — had done work for almost everyone on the street.

- ✔ **Do your work on budget and on time.** What are two things that your clients hope they'll never hear from you? That you're going to be late and that the project is going to cost more than you originally estimated. One of the best ways to keep your clients happy and ensure that you're on the top of their list of referrals is to do your work on time and at the price you originally agreed on. But what if you underestimated the price to do a consulting job? Shouldn't you try to recover the additional cost? Our advice is — depending on your contract — probably not. When you quote a firm price — and sign an agreement to provide a defined amount of work for that price — then you should honor it, regardless of what the project ultimately costs you to complete. Honoring your commitments builds strong bridges of trust with your clients and, for most consultants, trust is one of the most important things they've got.

  Of course, few clients will fault you if *they* do something to make you go over cost or deliver your results late, and, in that case, you should pursue remedies according to your contract terms and conditions. But even if they do something that creates a problem for you, do everything *you* can to keep things on track. You'll be a hero!

- ✔ **Keep your clients well-informed.** When you're working on projects for your clients, you can earn their undying affection (and their continued business) by taking the time to keep them informed about your progress and notifying them if you encounter problems or difficulties that require their attention. Indeed, consultants who make a habit of surprising their clients with bad news are consultants who soon find that they have a lot fewer clients than they had the year — or even the month — before.

✔ **Be reliable and dependable.** If anything turns on a client, it's being reliable and dependable. On the flip side of the coin, one of the biggest turn-offs for clients is a consultant who is unreliable and who can't be counted on to do what they say they'll do. If you promise your clients that you're going to do something, then they expect you to do as you have promised — nothing less and nothing more. Believe us: There is a very real shortage in this world of consultants who do what they say they will do — who meet their deadlines at the high level of quality and at the price that they promised they would. If you're reliable and dependable, you'll have more business — and more referrals — than you can imagine. However, if you aren't, you'll have plenty of spare time on your hands to do other things (maybe look for a new way to make money, for a start!).

✔ **Be flexible.** In any business, change is usually the rule and not the exception — especially in these days of fast-changing global markets, and even faster-changing telecommunications and computing technology. It seems that if you're not changing, you're not going *anywhere* — and you probably aren't. The best consultants are able to quickly adapt their approaches, schedules, and project staffing when required to meet their clients' needs. As a result, not only do they earn their clients' gratitude, but also their ongoing business — and their referrals.

✔ **Thank your clients for their referrals.** Be sure to thank your clients whenever they refer you to a prospective client — whether or not you end up doing business with the prospect. This gesture of gratitude demonstrates to your clients that you have taken note of their assistance on your behalf, and that you appreciate it.

Your good work sets the stage for more work with the same clients *and* for your clients to refer others to you. When you do good work, your clients will want to tell others about you. When you do bad work, your clients will be sure that others know about that, too. Do everything you can to keep your current clients happy with the work you do for them, and you'll be a very busy consultant indeed.

How to Get Referrals

You can either wait for your associates and acquaintances to refer new clients to you, or you can actively seek them. In our humble opinion, actively seeking them is always best. Referrals are great for any business to have because they are much easier to sell and cost less to obtain. You can increase the number and quality of your referrals by pursuing them through a variety of different techniques.

The following sections describe a few different approaches for you to try in your quest for new clients.

Use the direct approach

In life and in business, the direct approach is often the best approach. Why beat around the bush when you can ask your clients and acquaintances *directly* to send you referrals? How? Simply tell your clients that you would like them to refer any of their acquaintances and business associates to you if they need services of the sort that you offer, and you would be grateful for their assistance. You can do this in person or by telephone, letter, e-mail, or fax. Figure 14-1 presents an example of a letter soliciting referrals from a client directly.

If you're doing good work for your clients, most of them will be very happy (and perhaps even honored) to refer others to you.

Keep in touch with your clients

How does the old saying go? Out of sight, out of mind? Everyone today is incredibly busy, doing more with less and doing it more quickly than ever. If you don't keep in touch with your clients, your clients will soon forget you as they turn their attention to the crisis of the day. Every salesperson worth his or her salt knows that keeping in touch with clients — both old and new — is a key approach for generating future sales. When you're between jobs with your clients, drop by their offices to say hello every once in a while, or send them a note, a newspaper or magazine clipping, or a link to a story or Web site on the Internet that they may find interesting. By keeping in touch with your clients, you'll be the first consultant they think of referring to a colleague who needs help with a problem or opportunity.

Reward your clients for referrals

Think for a moment how you feel when someone takes the time out of their busy day to thank you for doing something to help them — makes you feel good, doesn't it? Now, imagine how your clients feel when you take time out of your busy day to thank them for something they've done. Guess what? It makes them feel good, too.

October 25, 20xx

Ms. Sara Blanc
Blanc & Associates
1330 Del Mar Avenue
Del Mar, CA 92014

Dear Sara:

I'm pleased to let you know that we successfully completed the redesign of the Laurel Canyon aqueduct, and we finished the project a week early. I have you to thank for helping us cut through wads of red tape at City Hall, and I am personally very proud of the partnership that we developed during the course of the project.

I look forward to our next project. Until then, if you know people who need the services of a good civil engineering consultant, I hope you'll send them my way. I'll be sure to make sure that they get the best service possible for the best price possible.

Thanks again for your help.

Best wishes,

John Adesanwo

Figure 14-1:
This letter
from
consultant
to client
includes a
request for
referrals.

You should always reward your clients when they refer business to you. The reward you select depends on the kind of consulting you do; it can range from a simple thank-you note — handwritten or delivered via e-mail — to a gift basket or bottle of their favorite beverage, all the way to a commission based on a percentage of the fee that the referral pays you. At a minimum, call your client and thank him or her personally. As an extra show of thanks, you can send a gift of nominal value — say, a coffee mug with your name and telephone number printed on it, or a nice flower arrangement — or you can extend your client a discount on your next job. In some cases — especially for a particularly valuable referral — you may want to pay your client a cash finder's fee (a flat amount) or a commission (an amount that varies depending on the size of the fee that you bill the client) for his or her consideration. If you decide to pay a referral fee, be sure you're not violating your client's company policies or the law by doing so. In some cases — for example, if your client is a government entity — the fee may be considered a bribe or a kickback, and that's the last thing you want to get wrapped up in. In such cases, a simple thank-you note may be the best, and safest, approach for all concerned.

Build a contact database

How many different clients and potential clients do you meet every year? 15? 150? 1,500? The problem is, after you meet with more than a few people, forgetting the personal details about each one is easy. This is where a contact database earns its weight in gold over and over again. After you set it up, you can target your referral efforts to specific clients with great precision. Your contact database should include your contact's name and title, company name and address, telephone and fax numbers, business needs, personal interests, and any other information you believe will help you in your efforts. While you can build such a database yourself relatively easily using programs such as Microsoft Excel, many terrific customer relationship management (CRM) software programs are available today. Do an online search for the latest-and-greatest CRM packages, and be sure to check out our discussion of CRM software in Chapter 15.

Make referrals yourself

Here's an important lesson that can help you both in business and in your everyday life: *What goes around comes around.* This is the idea of *karma* — that a person's deeds actively create their past, present, and future experiences. What does this digression into Hindu and Buddhist philosophy have to do with getting referrals? A lot. Just as you hope that your clients will refer you to *their* associates, you can (and should) refer your clients to *your* associates. Say you're a travel consultant and you're doing work for an accounting firm. If an acquaintance tells you that he's looking for a good accountant, then it only makes sense to refer your acquaintance to the accounting firm for which you are doing work — assuming, of course, that it's a quality firm. Of course, the accounting firm will be grateful for the referrals that you make to them, and they will likely make even more referrals of their clients to your own business. It's really quite simple: The more referrals you make, the more referrals you'll receive.

Following Up on the Referral

After you receive a referral, you need to follow up on it to determine whether you have a qualified prospect or just a dead end. Leads are kind of like a loaf of bread sitting on your kitchen shelf. The longer your leads sit on a shelf while you take no action to follow up on them, the staler they become. Eventually, when they start to grow green hair and smell bad, you have to throw them in the trash.

Referrals are an important part of your new business and your future. Do the following to ensure that you'll have plenty of referrals far into the future:

- ✔ **Follow up with your referrals.** Whenever you get a referral from a client, friend, or acquaintance, be sure to follow up *immediately*. Get on the telephone and return the call — right now! Nothing is more embarrassing to a client who has made a referral than to hear that you never returned the call or responded to the message. You can bet that *that* client won't bother making any more referrals to you!

  When you reach the referral, provide a brief summary of what you offer and then press for a face-to-face meeting to define the problem. Respect your referrals *and* your clients by responding to referrals quickly. Even if you can't help, you at least leave the door open for future referrals from your clients and also for future business with the referral you couldn't help out this time.

- ✔ **Follow up with your clients.** Keep your clients in the loop about how the work with their referral is going. They'll appreciate the update, and the communication helps remind them that you're ready, willing, and available for additional assignments.

Try an approach like this:

> **You:** "I just wanted to thank you for sending me the referral for Text3000 Corporation — I landed a nice job with them as a result."
>
> **Client:** "No problem. You do such great work for us; I thought I should share the wealth. I have a lot of business associates who are in desperate need of someone who is smart and experienced and has been around the block a few times. Keep your eyes open — I'll be sending more business your way soon."
>
> **You:** "Fantastic. I always have room to accommodate a few more great clients like you. I'll make sure that I treat them just as well as I treat you."

Chapter 15

Building Business with New Clients

*A*ttracting potential clients to your business is a definite must if you expect to sell them on your product or service. (Chapter 13 details the kinds of things that you need to do to bring potential clients to your door.) Now that they're at your door — or on the phone, or in your e-mail in-box — what do you do next?

The next step is to convince your clients that they need to do business with your consulting firm. Or rather, that they've got a problem that needs to be solved, and you — and perhaps only you — can best help them with their needs. So much so that your business has the clear edge over all your competitors.

In this chapter, we explore exactly what you need to do after you get the attention of prospective clients. We tell you about the importance of the personal introduction and the significance of quickly establishing good rapport and a firm basis of trust and goodwill. We walk you through the process of making a pitch to your clients and then following up — and we talk about the importance of keeping your commitments.

Giving Your Introduction a Personal Touch

In many ways, the personal introduction of a prospective client to your business is one of the most critical points in the process of selling your services. Blow it here, and you probably won't have to worry about seeing *that* client again. However, if you make the right impression, you'll have a client for life.

We know that you're not necessarily in business to make friends. You're in business to make money. But you have to remember that business involves much more than just dollars and cents (or pounds, euros, yen, or whatever your monetary persuasion). Consulting is first and foremost a *social* activity, and it is built on a foundation of one-to-one relationships.

In the sections that follow, we consider the things that go into this most important beginning phase of your consulting relationships: the personal introduction.

Making a great first impression

The first experience that a potential client has with your consulting business may be anything from leaving a message on your voice mail to visiting your Web page to meeting you personally through a mutual acquaintance. We can't emphasize enough the importance of a potential client's first experience with your business — in many cases, it may be your only opportunity to sell that client on the benefits of working with your organization. Consider these two scenarios:

- ✔ **Scenario A:** The client of your dreams calls the toll-free phone number listed on your Web site. The creaky old answering machine in your home-based office picks up, "Hi, this is the Acme Consulting Group. Sorry, we can't take your call right now, but leave a message and we'll get back to you as soon as we can." The client of your dreams leaves a brief message expressing his urgent need and asks you to return the call as soon as possible. Unfortunately, you're halfway across the country at the time, working with another client, and you don't get the call until you return home several days later. When you finally return the call, the client of your dreams has already found someone who can meet his urgent schedule.

- ✔ **Scenario B:** One of your best current clients refers the client of your dreams to you. When the prospective client drops by your office unannounced, she is warmly greeted by your receptionist — who offers a cup of coffee or soda — and is steered to the waiting area while you are paged. Because you *always* have time to meet a new client, you drop everything and come out to the waiting area to greet your client-to-be. After you take her on a brief tour of the architectural models of some of your most involved and successful projects and then review her needs and make a rough pricing estimate, your new client asks how soon you can start.

What kind of initial impression does *your* organization make with your clients?

There has never been a valid excuse for sloppy service — and there still isn't one today. What's more, in these days of e-mail–enabled mobile telephones and more, you have less of an excuse than ever before to be hard to reach — even if you're a one-person organization. If you can't get your introduction right, why should a client trust you to get *anything* right?

If you want a quick reality check on the first impressions that your organization is making with your clients, pretend that you're a new client and do the following:

✔ **Call your business phone number and see what happens.** Does someone answer the phone on the first few rings, or does it take longer? Is the initial greeting upbeat and cheery, or is it the kind of greeting that makes you feel like the receptionist would rather be doing something — anything — else rather than taking the call? If the receptionist is out, does another employee pick up the phone quickly and courteously? Do you end up in voice-mail hell with no chance of escape?

✔ **Take a close look at your facilities.** If you're a freelance advertising copywriter, your clients may not be surprised (or disappointed) to visit an office that is located in a spare bedroom of your home. However, if you're a tax accountant, your clients may prefer to see that you have a real office in a real office building with a real employee or two — indicating that your practice is financially stable and viable.

✔ **Take a close look at your marketing materials and work output.** Does your Web site look professional and modern, or does it look like something your 9-year-old child put together for you? Are your company brochures and other marketing materials of high quality? Are your letters and work samples laser-printed on high-quality paper? Would *you* pay your hard-earned dollars for your products?

✔ **Take a close look at yourself.** It probably goes without saying that you should be well groomed and dressed appropriately for the kind of consulting you do. Although your clients may expect their investment advisers to wear pin-striped suits, the same clients may expect their computer consultants to be dressed in polo shirts and khakis.

Seriously consider the answers to these questions and then make any changes needed to ensure that all your clients and prospective clients have a positive first impression of you and your organization. Don't forget: You have only *one* chance to make a first impression!

Asking and listening

The best professional salespeople know that their primary responsibility is to help potential clients find the best solutions to their needs. This means asking questions and then listening — *really* listening — to the answers.

In his book *Selling For Dummies,* 2nd Edition (Wiley), master salesperson Tom Hopkins presents a very useful rule:

> *Listen twice as much as you talk and you'll succeed in persuading others nearly every time.*

Think about why this is true.

- ✔ **Everyone likes to be listened to.** Not only does listening show respect, but it also makes the speaker feel important. However, good listening skills go *way* beyond simply stroking a client's ego.

- ✔ **Good listening helps you do your job better.** Why? Because when you listen, you *hear* exactly what your clients want, and you can respond with the exact answers that your clients need.

The simple fact is that you can't possibly understand what your potential clients need unless you give them the opportunity to *tell* you. And you can't possibly *hear* what your client is telling you unless you take the time to listen! To make sure that you ask clients the right questions *and* listen to their answers, we have developed the following four steps to effective asking and listening:

1. **Ask open-ended questions that define the boundaries of the opportunity.** When you first meet potential clients, you really have no idea what their needs are, how extensive those needs are, and what addressing them will require. Therefore, your first task is to ask the kinds of open-ended questions that help you define the big picture, the rough boundaries of the opportunities it presents, and, thereby, the rough boundaries of your solutions. For example, you might ask, "What results do you want to see from this management training?" or "Exactly what would you like our firm to do for you?"

   Avoid asking questions that may introduce an element of trepidation into your relationship. Questions along the lines of, "Do you realize how incredibly expensive it's going to be to straighten out this mess?" or "Who's the loser responsible for running this department?" are to be avoided at all costs.

2. **Use active silence.** When it comes to listening, silence is golden — not the disinterested silence that comes from having more pressing matters on your mind, but the active silence that tells your clients that you're involved in what they have to say and are interested, thinking, and

putting your all into understanding their issues and perspectives. When your clients appear to have ended a thought and seem ready for you to respond, first prod them to give you deeper understanding with a nod of the head or by asking "Is that all, or is there more?" before you launch into *your* side of the discussion.

3. **Ask clarifying questions.** Clarifying questions take you from the big picture to the little picture and help you to refine your understanding of your clients' opportunities. For example, asking, "Do you really want a full review of your entire quality assurance system, or do you think that a random sampling of products might accomplish the same goal?" is a good way to help define the extent of the effort required to accomplish a task.

4. **Confirm your understandings.** An important part of the process of asking questions and listening to their answers is periodically confirming your understandings with your clients. For example, you might say, "Now here's what I'm hearing that you would like me to do . . ." or "Correct me if I'm wrong, but I believe that what you would like me to do is to create a Web site for your firm that illustrates and explains all your products and then to update it on a regular basis — am I right?"

Never forget to listen before you leap! You'll have plenty of time to do plenty of talking after you land your client. For now, content yourself with asking a few questions to help draw your client out, and listen, listen, and listen some more.

Talking about yourself

Your clients want the best service that their money can buy. Your job is to give it to them. However, before you get the opportunity to do so, you have to *prove* that you've got the right stuff. You don't want to overwhelm your potential clients at this point in the process — you just want to set the stage for your relationship. And just how can you do that? Consider the following factors to get things rolling:

- ✔ **Related experience:** Of the firms you've worked with, whose needs were most like those of your client-to-be? How large or small were the firms, and what was your part in the project's success? Why will this experience help you deal with your prospective client's needs?

- ✔ **Personal credentials:** What are your *personal* credentials for doing the job that your client needs to get done? What firms have you worked for and with? What college and professional degrees do you have? What major projects have you been personally responsible for, and what are the quantifiable measures of their success?

- ✔ **Company credentials:** Who are the key clients of your business? What do you do for them, and how long have they been associated with your company? What are some of your business's most prominent successes, and what was your role in bringing that success about?

Building Relationships with Prospective Clients

Because of the nature of person-to-person interactions, every consulting relationship involves a certain amount of chemistry. If the chemistry is good, a consulting relationship can be long-lasting and beneficial to all. If the chemistry is bad — like a high-school lab experiment careening out of control — you can count the length of the relationship in nanoseconds instead of years.

Consulting relationships are built on trust and on an honest desire to help clients succeed. Sure, every consultant has something to sell, whether it's dragging a company kicking and screaming through a long-range planning process, conveying a lifetime of expertise in finding underground oil deposits, or setting up a company's Web page. But the best consulting relationships come first from a place of wanting to share your unique skills and expertise with someone who needs them.

In this section, we consider some techniques to help you establish good relationships with your potential clients. We discuss how to build rapport with your clients-to-be, get your clients what they need, and build a firm foundation of trust to carry your relationship forward into the future.

Establishing rapport

Before you enter into a business relationship with prospective clients, you have to establish some degree of rapport with them. *Rapport* is the connectedness that individuals in a relationship feel for one another. Rapport comes from shared experiences. A shared experience can be as simple as a shared joke or as complex as a common lifelong interest. In some cases, a relationship is established between people instantly; in other cases, a relationship never really blooms. If rapport doesn't develop between the parties of a relationship, you can bet that the relationship won't last.

We both grew up in homes where our families were transferred from one place to another every few years. Although this lifestyle did disrupt more than a few friendships as we grew up, all the moving around also taught us how to feel comfortable with all kinds of people. Whether it was the suburbs of Washington, D.C.; a small town 100 miles south of Atlanta, Georgia; or Paris, France; we learned how to adjust to new circumstances and make friends quickly with an incredibly diverse range of people around the world.

Fortunately, if you weren't lucky enough to discover the art of establishing instant rapport when you were growing up, it's not too late to find out how:

- **Be friendly.** Everyone likes people who are friendly and who seem genuinely interested in them. When you take the first step to reach out to someone, they're likely to reach back.

- **Assess your client's personality.** Does your client want to chat and socialize for a bit before getting down to business, or does he want to skip all that and keep business at the very top of the agenda? If your client is oriented to socializing first, allow plenty of time for getting to know one another before getting down to business. However, if your client is the kind of person who wants to forgo social pleasantries and get right to business, do that.

- **Find something in common with your client.** Do you share a common interest or hobby with your client — perhaps ice fishing, playing Bach fugues on the harpsichord, or collecting bottle caps? Common interests can break the ice between you and a client faster than a Russian icebreaker at 30 knots. You never know until you ask, so ask!

- **Be sincere and down to earth.** Don't try to pretend to be someone you're not. Just relax, be sincere, and, above all, be yourself.

Helping them get what they want

Helping your clients get what they want is really your number one job, and you have to be particularly vigilant to avoid letting *your* needs take priority over *theirs*. It's not uncommon for a consulting business to develop certain assessment or training tools or products and to then feel a lot of pressure to make clients fit these tools or products — even if it means pushing the clients into a box that really doesn't fit.

For example, a business that conducts long-range planning sessions with the top management teams of for-profit corporations may have developed an assessment model that works great in the private sector. When a local nonprofit agency asks for help in *its* long-range planning, the consulting business decides to apply its standard for-profit assessment model to the nonprofit organization — despite the fact that the fundamental nature of each organization is quite different. Although this tactic makes perfect sense from the consulting practice's cost perspective (why spend the money to adapt the assessment tools for a one-off project, after all), it may make no sense at all from the perspective of getting the best results. In a case like this, if the consultant is unwilling to take the time or spend the money to tailor his approach to the needs of the client, it would really be better for all concerned to refer the work to someone else.

Some consultants allow their egos to get in the way of building relationships with clients. If you see that ego is starting to get in the way — either with you or with an associate — step back for a moment and take a close look at what your clients really need. Then push that big bad ego out of the way, if only for a few moments, to determine whether what you're offering is really what your clients need. If it is, great — you're on the right track. If it's not, go back to the drawing board and come up with an approach that *does* meet your clients' needs.

On the flip side of this coin, you may need to tell your clients things that they just don't want to hear but that reflect the truth of a situation. For example, while speaking with your client about a problem he's having with the response rate for direct-mail advertising, you may quickly realize that the problem is the poor quality of the advertising piece that the client's firm is sending out. Even if your client disagrees vigorously (after all, he created the ad personally and *knows* what works and what doesn't), you have to call it like you see it. To do any less would be to do a disservice both to you and to your client. A good consulting relationship is built on trust, and part of building trust is being honest with your clients — even if, occasionally, the truth hurts.

Building a foundation of trust

Although many things go into making a good consulting relationship, trust is probably the most important factor of all. Trust is the glue that holds a relationship together. Without it, a relationship quickly falls apart — crumbling into little bits and pieces before your very eyes.

So how do you build trust in a consulting relationship? At this early phase of the consulting relationship, doing the kinds of things that set the stage for the development of a strong, long-term relationship is most important. Here are some quick and easy ways to build trust with your clients:

- **Make commitments — and keep them.** One of the easiest ways to build trust in a relationship is to make commitments and then keep them. If, for example, you tell a client that you will be available at 3 p.m. on Wednesday for a conference call, then, when you're ready and waiting for the call at 3 p.m. on Wednesday, you're sending a message to your client that you are reliable. Whether the commitments that you keep are big or small, they add up to increased trust. Make commitments and then keep them.

- **Give your honest opinion.** If your clients have a problem, tell them so. Sometimes you may be tempted to sugarcoat problems in the hopes that your clients will find them easier to swallow. However, this tactic can backfire when your clients finally realize (and most eventually *do* realize) the full extent of their problems and wonder why you kept them in the dark. Trust is built on honesty. Be honest with your clients at all times.

✔ **Keep secrets.** When you're hired as a consultant, you may have access to some of the organization's most important information and secrets. *Never* disclose this confidential information outside your business or outside the circle of individuals with whom the client designates for you to work. Not only can leaking confidential information destroy the trust you have worked so hard to build, but it can also expose you to an expensive lawsuit. By keeping secrets secret, you prove your trustworthiness every day.

✔ **Do great work.** When you do a great job for your clients, you demonstrate that you value their work and their organizations and that you can be trusted with taking on even more important responsibilities in the future. Do great work, and the trust that you've established with your clients will continue to build.

Keep in mind, however, that it's important to keep your objectivity, which sometimes means avoiding becoming too friendly or "one of the boys" (or girls). One of your key advantages as a consultant is your ability to look at an organization — and its issues, challenges, and opportunities — with a fresh and unbiased perspective. Maintaining an objective distance between being one of the gang and being a consultant often serves you and your client best.

Meeting Clients

Your first contact with a potential client is likely to be by phone, e-mail, letter, or another mode of communication rather than in person. However, after you get past the initial introductions and find a clear mutual interest to proceed, you have to take the relationship to the next step, which usually means a face-to-face meeting. Don't get us wrong — we're not saying that flying across the country for a meeting whenever a prospect calls is mandatory. In fact, both of us have established relationships and done business with clients without ever meeting them in person.

Your decision to meet face-to-face with a client depends on many factors. But, as we've said before, consulting is a people thing. Although you can establish and carry on a long-distance business relationship with your phone company or with a mail-order bookstore for years without a face-to-face meeting, consulting is a different animal.

Determining whether to meet in person

The world is a big place. We understand that the potential rewards of a business relationship don't always justify the expense of setting up a one-on-one meeting. And we also understand that the Internet, e-mail, voice mail, cellphones, and all those other nifty technologies make it easier than ever to communicate with anyone you want, anytime you want. But despite all these great innovations, *nothing* can replace the power of a face-to-face meeting.

The question is not *should* you meet with a prospective client. The question is: *Do the benefits of meeting outweigh the costs?* For example, it may make sense to jump on an airplane and fly halfway across the country to meet with a client who might hire you for a $50,000 job — with the promise of more work to come if the project is a success. However, it may not make sense to jump on an airplane and fly halfway across the country to meet with a client whose job is a one-time deal for just $1,000. When you consider your options, take the time to weigh the potential benefits of a face-to-face meeting with your potential client against the costs.

Using software to manage your customer relationships

Customer relationship management (CRM) is a computerized database that tracks information about customers. Years ago, important customer information — names, addresses, phone numbers, and so on — was filed away on Rolodex cards or on sheets of paper stapled into file folders. No longer. Today there are loads of computer-based systems available that allow you to quickly and easily capture, store, and analyze customer information.

What can a good CRM software package do for your company? Plenty. Here's a list of the functions you'll find in a typical CRM system:

- Company and contact management (keeping track of company and buyer names, phone numbers, addresses, e-mail addresses, and so forth)

- Lead management (keeping track of hot, warm, and cold leads, with status updates as they occur)

- Activity management (keeping track of the contacts and other actions taken to sell potential clients)

- Charting (graphing of sales information, such as value of sales each month)

- Reporting (summaries of various sales-related information, such as number of active clients)

- E-mail marketing and mailing lists management (bringing sales prospect e-mail lists together in one place)

- Sales forecasting (providing estimates of future sales activity)

As your consulting business grows, a good CRM system can be a real asset. Choosing the right CRM software is a critical decision for your business, so take your time when scouting out the right product for you. Ask your colleagues or industry contacts what system they use, or read the reviews on the Internet. Finally, when you select a system and implement it, monitor the rollout closely to make sure it's doing exactly what it's supposed to do.

In the following list, we present some of the things to consider when deciding whether to fly out to meet with a prospective client. If the pluses outweigh the minuses, pack your bags and get going!

✔ **The travel experience:**

- **Plus:** Traveling may be the only way you'll get the opportunity to meet your client in person. You may also meet some additional prospects on the airplane or in the waiting area.

- **Minus:** You may get stuck in the airport in a blizzard and your bags may get lost. Also, a cramped airline cabin is not exactly the best place in which to get work done, and the food isn't exactly anything you'd want to write home about either.

- **Net Result:** Make the trip if the potential benefit outweighs the cost of the trip, but bring your own food.

✔ **Time:**

- **Plus:** You can catch up on your work and return phone calls while you wait for the snowplows to clear the airport runways.

- **Minus:** Nowadays, with all the extra security, crowded airports, and flight delays, you can almost be certain that you'll spend many more hours en route to and from your destination than you planned.

- **Net Result:** Your time is worth money. Do the benefits of the trip equal or exceed the opportunity cost of staying home? If so, then keep that reservation.

✔ **Cost:**

- **Plus:** If you make your reservations far enough in advance, you'll find that the cost of airfare can be quite reasonable. Also, travel costs are generally tax deductible.

- **Minus:** The trip could end up costing you a lot of money, especially if the client is far away or if you have to travel on short notice.

- **Net Result:** The money you make on the deal should exceed the amount of money that you spend trying to get it — ideally, *far* exceed it.

✔ **Future work:**

- **Plus:** This meeting may lead to a long and fruitful consulting relationship that allows you to get your kids through college.

- **Minus:** This meeting may turn out to be a complete waste of your and your client's time.

- **Net Result:** You don't know until you give it a try.

Finessing successful face-to-face meetings

Personal, face-to-face meetings can be a particularly effective way to sell yourself and your consulting business. However, to take full advantage of the benefits of face-to-face meetings, you have to be sure you're meeting with the right person at the right place at the best time. Here are some tips to help you make your face-to-face meetings all they can be.

Whom to meet

This is quite simple. The best person to meet with is the one who can decide whether or not to hire you or your firm. Why? Because if you're dealing with anyone else, you may be wasting your time. However, the next best thing to meeting with the person who can make the decision is to meet with the people who can favorably *influence* the person who makes the decision.

Who are some of the people you should meet with? Before you schedule your next meeting with your clients-to-be, make sure you see how they stack up according to the following list:

- ✔ **The boss:** Whether this person owns the company or is a top executive or manager, this man or woman usually has responsibility for a budget and the authority to hire you. Not only that, but, after you're hired, this person can clear-cut a path through the organization's obstacles for you, making it *much* easier to get your job done.

- ✔ **The executive assistant:** Because they've earned the trust of their bosses, executive assistants wield tremendous power in their organizations. If you can't get to the boss, his or her executive assistant is definitely a close second in priority.

- ✔ **Employee committees:** In these days of self-managed work teams and employee empowerment, employee committees have gained a large measure of power and authority within their organizations. Many control their own budgets and can decide whether or not to contract for your services. Although convincing a committee of multiple individuals to hire you can be significantly more difficult than convincing just one person, your time working with employee committees can be time well spent.

So how do you get to the right person or group in an organization? After you select your target, simply pick up the phone and call. In our experience, you save a lot of time and money by sidestepping staff and using your phone to go directly to the person or group in charge. E-mail is also a great tool for getting to the right person. We have found that, in many cases, a person who won't return a phone call for days or weeks (or ever!) will reply to an e-mail in minutes. You may have to spend a little time with the receptionist or other employees while researching who's who in the organization, but, after you find out, be deliberate and assertive in your efforts to contact the right people.

Where to meet

You have the option of meeting at your place, the client's place, or somewhere in between. The selection depends greatly on the nature of your business, on whether you're traveling a great distance for the meeting, and on your client's time constraints. Consider the pluses and minuses of each option.

- ✔ **Your place:** Meeting at your place may make the most sense if you have a nice place to meet, or if the nature of your meeting is extremely sensitive and confidential. You have another reason to do so if your business requires you to demonstrate a product that isn't easy to carry around. For example, a firm that provides custom computer hardware and software solutions on large office servers and networks may have a difficult time lugging the appropriate equipment to a client's site for a demonstration. In such cases, bringing the client to your site, where the equipment is already installed, configured, and up and running, makes more sense.

- ✔ **Their place:** This is often the preferred choice — especially if your client-to-be is too busy to get away from the office or if you need to meet with more than one or two people at a time. The advantages are that your clients are on their own turf, and they're probably more comfortable meeting with you there than in an unfamiliar setting. The disadvantages include clients who answer their phone every time it rings or who spend time chatting with everyone who walks through the door.

- ✔ **In between:** Think of a favorite restaurant for lunch or dinner. The location is neutral, and you get the opportunity to get away from the moment-to-moment demands of a busy office.

Most busy clients prefer for you to meet them at their office. Ultimately, where you meet with a particular client really depends on whether you can effectively demonstrate a solution to your client's problem at her site and whether the cost of getting to your customer exceeds the expected financial benefits of doing business. When in doubt, err on the side of going out of your way to meet your client at the place of her choosing.

When to meet

Should you try to set up a meeting as soon as possible, or should you take things slow and easy? Although some people say that good things come to those who wait, this is not necessarily the case when it comes to consulting. The truth is that consulting is a very competitive field, and the more appropriate adage is likely, "You snooze, you lose."

When you press for immediate meetings with prospective clients, you not only impress them with your obvious interest in meeting their needs, but you also help to ensure that your firm is selected before other consultants have an opportunity to get their foot in the door.

So what is the correct answer to the question of when to meet? Now! Not enough time or not enough notice to meet today? Then set up a meeting for first thing tomorrow. The point is, the sooner you get your meeting scheduled, the better chance you have of landing the deal.

Following Through Is Everything!

Despite successfully making it through all the hurdles of getting to know new clients and winning their trust and confidence, many consultants ultimately lose their deals when they fail to follow through with their clients. Though you may prefer to think of consulting as the art of performing the services in which you're expert, the one thing that makes the world of consulting go around is ultimately your ability to sell yourself to the people and organizations who can afford to pay your bills.

If you can't sell yourself, you can't sell your services. It's that simple.

After you make your sales pitch, the next step is to set up a system of follow-through with your prospective client. As a consultant, you find that many of your prospects are very busy people, and they can easily lose your proposal among all the other priorities that they're charged with juggling. The purpose of follow-through is to keep your proposal fresh in your client's mind and make sure that he doesn't forget about you.

However, don't forget the number-one rule of following up with your clients: Don't be a pest. Proper follow-through walks a fine line between an occasional reminder that keeps your name in mind and a full-court press that makes you more trouble than you're worth. Be sensitive to the needs of your clients when you decide on your follow-through strategy. Although every situation is different, you can't go wrong by applying the follow-through techniques presented in this section.

Setting a date for the next step

What is the next step in selling yourself to your client? Another meeting? A technical demonstration? E-mailing a copy of an article that you authored? A phone call to see whether you're going to be selected to do the proposed job? Until you land your consulting job, make sure you always decide on what step is required next to get you closer to your goal, and set a date and time for its completion.

Whatever the next step is — no matter how trivial — make a note of it in your calendar. If the event is set for a definite time, make sure that you make a point of recording the time, too. The point is that you don't want to take the chance of forgetting what you need to do to land your consulting job. Two of the key tests that you have to pass for your clients are punctuality and reliability. If you say that you'll call to follow up at 9:00 a.m. on September 30, then you'd better be dialing the number at 8:59 a.m. that day.

Mastering the art of the thank-you note

A thank-you note can do wonders to get you planted squarely in the middle of your client's good graces. Just as a post-interview thank-you letter makes a positive impression on a company that is hiring a new employee, a sincere thank-you note makes a positive impression on the individuals who decide whether you get a contract for your services.

Writing good thank-you notes is an art. They should be sincere and from your heart, and they should leave the reader with a positive impression of both you and your business. Whenever you write a thank-you note, make sure that it does the following three things:

- ✔ Personally thanks your client for her time and interest

- ✔ Firmly expresses your interest in doing the proposed work for your client

- ✔ Includes any additional information that the client may need to make a decision in your favor

So when should you take the time to thank a potential client? Consider sending a thank-you note whenever you find yourself in the following situations:

- ✔ **You want to thank a client for agreeing to meet with you at some future time.** This thank-you note also serves to confirm the date and time of your meeting.

- ✔ **You want to thank a client for having taken time to meet with you.** Not only do you get to express your sincere thanks to your client, but you also get to reiterate the many compelling reasons for selecting you or your consulting business.

- ✔ **You want to thank a client for the business.** After you're hired, a thank-you note expressing your gratitude is certainly in order.

Your note can be sent via e-mail or via the post office. You don't have to write a book — all it takes is jotting down a couple of sincere sentences of thanks and then dropping your note in the mail. When in doubt, send it out!

Following up via phone, e-mail, or letter

The medium that you select to follow up with your clients is not as important as making sure that you *do* follow up. Each possible way of following up with clients has its pluses and minuses, and which one you choose depends on your style of doing business and on what seems to work best with a particular client. You always have the flexibility of selecting one method or a combination of methods of follow-up. Ultimately, the decision is up to you.

Consider the advantages and disadvantages of several media for client follow-up:

- ✔ **Phone:** The most personal form of follow-through besides a face-to-face meeting is a personal phone call. When you phone your clients, you demonstrate that their business is important to you and that you are very interested in winning it. On the plus side, you can make a phone call from anywhere, most anytime you like. On the minus side, playing phone tag over a prolonged period of time or getting lost in voice-mail hell is certainly not unheard of.

- ✔ **Electronic mail:** Computer e-mail is a bit less personal than either a letter or a phone call, but, when used properly, it can still be quite effective. On the plus side, e-mail offers the ultimate in flexibility and convenience. On the minus side, if you get the address wrong, your message may bounce right back to you undelivered.

- ✔ **Letter:** You can easily hand-write or type up a letter anytime or anyplace. Although a personal letter delivered by messenger, by overnight delivery, or by mail is the most impressive to potential clients, you can also send it via fax. On the plus side, letters are convenient and effective. On the minus side, letters can get lost in the shuffle of busy executives.

However you decide to thank your clients for their time, you need to keep one key rule in mind: Be sure to *thank* them. Not only do you leave a positive impression in their minds that may help you land the deal, but you'll also be remembered for future opportunities even if you don't do business this time.

Moving On

In the process of selling your services to potential clients, you have to decide which ones have the greatest potential of doing business with you or your firm and which ones have the least potential. Although being able to put your all into pursuing every single lead that you get might be nice, it just isn't realistic from a cost perspective.

Following through with clients takes both time and money — and lots of it. Because both time *and* money are available in limited amounts for most consultants, the wise thing to do is to split your client list into two groups, active and inactive, and put most of your resources into the former. Consider the differences between active and inactive clients:

- ✔ **Active clients** are the clients who have shown a definite interest in hiring you or your firm. Because they are the most probable source of future work, they should get most of your attention. Make sure that you place them on a schedule of regular follow-up communication — phone calls, e-mails, product brochures, newsletters, and more — from your firm that keeps you and your services in their minds.

- ✔ **Inactive clients** may have once expressed an interest in your business, but your repeated attempts over a prolonged period of time (six months or more, depending on your own criteria) have failed to land a deal. You should downgrade such clients from active to inactive status and also decrease the amount of resources you devote to them. A good way to keep in touch with inactive clients is to add them to the mailing list for your firm's electronic newsletter. For little or no cost, you keep open the possibility of doing business in the future.

In our experience, considering both active and inactive clients as potential clients is always wise. You never know when a client who has been inactive for months or even years will suddenly spring to life and want to hire you for an important job. We've seen this happen time and time again. Always *build* bridges with your clients — never *burn* them. After all, in consulting, it's not always *what* you know, but *who* you know — and what they think about you — that can make the difference between success and failure.

Part V
Taking Care
of Business

By Rich Tennant

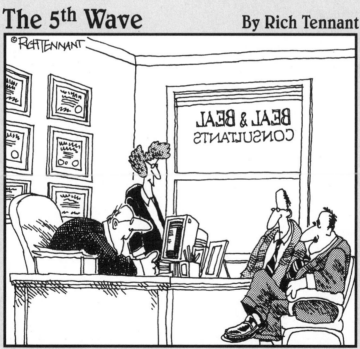

"Our goal is to maximize your upside and minimize your downside while we protect our own backside."

In this part . . .

Despite rumors to the contrary, becoming a consultant is not quite as easy as simply printing up a set of business cards and waiting for clients to come walking through the front door. Consulting is a business, and there are right ways and wrong ways to set up a consulting practice. In this part, we talk about the right ways to negotiate contracts, track your time and your money, communicate with clients — and prospective clients — and troubleshoot a variety of common business problems.

Chapter 16

Contracting for Business: It's a Deal!

. . . .

In This Chapter

▶ Defining contracts

▶ Reviewing the different kinds of contracts

▶ Negotiating contracts and agreements

. . . .

*M*oney makes the world go around in business, and contracts determine *how much* money you're paid, *when,* and for *what,* in addition to clarifying other expectations — little things like what you'll deliver and when you'll do it. Contracts are the basis for most business transactions and, heaven forbid, if you ever have to take your client to court to get paid, the first thing the judge will ask to see is a copy of the contract. For these reasons — and many more — *every* consultant should be *very* familiar with them.

This chapter is all about contracts — what they are, why you enter into them, and which kinds you're most likely to encounter during your career as a consultant. We also address another very popular topic that is near and dear to consultants from all walks of life: negotiating.

Getting the Lowdown on Contracts

What exactly is a contract? A *contract* is nothing more than an agreement between two or more parties to do something (or *not* do something) in return for something of value — called *consideration* among those who make a habit of practicing contract law. Contracts can be oral or written and range in size from simple one-page agreements to incredibly complex documents as thick as the Manhattan Yellow Pages. The details and complexities of a contract depend on the nature of the agreement and often the number of lawyers who are involved in drafting the contract. (Peter Economy's Third Law of Contract Dynamics states that the size of a contract is directly proportional to the number of lawyers involved, multiplied by the number of days they are given to work on it, squared.)

In some cases, oral contracts may be just as valid as written contracts. However, written contracts offer a variety of advantages over oral contracts, and you should insist on them whenever possible. Although some consultants are willing to work on a handshake (and many of them are doing *very* well, thank you), most have discovered that, in the long run, it pays to get agreements in writing and not rely on memories — or the continued goodwill of others — for something as important as the financial future and continued health and viability of a business, or you and your family.

In this section, we review the key elements of a contract and tell you about the many different kinds of problems that can make a contract unenforceable. And believe us, there are more than just one or two! That said, this chapter is written to give you a general overview of the principles of contracts and negotiation. Because every contracting situation is unique, our advice is to seek out competent legal counsel before entering into *any* contract.

Honing in on key contract elements

Good morning, and welcome to Business Law 101 — thanks for dropping by. Today, our topic concerns what constitute the key elements of a contract.

Every contract — written and oral — has three key elements. Each of these elements has to be in place for a contract to exist. If even one element is missing, then the contract is not valid. Without further ado, here are the key elements of a contract:

- ✔ **Offer:** An *offer* is simply a proposal — either oral or in writing — by one party to undertake an action on behalf of another party in exchange for adequate consideration. For example, you may offer to provide tax consulting services to local businesses in exchange for a fixed monthly fee. To be valid, an offer must be serious and must contain definite terms. What is *adequate consideration,* you ask? Keep reading to find out.

- ✔ **Acceptance:** An *acceptance* is a party's agreement to the terms of an offer as evidenced by an oral or written promise to pay the agreed consideration. (Still don't know what consideration is? Keep reading.) Acceptance can be made only while an offer is still open. If the offer is withdrawn before acceptance or rejection, then the offer has expired. If there is no acceptance, then there is no contract.

✔ **Consideration:** *Consideration* is something of value given in exchange for performance, or a promise of performance. Examples of valid consideration include money, goods, services, the promise to do something that there is no legal obligation to do (for example, build a Web site for a client at some future time), or the promise *not* to do something that there is a legal right to do (for example, take a client to small claims court for nonpayment of a bill for services rendered). *Adequate* consideration is generally whatever the two parties agree to, unless there is evidence of fraud or duress.

When these three elements are in place, you have a contract. Congratulations — you've made a deal! However, that's not necessarily the end of the story. After a contract is in place, several issues may make the contract unenforceable. We take a look at these in the next section.

"Unmaking" a contract

So you have the three essentials of a contract: an offer, an acceptance, and consideration. Everything's cool, right? Well, maybe. A number of circumstances can affect the validity of a contract. After a contract is formed, either party can raise certain issues to try to break it. Chances are, you'll never encounter a situation where your client will try to legally unmake your contract, but what's the old Scout motto? Be prepared. The key considerations that can ultimately impact the ability of someone to challenge the validity of your contract include the following:

✔ **Capacity:** This means that the parties who enter into a contractual agreement must be of legal age, sane, and sober for the contract to be valid. If not, you've got a *big* problem (and, likely, in more ways than one!).

✔ **Duress:** One party of a contract must not use undue pressure — either mental or physical — to force the other party to agree to the terms of a contract. If this situation exists, the contract could be in jeopardy.

✔ **Form:** Due to the Statute of Frauds, certain kinds of contracts in the United States — for example, home improvement contracts and sales of goods worth more than $500 — *must* be in writing to be enforceable. Depending on your locality, oral contracts for these kinds of transactions may be unenforceable. Check your state laws or seek adequate legal representation if you are unsure what your situation is.

✔ **Fraud:** If a party to a contract intentionally misrepresents an issue of substance in the contract, this is considered to be fraud, and the contract may be unenforceable. Above and beyond the issue of fraud, anyone in business who intentionally misrepresents him or herself—or their business—is someone you would not want to deal with in any circumstance.

✔ **Constructive fraud:** This occurs when one or more parties to an agreement knowingly omits an important piece of information by failing to fully disclose a key fact. An example of this is if you sign a contract to buy a commercial building from a broker who happened to "forget" to tell you that the owner received a notice from the city — *before* you signed the contract — that the property was going to be condemned to build a new shopping mall. Again, a contract made under these conditions may be unenforceable.

✔ **Legality:** The contract must be for a legal purpose. For example, a contract to provide consulting services on how to smuggle diamonds into the country or use fake credit cards to make unauthorized cash withdrawals from bank ATMs is not legally valid. Contracts for illegal purposes are automatically considered void and unenforceable and they can be unmade.

✔ **Mutual mistake:** Although a mistake by one party to a contract may not make a contract unenforceable, if *both* parties make a mistake on an important issue — say, where both parties relied on a faulty sales catalog that priced an item at $4,500, when it was actually $45,000 — then the contract may be unenforceable.

Did *your* contract survive all the tests? Yes? Great! Now maybe you can sleep a little easier at night. Next we take a look at the different kinds of contracts, along with the good and bad points of each.

Dealing with Different Kinds of Contracts

Although in some situations, both oral and written contracts may be equally valid in the eyes of the law (with the exception of those jurisdictions in the United States that, in accordance with the Statute of Frauds, require written contracts for certain kinds of transactions), each has its own set of pluses and minuses. Oral contracts are unintimidating and friendly, but they can be easily forgotten and hard to prove. On the other hand, written contracts can be easily understood and enforced, but they can also be complex and bureaucratic.

Ultimately, the choice of what kind of contract you use is up to you — it's *your* business, after all. However, many of the clients you deal with will want you to sign a contract — *their* contract — whether or not you want to do business that way. Our advice is for you to develop your own written contract form — meet with your legal adviser to hammer out the details — and then use it for all the work you do. In many situations, a client will sign your agreement with few or no comments or changes.

If you *do* decide to accept your client's contract form, read it carefully before you sign it. If you have any questions about any of the provisions, ask your client to explain them. And don't forget: Have your lawyer look it over *before* you sign — not after.

Oral contracts

Most people are involved in an incredibly wide variety of transactions every day — both business and personal — that are conducted on the basis of oral, or verbal, agreements. A kid in your neighborhood agrees to shovel the snow off your driveway and sidewalk in exchange for a nice, crisp $10 bill. She completes the job, and you pay her the agreed amount. The counter person at the deli down the street says that he'll make you the best ham and cheese sandwich you've ever had if you'll pay him $5 for it. You agree. He makes the sandwich, you pay him the money, and you're on your way. Think about all the other agreements that you enter into on an oral basis each and every day of your life.

Here's how an oral contract might be formed between you and a client during the course of a face-to-face meeting in her office:

> **Consultants R Us (You):** I've taken a good look at my schedule, and I can commit to develop a marketing plan for your new product line within two weeks. How's that sound?

> **Acme Fashion Warehouse (Client):** Great! That should fit the roll-out schedule perfectly. How much will you charge me to develop the plan? Don't forget — we're your number-one client, so I'm expecting you to sharpen your pencil!

> **Consultants R Us:** Right, how could I ever forget that? You know that I *always* give you my best rate. I can do the job for $4,500. We can go with our usual arrangement of one-third, or $1,500 upfront, and the balance to be paid within 30 days after I deliver your marketing plan.

> **Acme Fashion Warehouse:** That sounds fine. So to summarize, you'll complete the new product marketing plan in two weeks for a total price of $4,500 — right?

> **Consultants R Us:** Yes.

> **Acme Fashion Warehouse:** And I can pay you $1,500 to start, with the balance due within 30 days after you deliver the plan to me?

> **Consultants R Us:** Correct.

> **Acme Fashion Warehouse:** Super! Let me give my bookkeeper a call and he'll cut a check for $1,500 to get you started. Stop by his desk on the way out. I'll see you in two weeks!

> **Consultants R Us:** Okay — see you then.

You and your client at Acme Fashion Warehouse have just entered into an oral contract.

In many cases, a court of law may consider an oral contract to be just as binding as a written contract. However, this doesn't mean that oral contracts are as good for your business as written contracts. Despite their ease of use, oral agreements often have a number of problems:

✔ **People forget.** Although your oral agreement may be very clear and precise at the moment you agree to it, either or both parties may soon forget the exact terms. And, even if they don't forget, anytime you've got two or more people in the mix it's easy for misunderstandings to occur.

For example, Peter once hired a landscaper to cut back four trees on his property. As they walked around the yard, Peter pointed out exactly which trees he wanted cut, and then left for the office. When Peter returned, he was shocked to find out that his landscaper had cut down one of his favorite trees — three were right and one was wrong. A written agreement along with a detailed map of the yard might have saved this particular tree's life.

✔ **People go away.** Sometimes people get sick or die, and the terms of any oral agreements that they were party to go away with them. You've seen how hard it can be to sort out a business disagreement when there are written contracts and agreements to guide the parties. Well, imagine how difficult it is trying to figure out who owes what to whom when one of the parties isn't there to give his or her side of the story. Unfortunately, enforcing an agreement can be *very* difficult when there is no proof or evidence that it exists.

✔ **Complexity begets confusion.** If an agreement goes very far beyond the simplest terms and conditions such as who, what, when, and for how much, the complexity of the contract grows quickly. As the complexity of your contract grows, so too does the potential for confusion and misunderstandings. Clearly, oral contracts are inadequate for dealing with complex terms and conditions.

✔ **You just may end up in court some day.** You never know. You can be going along for years doing jobs simply on the word of your clients and a handshake when, suddenly — *bang!* — a client refuses to pay for a project that you toiled many long hours over. Now, if it's a $50 job, no big deal – you're probably not going to lose your business over it. But if it's a $5,000 job, or a $50,000 job, then you have a problem — a problem that can potentially put you out of business. Though most people never plan to end up in court, many do. And if you do, an oral contract is much more difficult to prove to a judge and enforce than a written contract.

✔ **You may not be able to recover your legal fees.** In many jurisdictions, you won't be able to recover the legal expenses that you incur to pursue a legal action against a client unless this provision is clearly spelled out *in writing* as part of a written contract.

If you decide that oral contracts are the way that you want to conduct business, then please take our advice. Only do so with trusted clients, and make absolutely sure that you use a letter of confirmation or a quick e-mail note when you reach agreement with a client (see Figure 16-1). The letter of confirmation or e-mail note briefly outlines *your* understanding of the key terms of the agreement and allows your clients to double-check *their* understanding of the agreement against yours. And if you ask your client to sign and return (by mail or fax) a copy of your letter acknowledging agreement to the terms — or reply to your e-mail confirming receipt — then you have that much more assurance (and written evidence) that both you and your client are working off of the same sheet of music. Remember: The business you save may be your own!

Written contracts

Like it or not, written contracts are here to stay. Despite the nostalgic longing that many people have for the days when deals were done with nothing more than a person's word and a handshake to back them up, most consultant business today is conducted with some sort of written agreement. If you're not convinced of the need to enter into written contracts with your clients, all it may take to change your mind is a couple of months — or even years — in court attempting to recover the thousands of dollars that a client owes you.

A written contract can be anywhere from a page or two in length to hundreds — even thousands — of pages.

Whew! Written contracts sure sound like a lot of work. Why bother? The main reason is that a written contract provides clear evidence of the *intent* of the parties to be bound to an agreement as well as exactly *what* the parties agreed to be bound to. In other words, a good contract clarifies the expectations of all concerned. In addition, a written contract often encourages discussion and an effort to clarify the definitions or terms in a contract. For example, a common contract term is "reasonable business expenses will be reimbursed." Okay, but is first-class airfare considered to be reasonable or not? Are color copies of reports (at $12 each) reasonable, or only black-and-white? Having these terms in the contract invites conversation, clarity, and agreement.

One more reason exists: the Statute of Frauds. Under this provision of the Uniform Commercial Code (UCC), any contract in the United States for the sale of goods that exceeds a total of $500 must be in writing. Not only that, but the contract must clearly state the key terms of agreement and must be signed by the customer. Many states and jurisdictions have their own versions of the Statute of Frauds.

June 14, 20xx

Sara Grosvenor
Tertiary Technologies, Inc.
4242 Chairman Way
Land O' Orange, FL 33333

Dear Ms. Grosvenor:

This letter confirms today's agreement for the design of a genetic
transporter and the delivery of a complete set of production drawings
and blueprints. Here is a summary of the terms of our agreement:

Delivery date: Draft plans will be delivered on or before November 30,
20xx; final plans will be delivered on or before January 31, 20xx

Total price: $75,000
Payment schedule: One-third upon start of work; one-third upon delivery
of draft plans; one-third upon delivery of final plans

Payment terms: Net/30 days

As always, it's a real pleasure working with you, Sara. I am confident that
we will surmount the challenges of this unique project and provide you
with the promised plans on time and within budget. If you have any
questions, please do not hesitate to call me anytime.

Please acknowledge your agreement to the above terms and conditions
by signing and dating the space below and returning a copy of this letter
to me as soon as possible.

Sincerely,

Felix Wang
Chief Innovator

_____
Acknowledged by   Date

Figure 16-1:
An example
letter of
confirmation
with
acknowledg-
ment for
your viewing
(and
contracting)
pleasure.

Although contracts *can* be very complex and lengthy, they don't *have* to be — especially for the kind of work that most consultants do. You certainly don't want to scare off potentially lucrative clients by pulling 50-page contracts out of your briefcase and requiring your clients to sign them in triplicate before you'll do work for them. The point of a written contract is to ensure that each party to an agreement understands what is required of each party. In most cases, for the vast majority of consultants, doing so takes only a page or two.

Written contracts come in many different forms. Here are a few of the most common.

Purchase orders

If you consult for larger businesses or the government, purchase orders are a regular part of your daily diet of written contracts. A purchase order is a written offer to purchase your services for a specified amount of money. In some cases, your clients will issue purchase order *numbers* in lieu of a written document.

A purchase order is technically considered to be a *unilateral* (one-sided) contract, that is, you accept the offer not in writing, but through your performance of the requested service or delivery of the requested product. For example, if your client issues a purchase order for you to produce an environmental impact report, a unilateral contract is deemed to exist if you perform by completing the requested work. A purchase order is considered a *bilateral* (two-sided) contract when both parties sign it before performance begins. Both types of purchase orders are equally valid.

Simple contracts

Simple contracts — normally one or two pages in length — are appropriate for the kind of work that most consultants do. Not only do they contain the most important parts of an agreement between consultant and client — such things as project definition, scope of work, performance requirements (sometimes called *deliverables*), price, delivery or completion dates, payment terms, payment schedules, and so on — but, because of their simplicity, they are easy to interpret and unintimidating to most people. Not only that, but if you end up in court, a judge can easily interpret the terms and conditions and make a decision relatively quickly and easily.

For many consultants, simple contracts are just what the doctor ordered. Figure 16-2 is an example of a simple contract that contains all the basic information needed for most consulting situations. Use it as a guide and feel free to modify it to suit your own individual needs. Whether you pick a version similar to Figure 16-2 or a variation of that format, be sure to have your attorney take a look at it before you start using it.

Sample only: Consult with competent legal counsel before entering into any contract.

AGREEMENT FOR CONSULTING SERVICES

Client's name and address: _____

Description of services to be provided to client: _____

_____

_____

_____

Start date: _____   *Completion date:* _____

Fees: $ _____ *per* _____ *(hour/day/other)*

Total estimated hours/days/other: _____

Total estimated fee: $ _____

Other costs: $ _____   *for* _____

Payment terms: _____

Additional terms and conditions, if any: _____

_____

_____

For _____(consultant)   *For* _____(client)

_____(signed)   _____(signed)

_____(date)   _____(date)

Figure 16-2:
A sample
simple
contract.

Complex contracts

In addition to the basic terms and conditions contained in simple contracts, complex contracts contain a slew of additional terms and conditions meant to address any and every problem or legal challenge that could possibly occur during the course of project performance and beyond. Instead of only the simple stuff, such as project definition, scope of work, performance requirements, price, delivery date, payment terms, and so on, suddenly you've got entire paragraphs or pages with such scary titles as "Warranties," "Termination," "Governing Law," "Force Majeure," and much, much more.

It's funny how things work. As the amount of consideration that you contract for increases, so do your clients' desires to enter into complex agreements. For example, a client who is happy to issue you a purchase order number for a $500 order may demand that you sign a 25-page contract loaded with any manner of complex terms and conditions when the price of your work crosses the $10,000 threshold. Every client is different, so you'll need to become an expert at what they will and will not accept — and decide whether you're willing to do business the same way.

Unless you are highly experienced and conversant in the terms and conditions of complex contracts, our advice is to bring in competent legal counsel when you're confronted with a long, complex contract filled to the brim with such terms and conditions. And don't automatically assume that, after you establish a precedent with an organization, all future contracts will reflect this precedent. Most organizations work with lawyer-drafted, lawyer-approved "boilerplate" (standard) contracts that are modified to reflect the particular terms and conditions of each deal. Every time you enter into a new contract with an organization, you're really starting from scratch. Read all new contracts closely to make sure that they match your expectations.

If you need to draft a complex contract, or you need someone to review any contract or agreement that a client has given to you to review and sign, then grab your Yellow Pages or Internet search engine, flip to the section or do a keyword search on "attorneys" and find a good lawyer to help you out. The legal review may cost you a couple hundred bucks, but the investment can save you a lot of heartache (and sleepless nights) down the road. Believe us — we've been there!

The ABCs of Contract Negotiation

What would a chapter about contracts be without a discussion of how to negotiate them? Although it would be nice if all your clients would just accept everything that you propose (yeah, we know — that would truly be Fantasyland), sooner or later you're going to have to negotiate terms and conditions with your clients. Don't worry, as you will soon see, anyone can become a better negotiator — it just takes preparation and the application of some easily acquired skills and techniques.

Without a doubt, each one of us negotiates every day for a wide variety of reasons and purposes. *I don't think I can make a 3:00 meeting — how about 4:30? $25 to do an oil change for my car seems too high — make it $15 and you've got a deal. There's no way that I can do everything that you want for only $25,000. Now, if you can raise the ante to $35,000, I think we may be in the ballpark. I said, you need to be in bed by 8:00 tonight — no ifs, ands, or buts! Okay — you can stay up until 9:00, but that's it!* In fact, it might not be exaggerating to say that life is one long series of negotiations.

As you may have noticed, there is no shortage of books available on the topic of negotiating. In this section, we distill the wisdom and tips gleaned from literally thousands of years of human negotiating experience into a concise package that fits neatly into your pocket. Well, it fits if you tear this section out and fold it a couple of times before you try to stick it in your pocket.

Carry on.

Anticipate the negotiation

No matter how simple a negotiation seems on the surface, or how trivial or small the amount of time or money involved, it always pays to think ahead and *anticipate* the negotiation on which you are about to embark with your client. Even if it's only to briefly outline your goals or do a little bit of research on your client's needs, the additional insight that you gain by anticipating your negotiation puts you in a position to better achieve your personal, business, and financial goals.

Although you can do many things to get ready to negotiate, you should always take these four essential steps before you open a negotiation:

1. **Prepare your goals.**

   If you don't have goals, then you never know where you're going, and you won't know when you've arrived. Goals are the ultimate targets that you're going to work hard to achieve in a negotiation. Take time *before* you negotiate to determine your goals and how important they are to you. Would you be willing to give up or modify certain goals in exchange for others? Know exactly what *you* need to achieve in your negotiation, and be prepared to get it.

2. **Research pertinent background information.**

   A wide range of information about the organization you plan to negotiate with is available. (Do a few different searches on the Internet, or check the business press for starters.) Use this information to help plan your negotiation strategies for achieving your goals. Consider the following:

- What do you know about your clients?

- Are they in the news?

- Are there pressing issues for the company or the industry?

- Can you determine what the pain is that you're being asked to eliminate?

- Is your client on the hot seat, under extreme pressure, or firmly in control?

- Who is making the purchasing decision on consulting services? Does your contact person have the authority to make the buying decision?

- What is the client's past experience with consultants? What have other consultants' experiences with the company been like?

- What is the company's budgeting calendar? Is the company at the beginning of its fiscal year and anxious to start spending the money that it budgeted for consultants? Or is the company at the end of its fiscal year, thus trying to pinch every penny and make money stretch as far as possible?

3. **Evaluate your client's positions.**

What do you expect your client's positions to be? Do you expect that the client may want to shorten or lengthen the period of performance? Or request that you cut your fee or increase or decrease the number of hours you have proposed to perform the project? Put yourself in your client's shoes for a moment and anticipate his or her positions. Can you estimate what the real value (maybe increased revenues or reduced costs) of your efforts will be as measured (in dollars and cents) by the client? After you do that, determine how you will counter your client's objections if and when your client introduces them.

4. **Prepare your own positions.**

Before you enter into *any* negotiation, prepare the positions that *you* will present and defend. Positions are the wants that you communicate to the other party in a negotiation — the interim stops along the way to achieving your goals. For example, your goal may be to make $50 an hour on a particular job, but your initial position may be to charge your client $60 an hour. Most likely you'll have already prepared your initial positions and submitted them to your clients in your proposal. However, before you negotiate, you should also prepare back-up positions in the event that your primary positions are not acceptable to your clients and you can't get them to see the infinite wisdom of going with your suggested plan.

Figure 16-3 presents a quick and easy worksheet that you can use to prepare for *any* negotiation.

Prenegotiation Worksheet

- What are your top three goals for this particular negotiation?

  1.

  2.

  3.

- What do you expect your client's top three goals for this particular negotiation to be?

  1.

  2.

  3.

- What do you expect your client's initial positions to be?

  1.

  2.

  3.

- What do you expect your client's backup positions to be?

  1.

  2.

  3.

- What are your initial positions?

  1.

  2.

  3.

- What are your backup positions?

  1.

  2.

  3.

Figure 16-3:
Use this worksheet as a guide to preparing for negotiations.

Be in keeping with the basic rules of negotiation

In negotiation, a number of basic rules have evolved over millions of years of human existence. Master these rules, and you'll be a real pro at negotiation. You'll always get *exactly* what you want, and your life will be full of unlimited success and happiness. Well, maybe not. However, if you ignore these basic rules, or fail to practice them effectively, we can guarantee that you'll end up with a lot less from your bargains than you hope for.

Anyway, here are the seven — count 'em, seven — basic rules of negotiation:

- **Be prepared.** Being prepared gives you a definite advantage in *every* negotiating situation — so much so that the downside of not preparing for a negotiation far outweighs the small amount of time and effort that it takes to prepare. And what should you be prepared for? For starters, go back to the preceding section titled "Anticipate the negotiation" and do the four things that we recommend there. Back so soon? Then go on to the second basic rule of negotiation.

- **Leave plenty of room to maneuver.** Nobody likes to be boxed into a position with no room for compromise or for flexibility in meeting the *mutual* goals of both parties. When you develop your negotiation goals and positions, build in enough flexibility to allow you to modify them to better achieve both your clients' goals and your goals.

- **Have lots of alternatives in mind.** For every possible reason that your client gives for *not* agreeing to one of your requests or positions, you should have one or more alternatives ready to go. For example, if your client says that four weeks is not an acceptable delivery schedule, then be ready with an alternative that gets your client the delivery in the two weeks that he wants, but with an increase in fee to compensate for the rush job. If an increase in fee isn't acceptable to the client, then consider redefining the scope of work to deliver less while meeting the minimally acceptable requirements and staying within his budget.

- **Keep your word.** In business, as in life in general, your word should be your bond. Negotiation is built on a foundation of trust and mutual respect. If you aren't willing to keep your word, then you'll quickly lose both trust and respect. It's one thing to make an honest mistake — most anyone can understand and deal with that — but if you can't keep your word, then what do you have left? (Here's a hint: Not much.)

- **Get the cost, time, and scope right the first time.** Clients don't want to hear a consultant come back for more money, more time, more this or that after the project has begun. Yes, there are legitimate times — sometimes many legitimate times — when you simply don't know how much work will be required until you get started. One technique for handling this is to build an assessment phase into the agreement so that you can properly scope out and estimate the amount of work, time, and money it will take to do the job right.

✔ **Listen more than you talk.** One of the most important negotiating skills is the ability to listen — *really* listen — to the other party. If you ask the right questions and then let your counterpart talk about the answers, you usually find out exactly what it will take to successfully negotiate and close a deal. Don't forget: When you're talking, you're not listening!

✔ **Don't give up too much too soon.** In our experience, it pays to not give up too much too quickly when you're dealing with a tough negotiator. Not only do you appear weak and perhaps a bit desperate (perceptions which don't work in your favor), but you also miss out on getting any significant concessions from your client. Take your time when you're negotiating with your clients. It's better for *them* to be in a big rush to close the deal than for *you* to be in a big rush to close the deal.

✔ **Learn to say no.** Telling a client no is a very difficult skill for many consultants to acquire. We all want to tell our clients yes to encourage positive client relations. However, when you're negotiating a deal, sometimes you have to say no if you want to achieve your own goals. For example, if your client wants you to cut your normal fee in half and you don't want to do so because you'll lose money on the deal, then just say no, but offer an alternative, such as a slight reduction in fee in exchange for payment in 10 days instead of 30, or a reduction in the amount of work you will perform.

Close the deal

Closing your deal successfully — that is, reaching final agreement on all terms and conditions and signing all the appropriate documents on all the appropriate dotted lines — is the ultimate goal of every negotiation. Countless business deals have lost their wheels and careened out of control and into the ditches of the backwaters of commerce when the parties couldn't reach final agreement and close their deals.

Closing is an art. The more you do it, the better you get. However, it's never too late to learn a few new tricks or brush up on old ones. Here are a few tips to help ensure that you close your deals efficiently and with a minimum of bumps along the way:

✔ **Give your clients lots of reasons to say yes.** The more reasons your clients have to say yes, the greater the chance that they will say yes. Find as many ways as you possibly can to make it easy for your clients to say yes. If you do, you'll *definitely* close a lot more deals.

✔ **Confirm your agreement.** To ensure that your understanding of the final agreement matches the other party's understanding, confirm your agreement — first verbally, and then in writing. If there's a problem, you'll undoubtedly hear about it very quickly!

✔ **Don't be surprised by last-minute surprises.** We have both been in many negotiations where we had reached (or at least *thought* we had reached) a final agreement with the other party, only to have them toss in a new demand or condition at the last possible moment. Be prepared for clients who use this negotiation tactic to wring additional concessions from you. If this happens to you, it's a good idea to calmly tell your counterpart, "No, this is not what we agreed to," and demand that he stick to the original deal. If your counterpart refuses, then it's up to you to decide if you need the business so much that you'll take the deal anyway, or whether it may be in your interest to just walk away. Sometimes walking away from a bad deal (and a difficult client) is the smartest thing you can do.

✔ **Follow up with a thank-you note.** Not only is sending a thank-you note a nice way to express your personal thanks to your client for hiring you or your firm, but it's also a great way to build rapport. The best business, after all, is built on long-term relationships with your current clients and the future clients that they refer to you.

✔ **Move on if you can't close the deal.** Despite all your efforts to reach a mutually beneficial agreement, some deals are just not meant to be. If this is the case, and there's nothing you can do to bring negotiations to a successful close, then simply tell your client that you can't do business and move on. By breaking off negotiations, you show your clients that you're serious, and they may very well make the final concessions necessary to close the deal. If not, then you can get on with your life and direct your efforts to more fruitful pursuits — such as lining up your *next* client.

Chapter 17

Keeping Track of Your Time and Money

*W*hen it comes right down to it, keeping track of the financial aspects of your business is really quite simple. There are essentially only two kinds of money that you need to focus on in your business: the money that comes in and the money that goes out.

This chapter is all about keeping track of your time — the hours of work for which you bill your clients — *and* your money. We start by talking about how to keep track of your time and how to track the work you do on specific projects for specific clients. Then we briefly consider the ins and outs of budgeting and the importance of staying on budget.

Tracking Your Time

Although some consultants bill their clients as they complete specific percentages of the project — say, every third or half — and some work on retainers where they are paid a fixed amount of money each month, many other consultants charge their services on the basis of some increment of time (usually hourly). Although you should seriously consider keeping track of the use of your time regardless of how you bill it (what better way to find out that you're spending more than half of each workday playing Solitaire on your computer?), you absolutely must do so if you're paid based on the number of hours you work on a particular project.

Although there are many different ways to track the time that you spend working on client projects (ummm . . . abacus? Post-It notes?), you'll probably find that most of your needs can be accommodated using just two different forms: the client activity log and the client time sheet. The following two sections examine exactly what each of these forms is all about.

The daily client activity log

If you're the kind of consultant who bills your time hourly or on another basis related to time, then the best way to track your time is to maintain an activity log. An *activity log* is a daily record of everything you do for your clients, broken down into your smallest billing increments — say, an hour, half an hour, or a quarter of an hour. By the way, some lawyers we know break their hours into six-minute increments.

Figure 17-1 represents a simple daily client activity log that is appropriate for almost any kind of consulting work that's billed in proportion to the amount of time you put in. It's up to you to decide the smallest increment of time you want to use to bill your clients. Most consultants use 15-minute blocks, but for simplicity's sake (and to keep the log from taking up two entire pages of this book), we have selected 30-minute increments for our example. You can select any portion of an hour that you like (and to which your clients agree!).

The first thing you may notice is that the client activity log looks very similar to an appointment calendar — in fact, an appointment calendar, either software or paper based, makes a great activity log — with every half-hour noted, from 7:00 a.m. until 5:00 p.m. Of course, you can tailor your client activity log to fit your exact schedule. If, for example, you start work at noon and work until midnight, you can set up your log on that basis.

As you can see from the sample client activity log in Figure 17-1, the consultant worked on projects for four different clients on February 8. The consultant worked on the Ramsey project from 7:00 to 8:00 and worked on a draft report for Willis from 9:00 to 11:00. Just before lunch — from 12:30 to 1:00 — the consultant made phone calls for Martinelli, another client. After a satisfying break for lunch, the intrepid consultant jumped into an Internet search for Speedway Associates from 1:30 to 3:30, and then finished the workday with another phone call to Martinelli from 4:30 to 5:00.

What's the point of going through the trouble of keeping a daily client activity log — isn't that a lot of paperwork to fill out every day (and who has time for that)? Before you decide that filling out an activity log every day is too much pain for you to endure, consider these advantages:

Daily Client Activity Log	
February 8, 20xx	
7:00	Internet search for Ramsey project
7:30	Internet search for Ramsey project
8:00	
8:30	
9:00	Worked on draft report of recommendations for Willis
9:30	Worked on draft report of recommendations for Willis
10:00	Worked on draft report of recommendations for Willis
10:30	Worked on draft report of recommendations for Willis
11:00	
11:30	
12:00	
12:30	Phone calls on behalf of Martinelli
1:00	
1:30	Internet search for Speedway Associates
2:00	Internet search for Speedway Associates
2:30	Internet search for Speedway Associates
3:00	Internet search for Speedway Associates
3:30	
4:00	
4:30	Phone call to Martinelli
5:00	

Figure 17-1:
Sample
client
activity log.

✔ **You're going to want to bill your clients someday.** Sure, working on all those fun consulting projects can be very satisfying in and of itself. However, you still have to pay your bills. And if you want to pay your bills, then your clients have to pay theirs! Keeping a client activity log makes it much easier to bill your clients when the time comes.

✔ **One sheet of paper is a lot better than lots of little sheets of paper.** The temptation to scribble your hours on a scrap of paper or a sticky note is often overwhelming, but you must resist this temptation at all costs! You can easily lose or forget about all those little scraps of paper, or your cat or dog may decide to eat them. Before you know it, you've done a heck of a lot of work for nothing because you can't bill your clients for it.

✔ **Your log has a better memory than you do.** You may think you can rely on your memory to keep the ten different projects that you're working on for seven different clients separate from one another and then bill them properly at the end of the month. Though you may be blessed with a memory that would make *Jeopardy!* fans around the world green with envy, we guarantee you that the memory in your client activity log is longer and much more precise — especially when you're considering 260-plus workdays in a year filled with a variety of projects for a variety of clients. Do yourself a favor and start using a client activity log to keep track of the time you spend on your consulting projects.

So, you may be wondering if we practice what we preach. In a word: yes. Bob keeps a daily client activity log on his computer in the form of an Excel spreadsheet. While he doesn't always have a chance to update it every day, he doesn't let more than a couple of days pass before he does, picking up client time from his appointment book and notes. Peter is also a big fan of daily client activity logs; however, his log is in the form of a spiral-bound notebook that he keeps on his desk to use for tracking work priorities and taking notes of conversations with clients. Every time he works on a client project, Peter notes the client name, the start and stop times, and a short description of the work done. Both Bob and Peter keep track of time in 15-minute increments.

Now that we've convinced you that it's in your best interest to use a daily client activity log to record your time (we *have* convinced you, right?), what do you do with all the information that you gather? This is the best part. You get to transfer all that information to your client time sheets. Coincidentally, that just happens to be the next section of this chapter.

Client time sheets

Eventually — perhaps once a month or maybe more often, depending on your client billing arrangements — you should plan to send an invoice to each of your clients for the work you did for them during that billing period. Believe us, this task is *much* easier and a lot more accurate when you've been maintaining your client activity log on a regular basis. (You *are* maintaining a client activity log, right?)

A client time sheet (see Figure 17-2) is simply a summary of the exact work that you do for a client, including how much time you spend on each task or project. Deciding what approach you want to use to present your information is up to you and your client.

Client Time Sheet	
Speedway Associates	
February 20xx	
Client consultation	20 hours
Internet searches	45 hours
Draft product marketing plans	10 hours
Focus groups	15 hours
Total hours	90 hours

Figure 17-2:
A sample
client time
sheet.

As you can see from the sample client time sheet, the consultant performed a total of 90 hours of work for Speedway Associates in February. This total was further broken down into specific tasks, including client consultation (20 hours), Internet searches (45 hours), drafting of product marketing plans (10 hours), and focus groups (15 hours).

Where did these numbers come from? They came directly from the client activity log that the consultant completed and maintained for each and every workday. Because the consultant bills his clients on a monthly basis, he goes through the month's client activity log and prepares client time sheets for each client at the end of each month. The client time sheet, which is merely a summary of the information contained in the daily client activity log, can then be used as the basis for the consultant's monthly invoice.

Billing Your Clients and Collecting Your Money

Although the entire topic of accounting is important when it comes to ensuring the financial health of your enterprise, the effectiveness of your billing and collections procedures probably has the greatest impact — whether positive or negative — on the health of your consulting practice. If you bill your clients quickly and accurately and then follow up to ensure that you collect your payments when they're due — or even sooner whenever possible — you do a *lot* to ensure the financial viability of your business.

Billing for your services

How you bill or invoice your clients for the work you do depends on your contract or, in the absence of a written contract, any other agreements you may have made regarding billing and payment. If your contract is set up to pay you as you achieve specific milestones — say, completing one-quarter of the project or submitting a draft report of recommendations — then you invoice your clients for the amount due upon completion of each milestone. However, if you work on an ongoing basis and bill your clients for the number of hours that you work plus expenses (photocopying, travel, and so on), then you collect the charges and bill them to your client at the end of the agreed-upon billing period, usually the end of each calendar month.

Figure 17-3 shows a sample invoice based on the Speedway Associates example used earlier in this chapter. As you can see, the number of hours for all the work done in February was simply totaled and multiplied by the contracted billing rate of $50 an hour for a total payment due of $4,500. If your client agreed to reimburse you for other expenses you incurred on behalf of the project — say, for example, a three-day trip to Atlanta, Georgia — then the actual cost of the airline ticket, hotel, food, and ground transportation would be added to the invoice.

Here are some tips on maximizing the effectiveness of your billing process:

- ✔ **Front-load your billing.** If you invoice on a milestone basis during the course of the project, try to load your fees into the front of the project rather than at the end. For example, push for an advance payment to start the project, or simply make your first couple of payments higher than those that are due later in the project. Doing so gives your project a financial head start that is very beneficial to the financial health of your practice while minimizing the risk if a client moves into a late-pay status during the course of a project.

- ✔ **Bill your clients often.** The more often you get paid, the better the effect on the positive flow of cash through your practice. Although monthly payments are pretty much the standard for consultants who bill hours and expenses, you can agree with your client to bill them more often than that.

Invoice	
Speedway Associates	
February 20xx	
Client consultation	20 hours
Internet searches	45 hours
Draft product marketing plans	10 hours
Focus groups	15 hours
Total hours	90 hours
Billing rate	$50/hour
Total amount due	**$4,500**
All payments due 30 days after invoice date. A prompt-payment discount of 1% will be granted for all payments made no later than 10 days after invoice date.	
Thank you!	

Figure 17-3:
A sample invoice.

✔ **Invoice immediately.** Immediately after you complete a milestone or reach the end of your billing cycle, send an invoice to your client. The sooner you send an invoice, the sooner your clients pay their bills. And the sooner they pay their bills, the better off your practice is financially. Peter tries whenever possible to send out invoices to clients within a day or two after the end of the month.

✔ **Use e-mail whenever possible.** In the good-old days of business, invoices would typically be mailed to clients, taking up to a week to arrive. However, many clients today welcome invoices sent via e-mail, which cuts the amount of time it takes to deliver an invoice from days to seconds. The sooner your invoice gets to a client, the sooner it gets paid. Make e-mail invoicing a regular part of the way you do business, and encourage your clients to do the same.

✔ **Offer a discount for prompt payment.** To help motivate your clients to pay early (or at least on time), offer a nominal discount — say, in the range of 0.5 percent to 1 percent — for paying their invoices within 10 or 20 days. You'll pay a nominal amount of money when you offer your clients this privilege, but the positive impact on your cash flow usually makes the cost a worthwhile one.

✔ **Monitor client payments closely.** Keep an eye on the status of your invoices and make sure your clients pay their bills on time. If certain clients don't, call them personally to see what the problem is. If it looks like you're going to have a hard time getting them to pay the amounts they owe you, act quickly to initiate your collection procedures.

What? You don't have any collection procedures? Then perhaps you should have a look at the section of this chapter titled "Collecting delinquent accounts."

Billing for reimbursable expenses

If business travel and other project-related business expenses, such as copying, phone calls, courier or overnight mailing service, postage, and so forth, are involved, it is often agreed in advance that the client will reimburse you for these expenses. (It should be in your contract — see Chapter 16.) In your contract, you should

✔ Be clear about what is reasonable and what is not going to be covered.

✔ Be in agreement about when you will be paid for these expenses.

✔ Be clear about what form the reporting of these expenses will take. Do you need to keep every receipt and do you need to fill out their forms or will yours suffice?

Billing your client for these reimbursable expenses is crucial and can occasionally be at times that are not related to the performance of the contract. For example, if you agree to fly to China for a client to interview his suppliers for a week, you can rack up some very hefty travel expenses. If your client doesn't pay for these in advance, you'll need to bill him. If this activity takes place at the beginning of a nine-month project — where the next milestone is at three months — you can be stuck holding the tab of several thousand dollars for three months. That crunches your cash and strains your business. You need to have an agreement that you will be paid for reimbursable business expenses as soon as possible — preferably "upon receipt of invoice."

Collecting delinquent accounts

No matter how great your clients are or how wonderful they are about paying their bills, eventually you encounter a client who either pays you late or doesn't pay you at all. Believe us when we tell you that we've had some of the best clients in the world, but even the best clients sometimes have not-so-great clients who don't pay them. Then they find themselves stuck in the middle, unable to afford to pay their *own* consultants and vendors. What should you do? Do you ignore this behavior and just be glad that you have the work, or do you take action? Our advice is to take action — *immediately.*

The action you should take to collect the money owed to you could probably be turned into a mathematical equation with variables for many things: the size of the job, the length of the relationship with your client, the total amount of money owed to your business, the number of days (or months) that the money is overdue, and more. When you decide to initiate your collection procedures, you need to weigh these factors in your decision. Whatever action you take, we recommend that you establish a clear order of precedence — starting with a simple phone call and then escalating your actions upward in intensity depending on your client's reaction — to guide you through the process.

If you decide that it's time to start the collections process, consider taking these steps as a part of your efforts:

1. **Call or send an e-mail to your client directly.**

   Politely mention that the payment is past due, and ask if your client can check into it. In some cases, you'll find that the client has forgotten to approve the invoice and submit it for approval. In other cases, the client's accounting folks may be sitting on the invoice, waiting for some additional bit of information from your client. Regardless of the cause, first start the collections process directly with your client. Your client likely has much more leverage being inside the organization than you do being on the outside. Therefore, your client probably will have more success getting your bills paid than you will if you call the payment department yourself. You often can solve the payment problem in only a few minutes with a call to your client.

2. **Send a past-due notice.**

   If the call to your client doesn't resolve the payment problem within a reasonable amount of time — say, a few days or a week — then send a written past-due notice to your client along with another copy of your invoice. Send these letters by regular mail — weekly or monthly — until you receive your payment. If the amounts are serious, and it appears that your client is trying to slip out of paying you, then be sure to send the letters by Certified or Registered mail, with a return receipt requested. Follow up your letters with phone calls to your client and to your client's billing department asking for help in solving the problem.

3. Stop work.

If you're not being paid, consider suspending your work until you *are* paid. Your work may be the only leverage — short of legal action — that you have to get your client to pay you. Of course, when you stop work, you risk angering your client and destroying your relationship, so be sure you take this step only after careful deliberation.

4. Call in a collections agency.

If the client continues to ignore your requests for payment, you can turn your delinquent account over to a collections agency. The agency will pursue the collections process for you for a piece of the money that is ultimately collected, usually somewhere in the neighborhood of 20 percent to 40 percent. Take this step only after you're convinced that your client isn't going to pay you, and the relationship you've built is effectively defunct.

5. Offer to take less and get on with your life.

If you're going to give 20 percent to 40 percent to a collection agency, you may decide to accept less than the full amount due to get the whole mess behind you. It's not preferable, and it can be a dangerous precedent, but it can also free you up to get on with the rest of your life and back to those clients that honor their agreements.

6. Mediate or arbitrate.

In lieu of going to court, both parties can submit to mediation, in which an independent third party helps you resolve your differences, or to arbitration. If both parties submit to arbitration, an independent arbitrator listens to both sides of the story and then makes a decision in favor of one party or the other. Check your contract to see if there is an arbitration clause.

7. Take the client to court.

Taking your delinquent client to court is the last remedy that you have. You can sue your client in small claims court, which allows you to sue without a lawyer for a very small fee, as long as the amount is within the limits of your state or locality — different states and countries have different limits for small claims actions. Check with your local court to find out the limits and procedures that apply to you and your business. If the amount owed exceeds the amount allowed by small claims procedures, then you need to hire a lawyer and file your lawsuit in a higher court.

Ideally, you'll never have to go to court to get your clients to pay you. The good news is that most clients will pay what they owe well before you get to that point. By monitoring your payments closely and contacting your clients at the first hint of trouble, you minimize your risk of exposure due to late payments or payments that are never made.

Building Better Budgets

A *budget* is an estimate of the amount of money you expect to bring *into* or pay *out* of your organization for whatever business activities you undertake. For example, you may estimate (and budget) that you'll bring in $25,000 worth of client billings in October. Or you may estimate (and budget) that you'll spend $300 in telephone charges in January.

Why should you consider developing budgets for your consulting business? You should do so because budgets provide you with a baseline of *expected* performance against which you can measure the *actual* performance of your consulting enterprise. With this information, you can diagnose and assess the current financial health of your business.

You can also use budgets to fulfill another important purpose: to provide a baseline against which you can measure your progress toward the successful completion of client projects. For example, if you are 50 percent of the way through a project but have spent 75 percent of the amount you budgeted, then you have an immediate indication that you may run out of money before you complete the project. This is not a good situation for any consultant. Either you've under-budgeted your expenses for the project, or you're over-spending. Whenever budgeted performance and actual performance disagree, your job is to find out why.

Differentiating between budgets

Depending on the size of your business, the budgeting process may be quite simple or very complex. You can budget almost anything related to your business, regardless of its size. While many home-based or small consulting firms get by with few or no budgets, larger firms are likelier to use a greater variety of budgets.

For example, although Peter works on a variety of projects every year and his business does well financially, the only budget he uses is a sales budget. At a glance, Peter can see his anticipated revenues and where they're coming from on a month-by-month basis, and identify shortfalls in future months that need to be addressed with additional marketing attention. Peter constantly updates the budget with new information as soon as it's available, including checks as they are received from clients, contracts when they're signed, and the addition of new proposals (as well as the deletion of failed ones).

Here are some examples of commonly used budgets:

- **Project budget:** A project budget is an estimate of all the different potential expenses that you'll incur during the course of a project compared to the amount of money your client intends to pay you.

- **Labor budget:** A labor budget is made up of the number and names of all the various positions in a company (if there are various positions in the company), along with the salary or wages budgeted for each position.

- **Sales budget:** The sales budget is an estimate of the total number of products or services that will be sold in a given period. You determine total revenues by multiplying the number of units by the price per unit.

- **Expense budget:** An expense budget contains all the different expenses you may incur during the normal course of operations. You can budget travel, training, office supplies, and other similar costs to your business within your expense budget.

- **Cash Budget:** This can be a simple budget that charts (weekly or monthly) when you expect to actually receive the payment (cash in) from your client and when you expect to have to pay your bills (cash out).

- **Capital budget:** This budget is your plan to acquire fixed assets (those with a long, useful life), such as furniture, computers, facilities, a physical plant, and so forth, to support your business operations.

Creating a budget

There's a right way and a wrong way to create budgets. The *wrong* way is simply to take a copy of your last budget and stick a new title on it. The *right* way is to gather information from as many sources as possible, review and check the information for accuracy, and then use your good judgment to guess what the future may bring. A budget is only as good as the data that goes into it and the good judgment that you bring to the process.

Here are a few tips to consider when you put together your budgets:

- **Gather data.** Retrieve copies of your previous budgets from your filing cabinets and then compare the figures that you budgeted against your actual experience. Look at this historical data to determine whether you overestimated or underestimated figures in any of your previous budgets and to see what previous years or similar projects cost your firm. Take time to consider whether you need to hire more people, lease new facilities, or buy equipment or supplies. Finally, consider what effect possible large increases or decreases in sales or expenses may have on your budget.

✔ **Meet with clients.** When you start the budgeting process, meet with your key clients to get a firm idea of the fees that you can expect your work for them to generate. You also want to get some idea of when the revenues will hit your system.

✔ **Apply your judgment.** Hard data and cold facts are an important source of information in the budgeting process, but they aren't *everything*. Budgeting is one part science and one part art. Your job is to take the data and facts and then apply your own judgment to them to determine the most likely outcomes.

✔ **Run the numbers.** Put your estimates of money coming into your business and money going out of your business into a budget spreadsheet and hit the calculate button on your computer. Review and modify this draft of your budget before you finalize it. Don't worry if the draft is rough or is missing information. You can always fine-tune it later.

✔ **Check results and run the budget again as necessary.** Closely review your draft budget and see whether it still makes sense to you. Are you missing any anticipated sources of revenue or expenses? Are the numbers realistic? Do they make sense in a historical perspective? Are they too high or too low? When you're satisfied with the results, finalize your budget and print it. Congratulations! You did it!

But you are not done! You need to review the budget regularly. Depending on how fast you collect and spend money, you may have to do this weekly. Others may have the luxury of giving it a sniff only monthly or quarterly.

Staying on budget

After you begin each client project, you need to closely monitor your various budgets to make sure you don't exceed them. If your actual expenditures start to exceed the amounts that you budgeted, you need to take quick and decisive action before you dig a financial black hole that quickly sucks up all your financial resources.

Here are some things you can do to get back on track if the money you send out of your business starts to significantly exceed the amount of money that you bring into it:

✔ **Freeze discretionary expenses.** Some expenses, such as computer repairs, telephones, and electricity, are essential to your business and cannot be stopped without jeopardizing it. You can curtail discretionary expenses, such as purchasing new carpeting, upgrading computer monitors, or traveling first-class, without jeopardizing your ability to complete client projects. Freezing discretionary expenses is the quickest and least painful way to get your actual expenditures back in line with your budgeted expenditures.

✔ **Freeze hiring.** Of course, you can cease hiring new employees only if your business is large enough to hire employees in the first place. By delaying the hiring of new employees, you save not only on the cost of hourly pay or salaries but also on the costs of any fringe benefits that you provide, such as medical care, and overhead expenses like water, electricity, and janitorial services.

✔ **Increase your rates.** Part of the problem may be that you aren't charging a high enough rate for your services to cover your reasonable and necessary expenses. If this is the case, consider raising your rates for new business that you bring in.

When it comes to keeping track of your money, budgeting is really just the tip of the iceberg. Whether you like it or not, as the owner of your own business, you need to have a basic understanding of the process that your business goes through in order to account for the money it makes and the money it spends. Even if you have the great fortune of being able to hire an accountant, it is your responsibility as owner to know what is going on with your business's books. Check out *Accounting For Dummies,* 3rd Edition, by John Tracy (Wiley) for all the information you need to know about the wonderful world of accounting.

Chapter 18

Communicating Your Way to Success

*I*f your goal is to be a successful consultant (and how could you wish for anything less?), you first have to be a successful communicator. Relationships are the foundation upon which you build your business with clients, and you can help build and strengthen your client relationships by becoming an effective communicator. If you communicate well with your clients, not only do they have more confidence in your abilities, but they also enjoy working with you more and are more likely to hire you for other jobs later.

Of course, some people are better communicators than others. Some people just have a knack for presenting their thoughts in speech or in writing. Others just ooze the kind of charisma that makes everything they say seem to be accompanied by the voices of angels. Fortunately, for those of you who still have a way to go before angels start providing backup to your words of wisdom, there's good news. You can learn to become a better communicator. How? All you need to do is follow some very simple advice and then practice, practice, practice. And when you're done practicing, practice some more. The more you communicate with others — whether in speech or in writing — the better communicator you'll become. And the better communicator you are, the more confident you feel communicating, the more you enjoy it, and the more effective you are with your clients.

One thing about communication and your clients: Make sure that the way you communicate with your clients is based on *their* preferences — not your own. If your client prefers a personal phone call over an e-mail message, then pick up the phone and call. If your client prefers to have one point of contact within your business instead of several, then provide that single point of contact. If your client prefers long meetings over lunch for project briefings, then do it that way — even if you hate lunch meetings. Be sensitive to your clients' communication needs, and your clients will have one more reason to send more business your way. Of course, you still have to do a good job on your projects!

This chapter is about communicating with others and, in particular, the *way* in which you communicate. We find out how to sharpen those rusty writing skills, and address the importance of communicating in person with your clients and asking the right questions at the right time. For detailed information on another important aspect of communicating with your clients — making presentations — see Chapter 10.

Putting It in Writing

Technology offers us a glut of ways to communicate with clients, including mobile and fixed-line telephones, e-mail, fax, voice over IP, instant message, mail, voice mail, and many more. We suppose that you could still use smoke signals or Morse code if you were so inclined. As a result of all these new-fangled ways to communicate, you may think that good old-fashioned writing is obsolete and soon to be replaced with something better. If that's what you think, you couldn't be farther from the truth.

The simple fact is that writing is more important than ever. Whether you're writing a proposal for new business, sending a thank-you note to a client, or responding to an associate's e-mail message, good writing never goes out of style; it's also an essential element of your success as a consultant.

What to put in writing

Although it looks like writing has many happy and healthy years ahead before it becomes obsolete (witness this 350-plus-page book and its many yellow-and-black-covered brothers and sisters, for example), it has turned into a bit of a lost art. Voice mail, e-mail, and the like have generally supplanted the need for a large amount of business correspondence that traditionally used to flow between consultants and clients, but writing still has a vital role to play in the world of business communication. In fact, because of its increasing scarcity, well-written business correspondence can set you apart from the rest of the pack.

So now that you may be thinking that writing is worth considering, what things should you write? Here are a few forms of communication that can help you foster good relationships with your clients:

✔ **Business letters:** Business letters — printed out and delivered by the postal service, by an overnight courier, or by fax or as an attachment to an e-mail message — are the traditional backbone of all business correspondence between consultants and their clients. Consultants write business letters to their clients for many reasons, including persuading, thanking, selling, apologizing, communicating good news, communicating bad news, asking questions, and seeking information. Crafting a good one- to three-page business letter takes more work than a two-sentence e-mail message, and the extra effort is usually worth it.

✔ **Notes:** Writing and sending notes to your clients and clients-to-be should be a central part of your writing campaign. Today, notes most often take the form of e-mail messages, mobile phone text messages, or instant messages (IMs). You can (and should) send your prospects thank-you notes after you meet with them or after you complete a project for them. And, yes, you can still write your notes out by hand and personally deliver or fax or mail them. If you write thank-you notes by hand, your clients will appreciate the thought, and you'll appreciate their business.

✔ **Proposals:** Very few clients will hire you without some form of written proposal of what you plan to do for them. Proposals require a very precise and organized style of writing that conveys not only the fact that you can do what you say you can do, but that you can do it well and cost-effectively. A well-written proposal can make the difference between being hired and being rejected. See Chapter 7 for detailed information on how to write winning proposals.

✔ **Reports:** For many consultants, reports — and the presentations that go with them — are the only products they deliver to their clients. Because of this, the contents of reports — and the way that reports are written — are critically important in the acceptance of consultants' recommendations by their clients. The next section addresses the important issues involved in writing good reports.

Composing two basic consulting reports

No matter what kind of consulting you are doing, in most cases you will use two different kinds of written reports to communicate with your clients: progress reports and final reports. In some cases, particularly in complex projects of long duration, you will use both types of reports. In others, especially with projects that are relatively simple and short in duration, you may need to submit only a final report.

Although you can choose to employ many different formats to get your information across to your client, perhaps the most important consideration of all is your client's expectation. If your client expects a short and to-the-point report, make sure you deliver a short report. If your client expects a long, detailed report, make sure you tailor your format to meet that need. It's not so much the size of the report that matters; it's the information within it. Many clients are very busy people who would prefer a five- to ten-page report filled with concise money-making — and money-saving — ideas that they can easily understand and put to work. Above all, don't make work if you don't have to. Time is money, both for you and for your client.

Progress reports

Progress reports — also known as milestone reports or project status reports — do just what they say: They report your progress on the way to completing a project. A progress report can be anything from a short, one-page update to a full-length, multipage extravaganza. Regardless of the length of your progress reports, make sure they are concise and to the point.

The exact length and format of your report are up to you and your client, but you should make sure your progress reports contain at least the following information:

- ✔ **Executive summary:** Write a brief but complete summary of the progress of the project during the reporting period, highlighting accomplishments and recommendations. This summary gives your busy clients a chance to get a quick overview of your progress without having to read the entire report.

- ✔ **Key accomplishments:** Your clients will be particularly interested in any notable accomplishments that you've achieved on the project. If you had any key accomplishments during the reporting period (and make sure that you do), make them known to your clients in the progress report.

- ✔ **Work completed during the reporting period:** Summarize the exact work that you completed during the reporting period and discuss how it relates to the overall project. Your progress report should be a snapshot of your activity during the period of time that you are covering in the report.

- ✔ **Percentage of completion:** This information is simply an estimate of the percentage of completion of your project during the period of the report. If, for example, you are approximately one-third of the way through the project, simply note your percentage of completion as 33 percent.

- ✔ **Work to be completed:** Briefly discuss the work to be completed during the next reporting period and how it relates to the rest of the project. If you anticipate any particularly notable accomplishments — or particularly problematic issues — highlight them in this section of the progress report.

✔ **Issues:** If you have encountered any problems or other issues that need to be brought to your clients' attention, list them here. Make sure you follow up this written presentation of project issues with personal, face-to-face discussions with your clients. You absolutely do not want to surprise your clients with project issues or problems. Bring up challenging issues as soon as you encounter them and ensure that they are promptly acknowledged and addressed. And if something serious comes up before your next progress report is due, inform your client immediately by telephone or e-mail. Don't wait until the next scheduled report.

How often should you produce progress reports? The specific answer to that question depends upon the exact nature of the project, how long the project is scheduled to last, the expectations of your clients, and the terms of your contract. If the project is a short one — say, only a few weeks' duration — you may not need to do a progress report at all. However, if your project runs for a month or more, progress reports are clearly in order. Although monthly progress reports are the norm for most consultants and their clients, there's no rule that says you can't do your progress reports on a weekly, quarterly, or any other basis that suits your needs and the needs of your clients.

Final reports

Your final report presents the results of your project and, as such, is the culmination and central focus of the efforts you have undertaken on behalf of your client. Depending on the exact nature of your work, your final report may be the showcase of the project, and it may form the basis for company-wide changes or restructuring.

In many cases, your final report will be the only product that your client will receive from you; its importance cannot be underestimated.

Final reports are different from progress reports in many ways. Here are the key ingredients that you always include in your final reports:

✔ **Executive summary:** Your clients are busy, busy people, and they don't have lots of time to wade through long reports. Briefly summarize the information you are presenting in your final report and highlight key project accomplishments and problems.

✔ **Project background and scope:** Some of the people who read your report may not know much about your project and why you were selected to do it. Make this part of the final report your opportunity to discuss the nature and scope of the project, how it came to be, and your role in it.

- ✔ **Methodology:** How did you approach the problem? Did you conduct a market survey? A statistical analysis? A review of the literature? Your readers want to know how you came up with the results and conclusions that form the basis of your report. The right answers to those questions add to your credibility and strongly support your recommendations. The wrong answers detract from your credibility and possibly create doubt about your recommendations.

- ✔ **Findings and conclusions:** This section of your report contains the results of your work and any conclusions you can draw from what you found out in your investigation. All your good news — as well as your bad news — goes into this section of your final report.

- ✔ **Recommendations:** Even more than your findings and conclusions, your recommendations are probably what your clients are most interested in reading. In this section of your report, you apply all your experience to develop and present your prescription to cure your clients' ills. Make sure your recommendations are concise and easy to understand and that they can realistically be acted upon.

- ✔ **Implementation guidelines:** Although your clients may not have asked you for specific guidance on implementing your recommendations, use this option to show your clients how your expertise can be of particular benefit to them. Do them a big favor by spelling out a step-by-step approach for putting your recommendations into place and include scheduling milestones and budgetary information. While you're at it, take the opportunity to propose your role in the implementation, along with a price and timetable to do so. Don't be shy — many consultants win a lot of business this way!

- ✔ **Summary of benefits:** Although your findings, conclusions, and recommendations may make perfect sense, most organizations need some sort of incentive to make any change to the status quo. Summarize the benefits of your recommendations in a way that shows your clients why they should be compelled to implement them. Increasing sales, decreasing expenses, getting new products to market quickly, avoiding litigation, improving customer satisfaction, and decreasing employee turnover are just a few of the possible benefits of your recommendations.

Improving your writing skills

Like anything else, the more you write, the better you'll get. So how can you write better? Dust off that old pen and paper or boot up your word processor and get to work! Here are eight tips for writing better that you can start using right now:

✔ **Know your point.** Before you write a single word, think about the point that you want to make. What's your point, and what kind of reaction do you want from those who read what you write? Keep your thoughts tightly focused and sharp.

✔ **Know your audience.** Just like when you give a speech or make a presentation, you should always know your audience before you put pen to paper (or fingertip to keyboard). You should consider that your report may go to others — both inside and outside the organization. Keeping your audience in mind will help you be clearer, minimize jargon, and more effectively sell your message.

✔ **Get organized.** Writing is difficult when your thoughts are a disorganized mess. The solution is to organize your thoughts before you start writing. One of the best approaches is to create an outline of what you want to say. An outline — or even a few notes — can help you pull your thoughts together into a coherent written product. As an additional aid to getting your thoughts organized, bounce your ideas off clients, business associates, or significant others.

✔ **Write the same way that you speak.** The best writing is natural, like everyday speech. Write the way that you speak. Don't be artificially formal or too businesslike and sterile when that's not your style. Not only will your writing be less accessible, but you'll squelch your individuality and personality.

✔ **Be concise.** Don't write just to fill up a sheet of paper with your words — every word should have a purpose. Avoid fluff and filler at all costs. When you write, make your point, support it, and then move on to the next point.

✔ **Simplicity is a virtue.** In writing, as in life, simple is better. Why waste your time writing a 300-word memo or letter when a 50-word note is sufficient? Why use jargon and indecipherable acronyms when plain English works just as well or even better? Make it your life's purpose to simplify, simplify, simplify.

✔ **Write and then rewrite.** There's no writer, amateur or professional, on the face of this green earth who doesn't need to rework much of what he has written until it's just right. We both have lots of experience in this regard — just ask Alissa Schwipps, our project editor for this book. When you write, first create a draft of what you want to say and then edit it for content, flow, grammar, and readability. You may need to write a few drafts before your work really shines, but the effort will be worth it.

✔ **Convey a positive attitude.** People naturally prefer upbeat, positive writing over writing that is negative and a drag to read. Falling into the negativity trap is easy, but don't let yourself become a victim! Even when you have to communicate bad news, be active, committed, and positive in the words that you choose and the way that you write. Your readers will really appreciate your approach!

If you want to find out more about how to write better, you can find plenty of books and classes to help you. Check your local library or bookstore for a wide variety of titles on improving your business writing skills. Contact your local community college, university extension office, or private training companies, such as The Learning Annex. People who write for a living and are quite good at it teach many of the classes offered in these outlets.

Harnessing the Power of the Spoken Word

Communicating occupies a large portion of every consultant's day. Whether you're trying to sell a prospective client on the infinite wisdom of hiring you to appraise her collection of Barbie dolls, or asking an accounts payable clerk about how he processes payments to vendors as part of your audit of his firm, your success depends heavily on your ability to speak and be understood.

In the following sections, we give you tips for saying what needs to be said and letting your personality shine through when you meet your clients face to face. We also discuss what questions need to be asked and why, and we provide some pointers on making business meetings as productive as possible.

Being an ace communicator face to face

In an increasingly impersonal world, filled with e-mail, voice mail, and text messages, faxes, and other technology-driven forms of communication, communicating in person — face to face — has become a rare commodity. And it is exactly because of its rarity that communicating in person is perceived to be more valuable — and therefore more powerful — than most other forms of communication that you could choose.

In a face-to-face meeting with a client, you rely on your ability to speak clearly and effectively. Most people consider speaking effectively with others to be something they do pretty well. However, even if you have a great deal of practice talking to clients, you can do several things to become an even better communicator:

> ✔ **Think before you leap.** Whether you're responding to your clients' questions or preparing to ask some questions of your own, you should stop for a moment to get your bearings before you leap into the breach. Reacting rather than reflecting can be tempting, but your first reaction may very well not be your best reaction.

✔ **Keep it simple and brief.** When presenting information to your clients, keep the information as simple as possible so that your clients understand it clearly and easily. Also make your statements as brief as possible while still conveying the information you need to convey so that you hold your clients' attention as you speak. Complexity begets confusion, and confusion makes it more difficult for you to control the outcome of your discussion. It is sometimes appropriate to use limited visual aids (we're not talking about a 20-slide PowerPoint presentation!) to present information. These, too, should be as easily understood and to the point as possible.

✔ **Ask lots of questions, and listen to the answers.** Not only does asking lots of questions show that you are genuinely interested in what your clients have to say, but it's also a great way to obtain information about your clients' needs and expectations. Vary the number of questions you ask, depending on the exact purpose of your contact and the amount of time available.

✔ **Be enthusiastic.** If you're excited by the prospect of doing a project for a client or providing an update of your progress, make sure your client knows it. The more enthusiastic you are about doing your client's project, the more enthusiastic your client will be about having you do it (and about paying your invoices when they come due!).

✔ **Be empathetic.** Your client will receive your message more favorably if you tailor it to the listener's individual needs. As the old saying goes, you should "walk a mile in their shoes." For example, if your client is too busy to spend more than a few minutes at a time with you, you need to present your message much differently than if your client seems to have all the time in the world and likes to philosophize for hours and hours.

✔ **Get personal.** A key component of consulting is building relationships with your clients. The best way to do so is to get personal with them. Although you should maintain a certain amount of professional decorum in your business relationships, you should get to know your clients as people, not just as customers. Get to know their likes and dislikes, whether they have kids, and what kinds of hobbies or other non-job interests they have that you may share (tennis, anyone?). Do business over lunch or dinner. Play a round of golf or racquetball together. However, before you dive in too deep, be sensitive to where you draw the line between your personal relationships and your business relationships with your clients. Although some clients may prefer to develop friendly, personal relationships with their consultants, others may prefer to keep some distance. Regardless, keep in mind that the rapport you develop with your clients helps you cement long-term relationships with them. And that's good for you *and* for your clients.

As you can see, you can do many things right now to increase the power of your personal touch. Give them a try. We guarantee that you'll see a marked difference in your client relationships almost immediately.

And don't forget: You won't always be able to be there in person. Some consultants have found in this situation that they can use a combination of the phone and presentation slides or worksheets to communicate effectively with their clients. They make their presentation on the phone while the client pages through it. Certain advanced software even allows the consultant to control which slides the client sees while talking on the phone. When you find yourself on the telephone with a client instead of there with him, the same advice for face-to-face interactions applies. In addition to the preceding tips, speak a little more clearly, a little slower, and a little louder so that your client will have a better chance of understanding you.

For more information on making the most of your business communication efforts, check out *Communicating Effectively For Dummies* by Marty Brounstein (Wiley).

Asking the right questions at the right time

If consultants should do one thing well, it's asking questions. Lots of questions. How much can you afford to spend to redecorate your house? When do you need this marketing survey completed? Did you know that my business has located more high-producing wells than any other in the valley? Not a day goes by that consultants don't ask clients — or clients-to-be — questions about something.

Because asking questions is such a big part of your job as a consultant, how do you make sure that you ask the right question at the right time? Before we answer that question, first consider exactly why consultants ask questions.

Asking questions: Why to do it

If you stop and think about it, consultants ask questions for many different reasons. Although you may at first think that the number-one reason to ask questions, such as why, what, when, and where, is to find out simple answers, asking questions goes far beyond those simple kinds of responses.

When asked the right way and at the right time, questions can give you direct insight into the heart and soul of your clients and provide you with a road map of where you should take your discussion. Here are some of the many different reasons that consultants ask their clients questions:

- **To obtain information:** You can solicit information from your clients by asking them questions along the lines of "Exactly what results are you hoping to achieve?" or "How soon do you plan to select a consultant for this project?"

✔ **To provide information:** You can use questions to inform your client about the capabilities of your consulting business and any number of other things. Try asking questions like "Did you know that, in addition to providing graphic design services, our consultants also produce press kits and other publicity tools?" or "Would you believe it if I told you that our largest customer is Apple Computer?"

✔ **To check comprehension:** Although your clients may be nodding their heads up and down throughout your presentations, do they really understand what you're talking about? You can check by asking questions like "Are you following me so far?" or "Do I need to explain anything we've discussed?"

✔ **To measure interest:** Of course, you want to quickly get a sense of whether your clients are interested in what you have to say or what you have to sell. Do so by asking your clients questions such as "Are you interested in contracting to have this work done?" or "Are you ready to make a commitment to this project right now?"

✔ **To encourage client participation:** Engaging your clients in your discussion is in your interest. You can encourage client participation by asking such questions as "What do you think about our approach?" or "What is the biggest problem that you're having with your current system of production scheduling?"

You have many more reasons to ask your clients questions than to simply find out when they plan to issue a contract or how much money they have to spend. Now that you know why consultants ask questions, read about the two kinds of questions they ask.

Asking questions: How to do it

Although you can ask your clients an infinite number of questions, there are only two key kinds of questions: open and closed. Just like you can open or close a door, you can either open up communication with your clients or close it down just by the kind of questions you ask.

There's a right time and place to ask open questions and a right time and place to ask closed questions. The type of question to ask all depends on the particular goals that you have set for your question-and-answer session. Following is a description of open and closed questions, including when you should use (and not use, as may be the case!) each kind.

✔ **Open:** Open questions require some amount of explanation to be answered. When you want to explore what your client thinks about a particular topic, you should use open questions. However, if you need a simple yes or no response, then open questions are definitely out. Open questions, such as "What suggestions do you have that can help make our proposal fit your needs?" or "How should we approach obtaining that particular information?" encourage your clients to go beyond simple yes or no answers and to open up and reveal their personal opinions and beliefs to you.

✔ **Closed:** Closed questions can be answered with a simple yes or no or another such specific response. Closed questions, such as "How many years have you been in business?" or "Do you like our proposal?" are great for getting specific responses and information, but they are lousy for getting your clients to open up and offer you any sort of insight into what they are really thinking. If you merely want to get specific answers to specific questions — and you want to avoid wasting time with a lot of needless discussion — then you should use closed questions.

We've delved deep enough into the whys and wherefores of asking questions. It's time to stop all this beating around the bush and find out the right questions to ask your clients. Determine the goals of your question-and-answer session before you start it and then apply the following rules when you ask your questions. Know where you want to go — and map out your route — before you start your journey, and you'll probably get there!

✔ **Do your research ahead of time.** Before you launch into your question-and-answer sessions, spend some time finding out about your clients and the kinds of issues they face and may need you to help them with. Don't waste your or your clients' time going through a list of issues that you easily could have obtained the answers to in advance.

✔ **Ask straightforward questions.** Don't beat around the bush or try to trick your clients. Ask your questions in a straightforward manner, and you're most likely to get straightforward responses.

✔ **Move from the big picture to the little picture.** Start with broad questions that give you a general sense of what your clients are thinking. As your clients answer your broad questions, use their responses to ask more precise questions that take you to the heart of the information you need to know.

✔ **Use answers as a foundation for more questions.** You frequently may have absolutely no idea where your questions will lead. Use the answer to each question as a bridge to your next question. Tailor your questions to the responses that you receive from your clients.

✔ **Try different angles.** If one approach doesn't work, don't be afraid to try another. You may have to ask your question many different ways before you find the one that gets the response you need.

✔ **Test your understanding.** Are you certain you understand exactly what your client wants or is telling you? Are you really sure? Test your understanding of what your client is telling you or the conclusions you are drawing from their answers. Ask questions along the lines of, "I'd like to double-check what I think I'm hearing . . . [fill in your understanding here]. Am I hearing it right?"

Making the most of in-person meetings

As you may have long suspected, meetings are a notoriously inefficient way of getting business done. Years ago, researchers determined that approximately 53 percent of time spent in meetings is unproductive, worthless, and of little consequence. And today, with the added distractions of PDAs and mobile phones competing for everyone's attention, our suspicion is that things are even worse.

But meetings don't have to be that way. By working the following five tips into your in-person meeting plans, you can become a meeting hero, instead of a meeting zero.

- ✔ **Be prepared.** Countless hours are wasted each and every day in meetings where the participants are unprepared. The good news is that you can choose to be prepared for your meetings, and you can help ensure that your clients are prepared, too. If there is material that your clients need to be knowledgeable about in the meeting, be sure to send it to them in plenty of time for the meeting. And be sure to let them know they need to review it!

- ✔ **Have an agenda.** Another big time-waster is meetings without specific direction. An agenda sets the topics you'll discuss, so it provides a framework on which participants can focus. Again, send it to your clients before the meeting so you can get their input and buy-in before you show up, rather than during the course of the meeting.

- ✔ **Start on time and end on time.** As a top-notch, highly professional consultant, you should always strive to be on time in all your client interactions. If you say you'll call at 3 p.m., then you should call at 3 p.m. This same philosophy extends to meetings. If you've ever waited for someone to show up for a meeting before it could start — and waited, and waited — you know how much time can be wasted when this practice is not adhered to. Keeping to agreed schedules builds expectations, discipline, and respect.

- ✔ **Maintain focus.** It's easy to drift off onto topics that have nothing to do with the purpose for your meeting — especially when the topics that you end up discussing are more interesting or entertaining than the business matters at hand. In most cases, topic drift is bad for meetings. When you're not focusing on moving the meeting agenda forward, then it's going to start taking a step or two or three backward. It is often helpful to state at the beginning of a meeting that if the group drifts you will respectfully stop the drift and move it back on track. This manages expectations and makes it easier to do it during the meeting.

✔ **Capture action items.** Be sure you've got a system in place for noting and keeping track of action items as they are discussed during the course of the meeting. You can have a great meeting, but if no one follows up and does what they promised to do, then maybe you didn't actually accomplish as much as you thought you did. Write down the action items, summarize them, and send copies to all attendees within a day or two after the meeting.

Become a better communicator and you will become a better consultant. Whenever you pick up the telephone, jot off a short note, or compose an e-mail message to a client, be conscious of what you're saying and how you're saying it. First impressions count, so be sure the one you make — and any subsequent interactions — are positive.

Chapter 19

Troubleshooting Common Consulting Issues

*W*hen you're a consultant, you either work for a consulting business or you own and operate your own consulting business. Either way, you find that — just as with any other business — issues, problems, and challenges arise that need to be addressed and solved. Sure, you can choose to ignore them, but in our experience, most of them don't go away when ignored. Instead, they often only get bigger, meaner, and harder to solve.

It's therefore in your interest — and in the long-term interest of your consulting firm, whether you own it or work for someone else — to identify problems as they arise and address them quickly. In this chapter we explore some very common consulting issues and problems and provide you with advice to help you identify them in your own organization and solve them.

Alleviating Poor Cash Flow

The old saying that money makes the world go 'round is nowhere more true than in your consulting business. The presence of cash can make it thrive, while the lack of cash will eventually break it. Every business needs cash to meet payroll, pay vendors for supplies, finance inventories, and more. The signs of poor cash flow are easy to recognize: The balance in your business checking account is getting lower and lower, and you're getting anxious about when the next payment from a client is going to arrive. When it gets really bad, you find yourself making vendor payments late because you don't have the cash to pay them.

Improving your cash flow is a quick and relatively easy way to improve the overall financial health of your consulting business — both in the short and long term. You can improve cash flow in four main ways:

- ✔ By speeding up cash receipts from customers
- ✔ By slowing down cash payments to vendors
- ✔ By increasing revenues
- ✔ By reducing expenses

Each of the following practices accomplishes at least one of those three things.

Requiring payment immediately (or sooner!)

Wouldn't it be nice to run a cash business, one where your customers paid you in cash when they purchased their merchandise or services? While relatively few businesses today run solely on a cash basis — even McDonald's and Starbucks take credit cards now — many do require immediate payment by way of cash, check, or credit card when an item or service is purchased. This is a near-ideal situation from the standpoint of cash flow. Instead of waiting 30 days (or more) after you send a customer an invoice to get your money, you have it in hand — right *now*!

Only one other situation is better: getting paid in advance. Many businesses require deposits, retainers, and other forms of advance payment as a normal part of doing business. Building contractors take deposits before they start work, authors receive advances before they start writing, and consultants may be paid a portion of their fee before they set foot in their client's building.

If you don't already do so, requiring payment on delivery, or even advance payment, is definitely worth your while. Don't forget: Happiness is a positive cash flow.

Paying no sooner than you have to

Every invoice has a due date. Though some businesses may require payment 30 days after delivering an invoice, others may require payment in only 15 days or less. *Always* pay your bills on time, but don't pay your bills sooner than you have to. If your vendor or supplier has agreed to finance your purchase for 30 days for *free* (which is exactly what is happening when you are sent an invoice with payment required in 30 days), then you should take full advantage of this free loan. By waiting to pay until payment is due, you have the benefit of your cash longer, and you positively impact your cash flow.

Making sure your invoices are right

A lot of companies simply reject invoices that have mistakes in them. And if an invoice is rejected, it won't be paid, and it may not even be returned to you for correction. After all, the company you invoiced is also taking advantage of the preceding tip (don't pay sooner than you have to). And by sending an invoice with a mistake on it, you're giving them an easy and semi-ethical way to extend the payment time.

Be sure that your invoices are absolutely correct before you send them out. And while you're at it, make sure they are addressed to the right place *and* the right person. When invoices go to the wrong place or to the wrong person, they tend to sit around unpaid or, worse, eventually find their way into the trash. If you want to get paid sooner rather than later, double-check all your invoices before they hit the mail, and make sure they're going to the right person at the right place.

Invoicing upon delivery

Some companies invoice all their customers on a set schedule, perhaps once a month. The trouble is that if an item is delivered on the first of the month but an invoice doesn't go out to the customer until the last of the month, 30 days of nonpayment are built into your cash flow equation — automatically. Then, if it takes your customer 30 more days to pay your invoice after he or she receives it, 60 days elapse between the time you deliver the item and the time you receive payment for it. Unfortunately, this is an easy recipe for cash flow disaster!

When you deliver a contracted item to a client, invoice your client that same day or no more than a day or two later. Check your contract for the method of invoicing, but always push for the method that is quickest — usually via e-mail or fax. The goal is to start the payment clock ticking as soon as you can. You'll get your money more quickly, and your cash flow will be better for it.

Billing more often

If you provide a service under contract over a long period of time, you may send out invoices after particular services have been delivered or after a set period of time — say, a month — has elapsed. If you are in this specific situation, an easy way to improve your cash flow is to increase your billing frequency. So, for example, if your current agreement requires you to bill monthly, you could renegotiate it to allow for billing twice a month, or perhaps even weekly.

The more often you invoice your clients, the better the impact on your cash flow. The payments are smaller, but you get your money sooner. And sooner is better when it comes to cash!

Managing your expenses

Cash flow is nothing more than the net result of the money that comes into your organization less the money that goes out. The less money that goes out, the better your cash flow. Every business has to spend money for things it needs to operate, but the timing of this spending can have a major impact on your cash flow. One way to reduce the amount of money that flows out of your organization — and to improve cash flow at the time — is to manage your expenses.

Only spend money when you absolutely need to. Need a new computer? Why not try to get another year out of your old one? FedEx raised its rates? Why not check to see what UPS, DHL, or the U.S. Postal Service charges? It pays to project your cash inflows (payments from clients) and to try to match them with your cash outflows (payments to vendors). For example, if you expect a big payment from a customer two months from now, you should defer all possible expenses until you have the cash in hand. That way you avoid the dreaded cash crunch that can occur when you spend more money than you have available to you.

Handling Clients Who Want Free Advice

Doctors have long known that once someone finds out the nature of their profession — say at a cocktail party or other social event — it won't be long before they're asked their advice about some physical ailment or pain. "Gee, Doc, I've had this pain in my back for years now — do you have any idea what it might be?" We're sure that many doctors avoid parties for this very reason.

Consultants often find themselves in the same boat when someone they meet or know finds out what they do for a living. Peter often experiences this when someone finds out that he is a professional writer. Many such new acquaintances instantly spill their guts about the book that they've long wanted to write, asking questions about the merits of the idea, what it would take to get the book published, and whether Peter has any interest in co-writing it. While Peter always enjoys talking books with people, there's a line between simply talking books and providing advice that Peter should be charging consulting fees to dispense. This line is not always clear-cut, and it's easy to give too much information away for free — removing the incentive for a client-to-be to pay for your services.

So, what should you do when someone asks you for free advice?

We've heard lots of good arguments on both sides of the issue. Some consultants argue quite convincingly that you should never, *ever* give out freebies. According to their way of thinking, to do so sets a dangerous precedent that will lead your client to expect further freebies in the future. But other experienced consultants argue just as convincingly that it can make perfect sense to give out freebies — especially if it will help you get your foot in the door for more business (or help ensure you keep it there once you have it firmly planted).

So, which approach is best?

Actually, giving free advice can be a good thing, especially when it leads to new business. For example, you may meet someone while you're networking who, based on the limited information you give him, decides to hire you to do a full-on consulting job. And it can definitely be a good thing when a current client wants to explore other areas of business that you can help with.

Our advice is to weigh the pros and cons of giving free advice in each and every case before you give it. Many consultants don't advertise their services, instead relying on referrals from happy clients to bring in new business. And if, for whatever reason, your clients aren't happy, then you're not going to get a lot of referrals to potential new clients. Giving some free advice is a kind of advertisement for your business, a marketing cost that should be anticipated, budgeted, built into your rates, and then happily extended when you feel the time is right. Always be prepared ask for their business card, to hand them yours, and to politely agree to follow-up with them later on the topic. Later when you're talking with them — either at their office or from your own office — you have shifted the environment to a professional setting where it is clearer that you are paid for this type of advice.

Of course, you can't do *all* of your work for free — that's a one-way ticket to a negative cash flow and bankruptcy. And, unfortunately, there are more than a few unscrupulous clients out there who would love nothing more than to have you do lots of work and never pay a dime for it. We've experienced that for ourselves more than once or twice. But for every lousy client like that, there are many more for whom an occasional freebie will work wonders, making it well worth taking a chance to give it. It all comes down to balancing your cost of doing the work for free with your assessment of the long-term potential of the relationship.

Getting That First Sale

If you've just started up your consulting business, you'll soon realize that you're not really *in business* until you have completed your first sale to a real, live client. Setting aside a bedroom as your consulting world headquarters doesn't mean you're in business, nor does printing new consulting business cards or setting up a Web site for your firm. Until you have your first client, and until you actually start performing work for her, you're just getting ready to do business.

Breaking the ice with a first sale, however, can be difficult for new consultants. While some consultants already have clients lined up before they make preparations to start up their businesses, others find that they hang out their nice, shiny, new consulting shingle and wait . . . and wait . . . and wait. So, what can you do if you're having a hard time getting that first sale? The following sections provide a few tips that will help you get out of the consulting parking lot, and into the fast lane.

Check your marketing

Say that you have the right product or service, and you have it for the right price. But, even so, you've yet to land your first client. What could be wrong? In this situation, it's likely that the news about your product or service is not getting to your target audience of potential clients, which means that your marketing efforts are falling short — *way* short. Take a close look at your marketing. What are you doing (or not doing) to publicize your consulting business and the services that you offer? Do you have a Web site? Are you networking with potential clients in your community or industry? Are you active in your local chamber of commerce or "leads" groups? Are you seeking opportunities to publicize your business through the local media or national bloggers? Do you have a marketing plan? If your marketing needs work, then plan to spend some quality time reading Part IV of this book for more direction.

Check your pricing

Okay. So you've got a great product or service, and you're getting the word out to a wide audience of potential clients that are very much in need of what you have to offer. All systems are "go," but you're still not getting that critical first client. Now what? Take a close look at your pricing. How much do you charge for your services, and how do these rates compare to those of your competitors? (If you don't know what your competitors charge, find out.) Are your prices significantly higher? If you're new to the market, you may find it difficult to get people to pay the same for your services as for consulting firms that have been around longer and have well-established reputations. Are you trying to compete on price alone, and neglecting to sell your clients-to-be on the value that you will bring to their organization, above and beyond the money that they spend? Consider dropping your price for your first few clients to break the ice and to begin to develop a stable of happy clients who will refer others to you and your firm.

Check your product or service

You may have a great price, and you may have great publicity and marketing, but you may simply have the wrong product or service for your target market. For example, you may have identified a great local target market populated with fast-growing, small technology firms. Only one problem: The consulting service you offer is of no interest to these fast-growing, small businesses. Be sure that your products and services are relevant to the market you want to enter. If they're not, then you can either change your target market or change the products and services you offer.

Check your competition

Your competition can teach you a lot, especially when it comes to landing your first sale. Before you offer your products or services to the public, you should definitely take some time to survey your competition. Find out exactly what they offer, at what prices, and in what time frames, and what your prospective clients like — and dislike — about working with them.

Check your expectations

There's one more thing to check if you're having problems landing your first client — your expectations. Have you quit your career and launched yourself headlong into a new consulting venture? If so, you may have put a lot of pressure on yourself, and your clients-to-be may sense that pressure — deciding to steer clear of you for now. Alternatively, have you kept your day job, and are you just dipping your little toe into the consulting waters? Again, your clients-to-be may sense that you're not fully committed to your business — and to their satisfaction — and they may be steering away from your offer to provide the services they need.

Are you hoping that becoming a self-employed consultant will rescue you from a life of quiet desperation working for someone else? (It may, but then again, it may not.) Are you expecting your consulting business to be a money-maker that will solve all your financial problems and keep the bill collector at bay? (It might, but probably not for months, or even years.)

Long story short, be sure you understand your own motivations and expectations for becoming a consultant, and then check to see how they are coloring your interactions with prospective clients. They can sense desperation a mile away, and they'll probably run — not walk — to your competitors when they sense it in you.

Dealing with Clients Who Are Slow (or Refuse) to Pay

There's not a consultant alive who hasn't run into a customer who either habitually pays late ("I'm expecting a big check this week — as soon as I get it I'll pay you!") or not at all. This is a problem for any consultant, but especially for those who own their own firms. You need a steady supply of cash coming into your business to enable you to keep it afloat.

When was the last time you took a close look at who owes you money, how much they owe you, and how far overdue their payments are? If you aren't keeping a close eye on your *accounts receivable* (the money that your clients owe you), you're leaving your business exposed to a potential financial disaster.

No matter how much we love our customers, some of them invariably don't understand how important it is to us that they pay their bills on time. A day or two late isn't a big deal. A month or two late *is* a big deal. Once your customers get in the habit of paying late, it can be almost impossible to get them to start paying on time.

Managing the money coming into your business is an important part of any self-employed consultant's job. (Even consultants who work for someone else should keep an eye on the money coming into their firm. If their clients aren't paying, these consultants may soon be out of a job.) When your clients don't pay you for your work when you deliver it, you are, in effect, granting them a loan. In accounting-speak, you're creating a *receivable* — an obligation for your client to pay you at some point in the future. While the generally accepted time for payment is 30 days after delivery of an invoice, that date can vary widely depending on the terms and conditions of your contract or agreement.

Knowing who owes you what

Unfortunately, getting your clients to pay their obligations on time and in the full amounts they owe can often make you feel like you're herding cats. While most clients will pay you on time, there will always be a few who will wander away from the pack and decide to do their own thing. The reasons are many — perhaps their clients are paying *them* late, or maybe their business has declined, or it could be that they haven't been managing their own business expenses as closely as they should. Whatever the reason, before you can collect on those late payments, you first need to *know* that they're late. You can do this by managing your receivables.

Here are a few tips for keeping on top of your receivables and helping to keep your late payers on track:

- ✔ **Create a system for tracking your receivables.** This system needs to list all outstanding client invoices, when and for how much each invoice was issued, and the date by which payment is due. If your consulting firm is large and you have many invoices outstanding at any given time, you may want to focus the majority of your effort on invoices for more than a certain amount of money, say $10,000. Or you may decide to focus on payments that are more than 30 or 45 days late.

- ✔ **Call or e-mail your balky customers when invoices are issued.** Let them know that an invoice is on the way, and be sure to ask them to let you know if it hasn't been received by a certain date or if there are problems or questions that need to be resolved before they will approve payment. Now is also a good time to ask your client when the invoice will be paid.

- ✔ **Call your customers a week before payments are due.** The idea is to ensure that your invoices are set up for payment on the date promised. If they aren't, ask what you can do to help ensure payment is made on time. Be sure to address any problems now, before they threaten to delay your receipt of funds.

✔ **When a payment is late — by even a day — call your customer immediately.** Ask why the payment is late and what can be done to expedite payment.

None of us enjoy calling clients to encourage them to pay their bills. However, if you extend payment terms to your clients rather than requiring them to pay you at the time you deliver your products or services, you'll eventually be faced with doing just that. And, when times get tough, this task is more important than ever.

Part of the overall job of managing your cash flow is the task of monitoring receivables, the money owed to your company by your clients and customers. A number of very capable business accounting software programs, including Quickbooks and others, have built-in receivables tracking reports that make the task easy.

Collecting your money when your client doesn't pay

Okay, so you've gotten the invoices out to your client, and confirmed that they are correct and acceptable for payment. You've been promised a date of payment, but that date comes and goes — as do many more. Now what? Now you need to get very serious about collecting the money that your client owes you.

Here are a few tips for collecting your money:

✔ **Make a call directly to your customer asking for his or her help.** Don't simply mark a copy of the invoice with one of those handy rubber stamps from an office supply store that says something like "We value your business — we hope you'll pay soon," or "Second notice — we would really like to be paid now," and mail it to your customer's accounting department. Ask your client to help you. Your payment will get a much higher level of attention if your client acts as your advocate inside the company than if you try to go it alone.

✔ **Ask what's holding up payment and find out what you can do to free it up.** Sometimes a payment gets held up because a client's accounting department lost an invoice, doesn't have proof of delivery, or can't find a signed copy of the purchase order or contract that authorized your work in the first place. Find out what's holding up payment and offer to provide it — as quickly as you possibly can.

✔ **As a last resort — and this is only if you aren't concerned about getting any future business from your client — turn the payment over to a collection agency or take the client to court.** If your client hasn't paid you what they owe on a timely basis and is ignoring or avoiding your phone calls and e-mail messages, then you have little choice but to take action quickly. This means turning your client over to a collection agency (which will keep a hefty portion of any collected fees — up to 30 percent or 40 percent — as a commission) or taking them to court. If the amount is relatively small (up to about $5,000 to $10,000, depending on your state laws), you may be able to take your client to small claims court. Higher amounts require taking them to superior court. Check your local laws to see which court applies for your specific situation. Keep in mind that once you take one of these actions, you can pretty much kiss this client goodbye, but in cases like this, that might not be such a bad outcome.

When your contract has multiple deliverables and payments are spaced out accordingly, but the client isn't paying you on time, then you may want to consider stopping work on the project, thereby using some leverage to get payment. But before doing this it's important to check your contract — and maybe consult an attorney — to be sure that by ceasing work, you don't expose yourself to counterclaims by your client. Whatever you do, when a payment is late, get on it right away. Don't wait for days or weeks (or months!) hoping it will come in. Chances are, something is wrong, so it needs your immediate attention.

Getting Clients to Pay You What You're Worth

We'll venture a guess that you probably think you're worth a lot to your clients. Indeed, you may very well *be* worth a lot. However, if you can't get your clients and your clients-to-be to agree with this self-assessment of your worth, then you've got a problem. The problem is that you'll end up either accepting jobs that are paying you less than you're worth or not landing any jobs at all. Getting your clients to look beyond the fees that you charge and to see the value that you bring to the table is a fine art — an art that you need to master if you hope to gain long-term success in the wonderful world of consulting.

When you find yourself in a situation where your client is more focused on the fee that you charge than on the value that you create for their organization, one of two things may have happened:

- ✔ You haven't done a good enough job linking the price you propose to charge to a strategic value proposition of the organization's overall business case.

- ✔ You're dealing with somebody who's not responsible for the organization's overall performance.

In the first case, you need to clearly make the case for the value that your consulting organization provides to your prospective client. How much will your client save each week, month, or year by putting you on the job? How many times is their investment in you multiplied by the more effective organization that you'll leave them? You can find more about the topic of value-based pricing in Chapter 21.

In the second case, be sure that you're talking with somebody who sees or is responsible for the big picture, rather than someone — perhaps a functional leader in the department — who is just looking at what you're going to cost. Your job is to move up your client's chain of command until you find the person who can see how your organization will provide value far above and beyond the fees that you charge.

In either case, avoid doing consulting work on an hourly fee basis. Once you set an hourly rate, it can become a trap that hamstrings your efforts to build a value proposition for your clients. Charging a flat fee for the work you do is far better, as it helps your client avoid getting hung up on hourly or daily billing rates. You can ease this approach by consistently producing value and building solid relationships with your clients. Become an essential partner for your client, and your value will be easy to see — and to sell.

Part VI

Taking Your Consulting Business to the Next Level

The 5th Wave   By Rich Tennant

"You notice how companies are demanding a lot more from their financial consulants these days?"

In this part . . .

One day — it may be weeks, months, or years — after you get your consulting business off the ground, you're going to realize that you're ready to take your business to the next level. In this part, we consider a variety of strategies to do just that, including how to use your current success to move into new areas, advanced pricing strategies that can make your business even more profitable, and a variety of approaches for enhancing your image and reputation.

Chapter 20

Building on Your Success

*E*very business goes through phases. There's an initial start-up phase where you're focused on the nuts and bolts of getting your business off the ground — setting up your office, establishing accounting and other administrative systems and procedures, obtaining a business license or filing articles of incorporation, and landing your first clients. Next, there is often a growth phase where happy clients start referring their colleagues to you, and your own marketing efforts begin to pay off with new business. How much and how fast you grow is pretty much up to you. You can do a number of things to expand your business if you like. Alternatively, you may be happy with things just the way they are, and see no need to grow. Either way is fine. It's your business, so you get to decide.

In this chapter, we consider a variety of different approaches for building on your success. Some of these approaches include consciously growing your business (for example, increasing your revenues over a baseline level of business — say, $1,000,000 in annual billings), understanding the keys to success, building partnerships, and giving back to your community. Even if you decide that you're happy with the status quo, keep in mind that you still need to keep a steady stream of new clients moving into your business as you complete projects with your current clients. To maintain your current revenue level, you'll need to do many of the same things that you would do to grow your business. To use a gardening analogy, your clients are, for the most part, annuals — they must be replaced each season. If you do good work — and you do it on time and on budget — you're almost guaranteed to have a very long line of clients clamoring for your services.

Tuning Up Your Growth Engine

To grow or not to grow? That is the question. If you own your own consulting business, at some time you'll have to answer this question. Of course, you can choose to ignore it, but by doing so you're actually making a decision. While some consulting firms may rocket into the stratosphere with little or no planning or action on the part of those in charge, the majority won't grow unless action is taken to bring in a steady stream of new business.

Deciding whether to grow

So we're back to our original question: To grow or not to grow?

To decide the path you should take with your consulting business, consider reviewing the following checklist:

- **What does your heart say?** Are you a driven, hard-charging entrepreneurial spirit who will stop at nothing to get to the top of the consulting heap, or are you a bit more laid back? If your heart is telling you to go slow, then perhaps you should listen — and proceed accordingly.

- **What kind of lifestyle do you prefer?** Many consultants find themselves on the road a lot, servicing clients across town, in different states, or even around the world. This means many long days and nights away from home. If you've got a family or have obligations back home, then a high-growth consulting business may be in direct conflict. Assess your lifestyle, and use the result to help you determine how much growth to pursue.

- **How are your finances?** Pushing a business into a high-growth mode usually requires a sizable investment of both time and money. It takes a lot of cash to market your services, to fly here and there, and to hire the extra employees you need to service all the new clients you get as a result of the growth process. If your finances are healthy and strong, then growth is a very real option. If your finances are weak and anemic, then you may be putting your entire business at risk by pushing growth too aggressively.

- **What's the state of the market?** Some consultants assume an unlimited supply of clients is just waiting to buy whatever it is they have to sell. While there may indeed be many clients who would be interested in buying these consultants' services, every pool of prospects has some absolute limit, and this limit varies depending on the market. Before you decide whether or not to fire up your growth engine, take a good look at your market and decide whether it can support your anticipated growth. If so, then growing is an option. If not, you may want to defer your growth plans until the market conditions are more favorable.

Only you can decide whether you want to turn your consulting firm into a high-growth operation — with all the good and bad things that growth entails — or whether you'd like to do something a bit more relaxed. Whatever choice you make, the good news is that you can always change your mind. Whenever you decide that growth is your number-one priority, you can start up your growth engine. And if you decide you want to step off the high-growth carousel, you can also do that anytime you like. The choice is yours.

Charting the stages of growth

Your consulting business is a living, breathing entity. It reacts to the environment around it and is always moving and changing — sometimes for the better, and sometimes not so much. According to Jana Matthews, founder and CEO of The Jana Matthews Group (www.janamatthewsgroup.com), a management consulting firm that specializes in working with growing businesses, most companies typically go through a start-up stage followed by three distinct growth stages. These stages are:

✔ **Start-up:** You're trying to figure out what product or service to offer that will meet the needs of the market and ways your company can provide value to its customers. If you are the CEO of a consulting business in the start-up stage, your role is to act as a doer and decision-maker.

✔ **Initial growth:** In this first stage of growth, your company is very sales driven as it tries to launch a new or different product, capture market share, and grow revenues. Company operations are fast-paced, highly flexible, even chaotic. People do whatever is necessary to be successful. If you are the CEO of a consulting business in the initial growth stage, your role is to be a delegator and direction setter.

✔ **Rapid growth:** In the second stage of growth, your company is trying to achieve widespread use of its products or services, gain a significant share of its chosen markets, ward off advances from competitors, and move into a market leadership position. Lots of new people need to be hired — rounds and rounds of them. Integrating them and aligning their efforts can be a daunting, never-ending task. If you are CEO of a consulting business in this stage of growth, your role is to act as a team builder, coach, planner, and communicator.

✔ **Continuous growth:** This final stage of growth comprises successive rounds of turbulence and periodic "reinventions" of the company. Rapid growth has led to many more customers and market opportunities, a much larger employee base, a more complex organization, and the potential to dominate the industry. But more of everything also includes more potential to spin out of control. If you are the CEO of a consulting business in the continuous growth stage, your role shifts to acting as a change catalyst, organization builder, strategic innovator, and chief of culture.

What stage is *your* consulting business in right now — the start-up stage, or one of the three stages of growth? Does your company culture match up with the descriptions of the different stages above? If not, what can and should you do to get them in synch?

Implementing growth strategies

You can pursue a variety of specific strategies to grow your consulting business, either alone, or in combination with one another. Some of the most common strategies include

- **Developing new products or services.** This strategy can be made easier by developing new products and services that are related to existing products and services. If they are related, they may give you the opportunity to revisit current and past clients — almost always the easiest path to more business.

- **Expanding into new markets.** Many consulting firms find that by expanding their geographic markets (including onto the Internet) they can grow beyond local markets, which may be saturated. In addition, expanding into entirely new industries (for example, an information technology consulting firm expanding from its base in the aerospace industry to the automobile industry) offers even more growth opportunities.

- **Going international.** Why limit your company to just one country, when you've got an entire world of them out there?

- **Hiring more employees.** When you hire more employees, you are growing by default (unless you're firing even more employees than you're hiring). However, when you're staffing up your organization, you must have work for them to do; otherwise, these employees will quickly become an expensive burden.

- **Creating strategic alliances.** It's true — one plus one can equal three. By finding the right organizations to align with — perhaps other consulting firms, or companies in a related industry — you can dramatically increase the reach and power of your firm. The key is to find the right allies — firms that aren't competing with you and that multiply your effectiveness rather than detract from it.

- **Pursuing corporate partnerships.** Putting together a corporate partnership is similar to creating a strategic alliance, but it is an even more formal (with written agreements) and potentially longer-term relationship between firms. We cover such partnerships in detail later in this chapter.

✔ **Pursuing acquisitions and mergers.** Companies have long pursued acquisitions and mergers as a relatively quick way to grow. However, while they can indeed help a consulting firm to grow and can lead to great success, they often fail as a result of mismatches between the cultures and values of the firms.

✔ **Executing an initial public offering (IPO).** There's nothing like a little bit of cash (okay, a lot of cash) from investors to fuel your growth engine. In an IPO, you raise money by selling stock in your company to the public. If your consulting firm happens to be the next big thing, then the amount of money you can raise — and the growth that money will support — can be substantial.

Whatever combination of growth strategies you decide to pursue, be sure to take the time required to plan your moves in sufficient detail before you execute them. The more planning you do (up to a point —it *is* possible to over-plan, after all), the greater your chances of success.

Using Nine Keys to Unlock Success

Many business owners, including the owners of consulting firms, wonder whether there is a secret sauce for success, some set of rules that will ensure their company is built to last. As it turns out, researchers have done a lot of work in this area, and they've found that successful businesses share certain characteristics.

One such researcher, William Bygrave, professor emeritus at the Arthur M. Blank Center for Entrepreneurship at Babson College and one of the nation's top experts on entrepreneurship, identified nine keys to success for an entrepreneurial business. Bygrave labeled these keys "The Nine Fs":

✔ **Founders:** Every startup must have a first-class entrepreneur. (If you're the owner of your consulting firm, that means *you*.)

✔ **Focused:** Entrepreneurial companies focus on niche markets. They specialize. (To be a successful consultant, you need to realize that you'll be much more valuable to your clients — and in demand — if you're an expert in some specific field, rather than a generalist in a wide range of fields.)

✔ **Fast:** They make decisions quickly and implement them swiftly. (But you should never make decisions so quickly that you don't have time to understand the alternatives before you take the steps required to implement them.)

✔ **Flexible:** Entrepreneurial companies keep an open mind. They respond to change. (If you run your own consulting firm and keep it small and nimble, you can respond much more quickly to changes in your business environment than much larger consulting firms.)

✔ **Forever innovating:** They are tireless innovators. (Successful consultants are always looking for new ways to bring value to their clients, while providing their own firms with advantages over the competition.)

✔ **Flat:** Entrepreneurial organizations have as few layers of management as possible. (When you're in charge, *you* decide how your consulting firm will be structured.)

✔ **Frugal:** By keeping overhead low and productivity high, entrepreneurial organizations keep costs down. (And when you keep costs down, your profits go up.)

✔ **Friendly:** Entrepreneurial companies are friendly to their customers, suppliers, and workers. (This builds tremendous client goodwill and loyalty.)

✔ **Fun:** It's fun to be associated with an entrepreneurial company. (Few things are more fun and satisfying in the world of business than being part of a growing company that is solving important problems for its clients.)

While there are no guarantees (sorry about that), we think that professor Bygrave is on to something here. You would do well to take a close look at your own consulting firm, whether you're an owner or an employee, and see how many of the Nine Fs you can check off. As the old saying goes, the more the merrier.

Forming Partnerships to Build on Your Success

Forming partnerships with other individuals — and other consulting firms — can be an excellent way to build on your success. How? Because forming a partnership can give you access to additional resources, expertise, and markets that you don't currently have access to. Not only that, but bringing an outsider into your organization can also give you a fresh perspective on your consulting firm — and its own opportunities and challenges — that you may not see for yourself.

Partnerships can be informal — just a handshake or meeting of the minds — or formal, complete with legally binding partnership agreements. Whichever approach you decide to take with your partnerships, getting in writing the understanding of who will do what — and how the resulting rewards will be divided —is always a good idea. Believe us: More than a few partnerships have crashed and burned as a result of misunderstandings of these kinds of business issues.

To keep your own partnerships from becoming casualties, here are a few tips for you to consider:

✔ **You have to have trust.** Sharing your consulting business with someone else requires a lot of trust. Without trust, you're unlikely to be engaged in the partnership at the level that's required to make it successful. Partner only with those you trust, and if that trust is lost, don't hesitate to cancel the partnership.

✔ **Be sure that your business can stand on its own.** The idea of forming a partnership is not to shore up a weak business; it's to build on the strengths of each business and then multiply them for the benefit of all. If your business is weak, be sure to fix it before you think about creating partnerships with others.

✔ **Focus on partnering with firms that bring value to your business.** While you don't want to partner from a position of weakness, you do want to find partners who will add value to your consulting firm by providing skills, knowledge, expertise, and resources that may be missing in your own firm. This is one of the key reasons for partnering in the first place.

✔ **Share the wealth — and the risk.** Partners should share the rewards of their success — in proportion to their participation — and the risk. Although gauging just how much each partner contributed to a consulting firm's success can sometimes be difficult, it's important to get close. Otherwise, one of the partners will feel like she was left holding the short end of the stick. Similarly, if one partner is stuck shouldering the majority of the risk for little reward, then she will not be happy with the partnership.

✔ **Put it in writing.** Even if you decide not to enter into a formal partnership, it's important for you and your partner to spell out your key understandings in writing. These understandings should include a summary of each party's responsibilities and a clearly spelled out division of the partnership's revenues and income.

✔ **Consider a trial relationship first.** Just as most couples date for a while before they get engaged and eventually married, you and your prospective partner should consider a trial relationship before you enter into a formal partnership. It won't be long before you'll know whether or not a longer-term relationship is in your future.

If you take time to find a good partner and you spell out your key understandings — preferably in writing — before you enter into your partnership, then it's likely to be successful. Of course, not every partnership is destined for success, no matter how great your consulting firm is or how wonderful your partner's business is. If it works, great. If not, you always have the option of dissolving this partnership and moving forward without partners, or finding another one. If you own your consulting firm, the choice is all yours.

Be sure to have the discussion about how you will end the partnership should it not work *before* you enter into a partnership agreement. Even better, make these terms — including the separation of assets, clients, employees, consulting tools, intellectual property, and more — a part of your formal partnership agreement. Having the discussion upfront helps eliminate untold amounts of time (distracting you from your consulting business) and money.

Giving Back

A time will come in your business life when you'll achieve a certain amount of success, and you'll start to feel the urge to impact your community — or to change the world. True success is not measured in dollars and cents, but in the satisfaction you feel in helping your clients, and in the respect and reputation you develop over time for your good work. And true success can also be measured by the extent that you make a difference in the lives of others.

For many businesspeople, making a difference is most effectively accomplished by giving back — getting out into their communities and participating in nonprofit organizations — as a volunteer, leader, board member, or contributor. As with anything else, some approaches work better than others. The Washington D.C.–based Institute for Educational Leadership (www.iel.org) published the following list of recommendations for businesspeople who plan to volunteer to lead community efforts:

- ✓ **Stay focused.** Identify an area that best suits your interests and abilities — affordable housing or improving workforce skills, for example — and focus on it. Avoid grand, all-encompassing approaches. Don't lose patience if your ideas don't instantly resonate with the people you're trying to help. Remember that their previous experiences with "outsiders" may have been dismal.

- ✓ **Avoid magic solutions.** Management systems, such as total quality management, reengineering, or virtual organizations, that work in corporate settings may not work for a government agency or a community. Be practical. Be clear about objectives and expected results.

✔ **Don't act like a "typical" CEO.** Top-down leadership doesn't work in community settings. Collaborative and collective leadership are more likely to succeed. Other pointers:

- You can't fire people, so don't try.

- Avoid self-promotion.

- Respect communities' realities, but make sure that the information you get stands up to tough criteria.

- Learn to coexist, at least temporarily, with racial tension while striving to eliminate or reduce it.

- Try to work within and around restrictive regulations instead of trying to change them, at least at first.

✔ **Use your best people.** Community activists can easily spot unqualified newcomers. Direct participation from the CEO, a top aide, or any other well-qualified member of the business is best. Whatever the approach, it's important that company representatives have strong, public backing from senior management.

✔ **Hang in there.** This work isn't easy. Expect the unexpected, because life in poor neighborhoods can be politically messy. Business leaders working with these communities encounter problems of a magnitude and a complexity beyond anything they have dealt with before. Resist the temptation to bail out when things get tough. Don't spread yourself too thin, and be flexible.

As we have seen in this chapter, many ways exist to build on your success. Some involve growing your business and bringing in more money, and some involve helping others — from your clients, to your neighbors, to the world as a whole. Remember: You don't have to be Bill Gates or Warren Buffett to make a difference. There are countless community-based organizations that would greatly benefit from your business experience and network of connections. By helping others, you find the kind of success that is especially precious, and particularly needed.

Chapter 21

Advanced Pricing Strategies

· ·

· ·

*I*n Chapter 6 we discuss the basics of pricing, including such topics as establishing your value to clients, structuring your consulting fees, changing your pricing, and knowing when to say "no." Depending on what kind of consulting you do and the nature and complexity of your projects, you may find that the material in Chapter 6 is all you need to set your prices and negotiate deals that are profitable to you and fair to your clients.

However, you may find that the basic information in Chapter 6 is *not* enough. Perhaps you provide services in a field that is highly commoditized — for example, house inspectors — and clients make their buying decisions primarily on price. You may be trying to figure out a way to increase your fees without losing business. Or maybe the projects you do are very expensive and specialized, and you need to find a way to help your clients look beyond your fee to see the value that they will receive as a result of the work that you'll do for them.

As it turns out, there are many different alternatives for pricing your consulting services in a way that clients may not find as objectionable as the good-old-fashioned hourly rate or fixed price — and that may actually encourage them to hire your consulting firm over the competition. In this chapter, we consider a variety of topics related to advanced pricing strategies, including the philosophy of pricing, value-based pricing, contingent fees, and performance-based pricing.

The Zen of Pricing

The psychology of sales — why people buy what they buy, when, and for what price — has fascinated researchers and salespeople (and the managers of salespeople) alike for centuries. It's no accident that there are countless books, seminars, workshops, online courses, and other teaching tools available for those who want to find out how to leverage the psychology of sales to their own advantage. And, truth be told, there is some validity to the gallons of snake oil these people are peddling. Why? Because people often make purchasing decisions based on their emotions and justify their purchases intellectually later on.

When you set a price, you don't do so in a vacuum. Sure, you need to cover your expenses — your salary, your electric bill, the cost of acquiring computers and office space, and much more — and you need to make a profit to grow your consulting firm, but setting a price involves much more than your side of the equation. You also have your client's side of the equation to deal with, which includes his or her emotions, attitudes, previous experiences with consultants, pressures from management, upbringing, personal values, available budget, level of authority, and much more.

In this section, we dive a bit deeper into the Zen — the basic philosophical underpinnings — of pricing for your consulting business. Whether you own your own consulting firm or simply work for one, this section applies to you.

Factoring in how buyers determine your price

Pop quiz: Who sets your price? You may think the answer to that question is obvious and straightforward. You set your price — right? Actually, the answer is not quite as obvious as you may think. While you may be the one who puts a price in a proposal to a prospective client or who publishes a price list for your consulting services, you have to be responsive to your client's needs and expectations.

So, who *really* sets your price? Your *client* does.

Here are some of the factors that enter into the psychology of your buyer, helping to determine how much he is willing to pay for your consulting services:

> ✔ **Demand:** If your service is in high demand — for whatever reason — then it will be more valuable to your prospective clients. This is especially the case when there is a shortage of talented consultants working in a particular area of expertise. For example, a presidential election

takes place every four years in the United States. You can bet that in the months — and even years — ramping up to the actual election, talented political and election consultants with proven results are in great demand. And you can also bet that the cream of the crop can demand almost any price they like.

✔ **Competition:** When you have a lot of competition, your buyers usually realize that they have many buying options; therefore, they are less willing to pay you a premium for your consulting services. Taken to its extreme, this can lead to your service being considered a commodity where potential clients use lowest price as their primary buying consideration.

✔ **Features:** Does your consulting service or product have unique features that other consultants don't offer? For example, perhaps you offer a money-back guarantee if your services don't bring about the promised results. If your competition doesn't have a similar policy, then your firm may be perceived as offering more value than they do — potentially allowing you to demand a higher price.

✔ **Benefits:** Benefits are what your clients really value, and they speak to their psychology. While *features* are characteristics of what you offer, for example, recommendations, reports, reputation, speed, guarantees, and so forth, *benefits* are measured in terms of increased profits, reduced expenses, less stress, more confidence, less drama, more success, less risk, and more. Knowing which benefits your clients truly seek is key to advanced value-pricing techniques.

✔ **Technology:** Some consultants ride on the leading edge of technology, and their clients are willing to pay them a premium for this.

✔ **Positioning:** Your positioning in the market can dramatically impact client expectations of your value, and thus the price they are willing to pay for your services. For example, if you're a legal consultant who specializes in working with high-profile, celebrity defendants, you'll be able to command a much higher price than someone who specializes in working with the homeless.

While these are some of the key psychological factors that enter into your clients' perception of your value and the price they think they should pay for your services, there are no doubt others. Be aware of the signals your client sends to you about what they value as well as the signals you send to them. Together, they add up to the value you bring and the price they should pay you. It's no coincidence that the best real estate agents quickly discover that the most important benefit to their client is the relief of having a great school nearby for little Suzie, and that they often drive luxury cars rather than beat-up old vans. They're listening to the signals their clients are sending them as well as sending prospective clients a message of value.

Delving deeper into common pricing strategies

In Chapter 6 we considered a variety of basic consultant pricing methods, including the hourly rate approach, the rule of thirds, the per-item or per-project approach, and retainers. However, when considering the actual philosophy behind your approach to pricing your products or services, it is instructive to take a close look at the most common pricing strategies used by all sorts of businesses, not just consulting firms.

We're not suggesting that you need to go through all of these pricing strategies each time you set a price for your consulting products or services. However, we *are* suggesting that you should consider them as you develop the pricing philosophy that you will apply in your business. As you've seen, many different approaches exist. Your job is to decide which one will work best for your firm — and for your clients.

Following is a list of the most commonly utilized pricing approaches:

- ✔ **Cost-based pricing:** When you use this pricing strategy, you simply add up all of your costs to provide a specific consulting product or service, tack on an additional amount for profit, and use the resultant number as your price. While this pricing strategy assures that you are compensated for all of your expenses, it doesn't take into account that other consultants may be able to trim their costs — enabling them to significantly undercut *your* price.

- ✔ **Demand-based pricing:** Your prospective clients are very likely to have expectations of how much they should pay for a given product or service, perhaps gained from previous experience or from talking to colleagues who have previously enlisted the services of consultants. By doing some market research, you can find out what prices your prospects are willing to pay, and price your consulting products and services accordingly.

- ✔ **Competition-based pricing:** In applying a competition-based pricing strategy, you look at the prices your competition is charging to determine your own pricing. You can actually proceed in any of three different directions with the information you gain by looking at your competitors' prices:
  - You can simply match their prices, dollar for dollar.
  - You can undercut them to become a more attractive option yourself.
  - You can intentionally price your products and services higher than the competition to achieve a premium aura of exclusivity.

- ✔ **Loss leader pricing:** You see this strategy at work when a supermarket sells milk, eggs, or some other basic food commodity at a very low price, hoping to bring people into the store where they will inevitably buy other — more profitable — products. Consultants often use loss-leader pricing when they offer some of their products or services at a particularly low price (sometimes free) to get their foot in the door with a client that it is hoped will lead to additional business. A management consultant may offer to perform an initial assessment of an organization's hiring process, for example, for a nominal fee — say, $500 — with the actual consulting services that are required to develop and implement solutions costing the prospective client much more.

✔ **Demand-curve pricing:** This pricing approach generally applies to manufacturers of products. Demand-curve pricing is offering a new product at a relatively high price when demand is high. As demand eventually lags and manufacturing costs are decreased due to economies of scale and other manufacturing efficiencies, the price is gradually decreased to generate ongoing buyer interest and additional incremental sales.

✔ **Skimming:** Imagine being a consultant who offers a service or product that no one else has, but that your clients — after they find out about it — really want. Believe it or not, it does happen. And when it happens, you can price your consulting products very high — at least until competitors enter the market and start driving your prices down.

✔ **Penetration:** Say you want to enter a crowded market, and you want to capture a lot of business as quickly as you can. To do this, you need to dramatically undercut the competition while getting the word out far and wide that potential clients have a great opportunity to obtain your services at a great price. As you build your business and land a solid base of clients, you can gradually increase your prices until they're in line with the rest of your competitors.

✔ **Psychological pricing:** Why is it that the price $19.99 looks significantly less expensive than $20.00 to many consumers? Researchers have found that such "odd/even pricing" results in higher sales volume. Buyers perceive they are getting a bargain with odd prices. Whatever the cause, such pricing does work. For a consultant, this may mean pricing a particular service at $499 instead of $500, or $9,999 instead of $10,000.

Taking a Closer Look at Value-Based Pricing

Value-based pricing has taken the world of consulting by storm over the past decade. *Value-based pricing* simply means basing your prices on the value that clients perceive they receive from your services and products rather than basing your prices on your costs to provide them.

A client's perception of value is related to three factors:

- **The supply of consultants available to do the necessary work:** The more consultants available to deliver a particular service or product, the lower the client's perceived value.

- **The intensity of demand:** The greater the client's need, the higher the perceived value of consultants who can do the necessary work.

- **The level of trust:** The more a client can trust a consultant to follow through on his or her promises, the higher the perceived value.

- **The level of risk:** The more a client trusts you based on past performance, the lower the perceived risk.

For example, say that you are an industrial energy efficiency consultant, someone who specializes in helping manufacturers discover and implement new, more efficient ways to use energy within their operations. You might do this through the application of onsite energy generation facilities (combining heat and power generation), improved and more efficient space heating and lighting, process heat recovery, measurement and control systems, and so forth.

As a consultant, you could choose to use a cost-based pricing approach, working up a fixed-price proposal for each of two phases of the project. The first phase would entail doing an assessment, and the second phase would involve making recommendations and helping with the implementation of the resulting plan. In this example, in which the fee covers your costs plus a healthy profit, the first phase of the project might be priced at $25,000, and the second phase, $50,000.

Alternately, you could decide to use a value-based approach. Say you've studied your potential client's operation, and you're certain you can wring significant cost savings out of the manufacturing plant — to the tune of $1.5 million a year for the next decade.

While a client's perception of consultant value includes more than just the money they can save, right off the bat the prediction of $1.5 million in annual savings — $15 million over the next 10 years — will certainly get their attention, and it provides you with the opportunity to use a value-based pricing approach. Instead of charging just $75,000 for both phases of your consulting job, you may be able to charge $500,000 or more based on the tremendous value that you bring to your client.

Now, which approach would you rather take — the cost-based approach for $75,000 or the value-based approach for $500,000?

Of course, the challenge is to convince your client that he or she should pay the higher, value-based price of $500,000. This can become particularly challenging if your client has received proposals from other consultants with cost-based pricing closer to $75,000 for the entire job. So, what can you do to help convince your clients that they should focus on value instead of cost? Here are a few tips:

- ✔ **Be ready to help your clients see the value of your work.** Your clients may not be aware of just how much value you can potentially bring to them — it's your job to tell them. Be specific, and point out the advantages in terms of time and money saved, processes streamlined, efficiencies gained, expenditures deferred, and so forth. Contrast these savings with the alternative scenario: that they do nothing at all. Take time to create clear and compelling ways — in writing, over the phone, in person — to express your firm's value proposition.

- ✔ **Focus on the performance of your client's business, not yours.** If you're running a business, sure, it's important to keep an eye on the bottom line. But if you're a consultant who hopes to sell your clients on the value that you bring them, then you've absolutely got to focus on your client's business rather than your own. What are the key challenges for your clients? What can you do to help solve them?

- ✔ **Point out the advantages of a value-based approach.** When you bill by the hour, there really is no limit to what you can charge except, ultimately, your client's budget. The number of hours you expect to deliver is an estimate at best, and you may actually provide more or less to complete the project. When you apply value-based pricing, you likely quote a fixed price which caps the investment your client has to make. Unlike the possible situation with a project that exceeds the estimated number of consultant hours, there are no surprises — your client can know exactly how much she will spend for your consulting services.

- ✔ **Create incentives for clients to make the leap.** Many clients are used to the tried-and-true cost-based pricing approach of hourly rates, and they may be reluctant — in fact, *very* reluctant — to accept a contract using value-based pricing. If you've been focusing throughout the selling process on the value that you will bring to your clients, then it shouldn't be too difficult for your client to make the leap. However, you may still need to provide your clients with incentives to switch from an hourly rate to a value price. One such incentive is a guarantee. In the instance of the preceding example, you might guarantee that, so long as your recommendations are followed, your client will experience at least $1.5 million in energy savings a year or no fee will be payable. Chances are, given a guarantee like that, your client may be very willing to give your value-based proposition a try.

Million dollar suggestions

Alan Weiss, author of the popular book *Million Dollar Consulting* (McGraw-Hill), pioneered the idea of value-based pricing for consultants. At his Summit Consulting Group Web site (www.summitconsulting.com), Weiss offers a list of 40 methods to increase and/or protect fees. Here is a selection of some of Weiss's suggestions:

✔ Establish value collaboratively with the client.

✔ Base fees on value, not on task.

✔ Never use time as the basis of your value.

✔ Don't stop with what the client wants. Find out what the client needs.

✔ Never voluntarily offer options to reduce fees.

✔ If you must lower fees, seek a *quid pro quo* (something in return) from the buyer.

✔ As early as possible, ask the key scope question: "What are your objectives?"

✔ It is better to do something pro bono than to do it for a low fee.

✔ Psychologically, higher fees create higher value in the buyer's mind.

✔ Always be prepared to walk away from business.

If competitive bids come in substantially lower *and* they offer exactly the same benefits, there may not be much you can do about it. Your competition hasn't yet read this book and is not value-pricing enlightened. However, if the stakes are high, you should try to confirm that the benefits *are* exactly the same. If they're not, you'll have to decide if the incremental benefits you offer are worth the difference — or perhaps you can adjust your price to reflect your incremental benefits.

Is there a value-based price in your future? Maybe. According to Kennedy Information, both time-and-materials and project-based pricing are on the decline, while value-based pricing is increasing in popularity (although only about 5 percent of current consulting jobs are being performed using value-based billing). Whatever approach you decide to take, value-based pricing is another tool for differentiating yourself from the competition while potentially boosting your bottom line. Not too shabby.

Considering Contingent Fees and Performance-Based Pricing

Are you willing to put some or all of your fees at risk in the event that you can't deliver what you promise? If the answer to that question is "yes," then you should consider using contingency or performance-based pricing. While both require you to put some amount of your fees at risk (which reduces your client's risk and increases your value), the upside potential if you are able to perform as promised can be considerable. Here is additional information for you to take into account as you consider these options.

Counting on contingent fees

Commonly used by law firms, a *contingent fee* is one that is paid only if you provide the results that are promised by your firm. Using the example of a law firm that is defending someone on a drunk-driving charge, in a contingent fee situation, the client pays only if he is acquitted of the crime. If the client is convicted, then no money is owed to the law firm.

Before you consider agreeing to contingent fees, be fairly certain that you will be able to provide the desired results. Obviously, if you don't have enough clients paying their fees, it won't be long before you go out of business. Carefully consider whether your firm would be better off adopting a more traditional approach to doing business.

Basing the price on your performance

Here's an idea: Why not base your price on some metric of improved client performance? For example, if your client is able to double the number of widgets he produces after your recommendations are implemented, then why not double the amount paid to you? Or, how about charging a flat rate regardless of performance, with an additional "award" fee based on improved performance? Or what about taking 15 percent of your client's net profits as your fee?

Each of these situations is an example of performance-based pricing, where some portion of your fee is based on the extent of your success. Here are some examples of common metrics that can be used to quantify your success — or lack thereof:

- ✔ Number of items produced per hour
- ✔ Weekly sales
- ✔ Monthly expenses
- ✔ On-the-job injuries
- ✔ Number of working customer installations
- ✔ Employee turnover rate

As with contingent fees, you need to be fairly certain you can deliver on your promises when you propose the idea of performance-based pricing to your clients (or when they propose it to you). If you're new to consulting and have not yet developed a steady track record on which to base your decision, you may want to avoid it. However, if your performance is steady and predictable, and you can minimize the potential risk, then performance-based pricing may be a viable option for you and your consulting firm.

One last thing before we run out of ink in this chapter: You need to be fairly certain that you and your client can measure and agree on the performance metric results. It's highly recommended that the metrics are simple, verifiable, regularly measured, and already publicly disclosed. This keeps the process clean and makes it easier to agree on the results.

Chapter 22

Enhancing Your Image and Reputation

A big part of finding success as a consultant is your ability to convince prospective clients that you and your consulting firm are the best choice for the job. Certainly, price and technical skill are both key factors when clients weigh the pros and cons of hiring various consultants. No one (at least no one in her right mind) is going to hire a consultant who is technically incompetent just because that person happens to offer the lowest price or dresses well or has a firm handshake. However, beyond price and technical expertise, something less tangible and significantly more subjective weighs very heavily into the decision whether to hire a particular consultant. This additional factor is image.

Image is the overall impression that others have of you. Many different things go into the mix that, when blended together, becomes your image. And make no mistake about it — image and reputation are very important factors in the impression that you make on your clients. They weigh heavily in their hiring decision.

A favorable image and reputation are important to most clients, and clients are generally more willing to hire (and to pay more for) consultants who possess these attributes. If you had the choice between hiring a consultant with good technical skills but a so-so reputation and image and hiring one with equally good technical skills but an excellent reputation and image, wouldn't you be willing to spend more for the consultant with the much better reputation and image? Most clients probably would.

The good news is that image and reputation are characteristics that you can work on and improve. This chapter is about creating a positive image with your clients and clients-to-be and building your professional reputation — and how you can do both by creating a winning Web site.

Creating a Professional Image

Though image isn't everything for a consultant, it's a big part of the selection process when clients go shopping. Many things add up to make your image. The way you dress, the way you speak, the way you carry yourself, the kind of office you work in, the brand and model of the car you drive — all these things influence the way others perceive you and the impression you make.

Fortunately, you can always change your image. Although the adage that you have only one chance to make a first impression is true, the impression that others have of you can change over time. Some things, such as the style of your business cards and the look of your office, are easy to change. Other things, such as converting your negative personality traits into positive ones, may take a bit longer.

Here are a few things you can do to enhance your professional image:

✔ **Get real.** The first rule of creating a professional image is to be yourself. Don't try to be someone you aren't. Take advantage of your best personal attributes — perhaps your ingenuity, your persistence, or your ability to perform under pressure — and amplify them. If you have any negative characteristics, whatever they may be, work hard to minimize them.

✔ **Look like a duck, be a duck.** If you look professional, your clients and clients-to-be will perceive you to be professional. Despite the old saying that you can't judge a book by its cover, clients do so all the time. If you're asking someone to entrust his or her multimillion-dollar company to your care — a company that your client spent a significant part of her life building up from nothing — then you're going to have a hard sell if you look like you just came in from your morning jog or you don't appear to be serious about your work and the way that you do it.

✔ **Build trust through action.** Actions speak louder than words. Although your proposal may rhapsodize enthusiastically about your commitment to quality, if you don't follow up these words with action, then your clients will think otherwise. Believe us: If you follow up your words with action, your clients will love you forever, and you'll soon have more business than you know what to do with.

✔ **Create an environment that matches the work you do.** If you're an investment adviser, your environment should be one that exudes an atmosphere of quiet success, conservatism, and stability. However, if you're a graphic artist or an interior decorator, your environment should be energetic, creative, bright, and full of life. The point is that when your clients come to visit your office, you want your environment to send the kind of message that matches their expectations for a high-quality consultant.

✔ **Make your media your message.** Your business cards, your report covers, your Web site, and other forms of business communication speak volumes about your professionalism and your commitment to quality. High-quality paper and printing; professional-looking brochures, newsletters, and mailers; and a well-done Web site send a message that you are the kind of consultant that your clients will want to hire — and retain far into the future.

Creating and maintaining a professional image can play a very important role in your ability to achieve the kind of success you're aiming for. Be aware that you are constantly being judged and assessed by your clients and your clients-to-be. With a little work, you can make your good image even better. And doing so translates not only into more business but also into better, higher-paying business to boot.

Enhancing Your Reputation

Just as a good reputation can enhance your image in the eyes of your clients, a bad reputation can tarnish it. And just as many different factors add up to your professional image, many different factors make up your reputation. The quality of the work you do, the time you spend in the public eye, the work you do for charity, and much more play a part in determining your professional reputation.

One thing about reputation: Enhancing and maintaining a good reputation is much easier than trying to rehabilitate a bad one. Once you develop a bad reputation, many clients won't bother to consider you for any sort of work, no matter how great your proposal or how low your price. And after your reputation is tarnished, many clients will never believe that your business has turned things around and changed for the better — even if it has. Turning around a bad reputation can take years. Therefore, doing whatever you can to enhance your reputation is clearly in your best interest. Your current clients will be proud to tell their associates that they are affiliated with you, and future clients will be more likely to seek you out.

With that point in mind, here are a few tips for enhancing your reputation or for helping to repair your reputation if you have fallen on hard times:

✔ **Do consistently great work.** Of course, one of the best ways to enhance your reputation is to do great work. And if you do great work consistently, that's even better. Your clients want and deserve the best you have to offer. Give it to them. Consistently deliver more than you promise.

✔ **Be easy to work with.** What's one of the most effective ways to get a bad reputation quickly and easily? By being difficult to work with. You can be a brilliant consultant and your price can be right, but if you're an incredible pain in the neck to work with, clients will avoid you like a swollen can of tuna. Be someone whom your clients look forward to talking to, not someone they have their assistants tell that they're in a meeting — even when they're not.

✔ **Keep your clients informed of your successes.** A great way to enhance your reputation is to keep your clients well-informed about your doings. If you land a big new contract with a high-profile client, let all your other clients know about it! If you successfully complete a highly visible project, get the word out! (But be sure to get a client's okay before you publicize your work for that client.) If your business has been featured in a newspaper or you have appeared on television, get copies to your clients. Newsletters, e-mail, voice mail, brochures, clippings of newspaper and magazine articles, podcasts, videotapes of television appearances — use all these methods to spread the word and raise your standing in the eyes of your clients and your prospective clients.

✔ **Get in the public eye.** Give speeches to community groups or groups of your peers. Write articles for trade magazines or submit op-ed pieces to your local newspaper or national publications, such as the *Wall Street Journal* or *USA Today*. Become an expert resource for your local newspaper or radio and television stations. Develop a press kit and a regular newsletter and distribute them to a wide variety of national media.

✔ **Teach.** Teaching at a local college or university can be a very effective way for you to enhance your reputation, broaden your skills, and expand your professional network. You may learn a few new things from your students, too!

✔ **Write a book.** Many consultants find their professional reputations greatly enhanced after writing and publishing a book. Not only can you enhance your reputation by writing a book, but organizations may hire you to present the ideas from your book to their employees. You may eventually find yourself making more money from activities related to your book than you do from consulting.

✔ **Work for free.** Many worthy nonprofit organizations — boys' and girls' clubs, environmental groups, churches, and more — could really use your expertise and skill but can't afford to pay for it. By offering to work for free for a few organizations that you really believe in, you are not only doing something good for your community but also building your reputation and network at the same time.

✔ **Work ethically and honestly.** It should go without saying that engaging in unethical and dishonest behavior is a sure way to destroy your reputation and lose all you have worked for. Because of the sensitive and confidential nature of the jobs for which clients often hire consultants, any hint of dishonesty or lack of ethical fortitude can be the death knell of a consulting relationship. Always work honestly and ethically. This topic is so important that we devote an entire section of Chapter 5 to it.

Work hard at developing and enhancing your good reputation and, at all costs, avoid doing the kinds of things that could tarnish it and destroy the client relationships that you have worked so hard to establish and nurture.

Building a First-Class Web Site

As many consultants have realized, one of the best ways to accomplish both goals of creating a professional image and enhancing your reputation is by putting together a Web site. Of course, to have the positive impact you want, it can't be just any old Web site — it has to be professional looking, it has to work well, and it needs to be a positive reflection of your own standards of excellence as a consultant.

When deciding to put together a first-class Web site, perhaps the first decision you'll have to make is whether to do it yourself, or to hire someone to do it for you. Each approach, of course, has its pluses and minuses.

If you decide to build your own site, you'll have ultimate control over the site and you'll likely pay less than hiring someone to do it for you. Unfortunately, unless you're pretty savvy at building Web sites, the results may look amateurish at best and reflect poorly on your business. Not only that, but while you're building the site, you'll be distracted from doing the things you normally do to make money — like consulting. On the other hand, while hiring a professional to create and maintain your Web site will likely get you a better-looking and functioning site, it may cost a lot of money. Not only that, but you may have to wait in line for your Web designer to make site updates for you.

Building your own Web site

All it takes is a basic knowledge of the Internet to create your own Web site and have a lot of fun in the process. There are a number of very capable Web site development programs available to you that are relatively simple and easy to use. In addition, some Web-hosting services offer templates that make putting together your own Web site a snap.

If you decide to build your own Web site, here are three steps to making it happen:

1. **Select a Web hosting service.**

   You'll need a Web hosting service to set up your Web site address (or URL), something like www.yourname.com. The hosting service then hosts your site on its computers where anyone with access to the Web can access it. You'll quickly find that there are many, many Web hosting services, and they vary considerably in price and level of service, so it definitely pays to shop around. Before you select a Web-hosting service, check with your friends and colleagues to see who they use, and read the reviews posted on Internet sites such as cnet.com. Peter's personal favorite hosting service is Dotster (www.dotster.com), but there are plenty of other ones around.

2. **Build your Web site.**

   Some Web site hosting services offer simple, built-in Web site creation software and templates as a part of their hosting packages. This is probably the best option if you're new to all this Internet stuff and you don't have a lot of time to waste learning about it. If your needs go beyond these basic templates, consider buying software specifically designed for creating Web sites such as Microsoft FrontPage, Macromedia Dreamweaver, or NetObjects Fusion. Also, Microsoft Word has the ability to save regular text pages as HTML (hypertext markup language, the language of the Web) documents.

3. **Maintain your Web site.**

   One good thing about creating and maintaining your own Web site is that you have full control over the content and when and how it is updated or modified. It takes just minutes to update your own site yourself, while it can take days or even weeks for someone else to get around to making even minor updates for you.

For more information on this approach, be sure to take a look at *Building a Web Site For Dummies,* 3rd Edition, by David A. Crowder or *Building Web Sites All-in-One Desk Reference For Dummies* by Doug Sahlin (both by Wiley).

Hiring someone to build and maintain your Web site

If you've got better things to do with your time than creating and maintaining your own Web site — or if you'd simply like to get the most professional-looking site possible — there are plenty of Web site design companies (many of them consulting businesses) that would love to design it for you. You'll end up spending anywhere from a couple of hundred dollars for a simple site to thousands for a much more complex one, but if it helps you enhance your image while providing clients with the information they need, then the investment will be well made.

Be careful who you hire to build your Web site for you. Some Web consultants talk a good story, but deliver far less than they promise. Here are a few tips for finding a great Web site designer:

- The very first thing you should do is ask your business colleagues if they know someone they would recommend. Put these recommendations on your short list.

- After you've got your short list of candidates, conduct interviews, get references, and thoroughly check out the sites they have built for other businesses.

- Be sure to compare the work of several different designers before deciding. Don't just go with the first one that walks through the door.

- If you're wandering the Internet and see a Web site that is just what you would like for your own business, find out who designed it and contact them. The designer's name is usually posted on the bottom of the home page, although sometimes you'll need to ask the site owner who they used.

Optimizing your site

After you've got a good-looking, professional Web site — then what? The next step is to get people to visit it — preferably the people who are your best prospects for future clients. You can attract and hold your clients' attention in lots of ways, including the following:

- **Make your site easy to find.** If it's hard for your clients to find you, they probably won't waste much time trying. If your company's name is the Susan Schwartz Group, your URL could be www.susanschwartz.com or www.schwartzgroup.com. Clients (and clients-to-be) who don't have your address at their fingertips can easily guess it, and it will show up at or near the top of most Internet search engine results.

Set aside some time to register your Web site with the five most-visited Internet search engines and directories: Google, Yahoo!, MSN, America Online, and Ask.com. Be sure your site is optimized to rank high in the search results by incorporating meta tags and other tricks of the trade. For more information, drop by The Art of Business Web Site Promotion site (`www.deadlock.com/promote`) for free advice on how to work the search engines to your advantage.

✔ **Promote your new address.** Plaster your Web site address everywhere you possibly can, including on your business cards, letterhead stationery, invoices, marketing brochures, your car, the side of your house — and anyplace else you can possibly fit it. For more ideas on reeling visitors in to your site, see the sidebar "Even more ways to promote your Web site," later in this chapter.

Don't waste your time with firms that promise to increase the traffic to your Web site by submitting your name to hundreds of search engines. Truth be told, most people use only the top few most popular search engines, and you're wasting your time and money by submitting your site to the also-rans.

✔ **Give your visitors a reason to visit.** If your site is boring, or if it takes too long to load, your client or prospect will click right back out of the site. One of the best ways to see how you stack up is to take a look at your competitors' sites. What have they done to make their sites *sticky,* that is, to keep visitors there once they arrive? Be sure to provide lots of fresh, value-added content in the form of news, reports, articles, surveys, industry trends, networking forums, and the like that will keep your clients and prospects coming back for more.

✔ **Capture contact information.** Once your visitors arrive on your site, encourage them to provide you with contact information so you can add them to your mailing list. One way to do this is by offering a complementary subscription to your client newsletter to anyone who is willing to give you their contact information. You can also encourage visitors to provide their contact information by way of contests, special offers, and surveys.

✔ **Keep close tabs on your site.** Make your Web site the home page for your Internet browser so that you visit it frequently. Have a look around and make sure all the pages are loading as they should and that all the links work. And check your site statistics regularly — the number of visitors each day, where they're from, how long they stayed, which pages they viewed, and which search engine (if any) referred them to your site — to get a feel for who is dropping by your site, and what they're doing once they get there. You'll be able to quickly identify which parts of your site attract the most (and the least) visitors and test visitor response to site changes on a real-time basis.

Even more ways to promote your Web site

While there are many ways to promote your Web site, some ways work better than others. Here are a bunch more ways to promote your Web site:

- Send announcements for your Web site (including a picture of your home page) to all your customers and clients, as well as to the media and targeted mailing lists of potential clients.

- Incorporate your Web site address into your standard fax cover sheet.

- Include your Web site address in your voice-mail system and in your on-hold message.

- Include your Web site address in all advertising.

- Visit Internet newsgroups and message boards, leave messages, and participate in relevant discussions.

- Seek out busy Web sites where you can volunteer to host online chats and conferences. Large sites, such as America Online and iVillage, are always looking for knowledgeable hosts who are willing to share their expertise with others.

- Trade links with your customers and clients and with other relevant Web sites.

- Create an e-mail signature for yourself and your employees that includes your Web site address. A *signature* is a short paragraph that's automatically included at the bottom of every e-mail message you send out. It usually contains a plug for your business, along with your address, phone or fax number, and a Web site address.

Part VII
The Part of Tens

The 5th Wave   By Rich Tennant

"Annuities? Equity income? Tax-free municipals? I say we stick the money in the ground like always, and then feed this consultant to the sharks."

In this part . . .

These short chapters are packed with quick ideas that can help you become a better consultant and build a more profitable and more effective consulting business. Read them whenever you have an extra minute or two.

Chapter 23

Ten Ways to Improve Your Cash Flow

*F*or businesses, cash makes the world go 'round. Without a constant inflow of cash, you can't afford to pay for the things you need to run your business. Anything you can do to improve your cash flow — the difference between the money coming into your business and the money going out — is guaranteed to have a positive impact on your business.

You can keep money coming into your business on a steady basis by carefully monitoring the status of unpaid accounts and doing everything in your power to encourage clients to pay up in a timely fashion. On the flip side of the coin, you can keep as much of the money you bring in from going out the door again as possible by budgeting carefully and minimizing expenses. The following ten tips help you manage both sides of the equation.

Manage Your Accounts Receivable

One of the most important things you can do to improve your cash flow is to keep a close eye on your accounts receivable — the money owed to your firm by your clients — and be sure that clients are making their payments to you the moment they are due, if not sooner.

Unfortunately, some clients invariably don't understand how important it is that they pay their bills on time. Receiving payments a day or two late isn't usually a big problem. Getting them a month or two late, on the other hand, can wreck your cash flow and have devastating, long-term consequences for your business. Once your customers get in the habit of paying late, getting them to start paying on time can be almost impossible. By managing your accounts receivable, you identify your late payers as soon as you can, and then take steps to get them to pay.

Budget Your Cash

How can you run a healthy consulting business (much less sleep well at night) if you don't know when cash will be received from clients, and when you'll need to make major expenditures in support of your business? Frankly, you can't. The solution is to budget your cash.

A *cash budget* is a detailed budget of cash inflows and outflows that takes into account payments you receive from clients and expenses you need to pay to run your business. The result is a statement that clearly shows the forecasted cash balance of your business at specific points in time. As the owner or manager of a consulting firm, your cash budget is perhaps your most important planning tool. By studying your cash budget, you're able to determine whether you have enough money to run and grow your business, or whether you need to push harder for new work — or squeeze your current customers to pay the money they owe you sooner. You're also able to figure out whether you'll be able to make major expenditures for capital equipment or to hire new employees at some future time.

Push for Advance Payment

When you run your own business, you get to decide the terms and conditions under which you accept work from clients. When it comes to payment, you could decide to do all your work for free. However, you probably wouldn't be in business very long with that approach. You could perhaps try letting your clients pay whenever they like, but some clients might not pay at all, and your business would certainly suffer. You could invoice as you do your work, and give clients 30 days to pay. That's not a bad approach, but there's something better yet: having your clients pay you in advance — before you actually start work. By getting a large payment up front, you jumpstart your cash flow, putting your business in a very positive financial position.

Hold On to Your Money as Long as You Can

You can improve your cash flow in two fundamental ways: by increasing the speed and size of cash inflows and by decreasing the speed and size of cash outflows. Holding onto your money as long as you can — by slowing down the speed at which you pay the money that you owe others — definitely improves your cash flow. But, don't get us wrong. We're not saying that you should pay your bills late. What we are saying is that you shouldn't get in the habit of paying your bills sooner than you have to. Some business owners as a matter of course pay their bills as soon as they receive them — regardless of the payment terms. If your vendor or supplier has agreed to finance your purchase for 30 days for free (which is exactly what is happening when you are sent an invoice with payment required in 30 days), then you should take full advantage of this free loan. By waiting to pay until the bill is due, you have the benefit of your cash longer. If your vendor offers a prompt payment discount, be sure to consider the savings for paying early against the value of hanging onto your cash for the full 30 days.

Make Sure Your Invoices Are Right

Some companies have a very simple approach to paying invoices with mistakes in them: They don't. They don't pass Go, and they won't send you $200. They won't even call to find out why you made the mistake. They just won't pay it. And if you're not managing your accounts receivable (see the first item in this chapter), you may not even notice that you haven't been paid yet.

Be absolutely sure that your invoices are correct before you send them to your clients. Make sure that the numbers are right, and that they are addressed to the right place and the right person. When invoices go to the wrong place or to the wrong person, they tend to sit around in someone's in-box — unpaid. Don't give your clients an excuse to pay you late — make sure your invoices are right.

Bill More Often

While some consulting engagements are short — perhaps just a week or two — many others run for months or even years. If your services are provided over a long period of time, then an easy way to improve your cash flow is to bill more often. For example, instead of billing your client $1,000 at the end of each month, you could bill your client $500 halfway through the month, and then another $500 at the end of the month. Or — even better — how about billing your client $500 at the beginning of the month, and then another $500 halfway through the month? While your individual payments are smaller, you get your money sooner, which has a positive impact on your cash flow. Believe us: Sooner is better when it comes to cash.

Give Prompt-Payment Discounts

There is a quick and easy way to encourage your clients to pay their invoices sooner, improving your cash flow at the same time. You can do so by offering a prompt-payment discount. A prompt-payment discount is when you allow a customer to decrease a payment by some set percentage — say 1 percent — for paying an invoice within a specific period of time, usually 10 or 20 days. We can already anticipate your question: Doesn't giving a payment discount decrease the cash you receive, resulting in a negative impact on cash flow? Actually, in many cases, the positive impact on cash flow that you experience by getting your money sooner exceeds the small amount of money that's lost in extending the discount. You have to weigh the impact for yourself, and then decide if it makes sense for you.

Start with the standard net/30 payment terms (which give customers 30 days to pay invoices without penalty) and analyze the average time your clients take to pay their invoices. (It may surprise you to discover that you're actually getting paid in 45 days on average.) Next, offer a minimal prompt-payment discount to your clients, perhaps one-half percent/20 days, and see what happens. Do payments come in sooner? How much sooner? Enough to make it worthwhile?

Manage Your Expenses

Your business's cash flow is impacted by two different things: the money coming into your business, and the money going out. Just as you can have an impact on the money coming in, you can impact the money going out. In fact, we would venture to guess that most business owners have a much greater impact on the expense side of the equation than on the revenue side. You're the one who decides whether or not to hire that new employee, or buy those new computers, or pay for first-class air travel instead of coach. Before you spend any money on behalf of your business, stop and ask the following question: Is this expense necessary? If the answer to that question is "Yes," then ask one more question: Is this expense necessary right now? Don't spend money just because you can.

Only spend money if and when you absolutely have to. Want a pretty, new desk or chair? Why not try to get another year out of your old one? Or find inexpensive used — but more up-to-date — office furniture on Craigslist (www.craigslist.com) or eBay (www.ebay.com).

Don't Be Afraid to Push for Payment

Rare is the consultant who doesn't occasionally have a client who pays late. Of course, an occasional late pay is usually not a problem for most consulting firms. However, when late payments become widespread or habitual, you have to make a choice: Do you put your clients on notice that they are late and demand payment, or do you just ignore it? The choice you make depends on a number of factors: the state of your consulting firm's financial health (a healthy firm can afford to wait longer for payment than one that is headed to the intensive care unit), how important the customer is to you and your business (you don't want to make a key customer mad), and the size and age of the invoice itself (the larger the size and the older the invoice, the more urgent payment becomes).

As soon as you decide that you've waited long enough for payment, don't be afraid to push your client to pay. In our experience, the most effective way is to personally pick up the phone and call your client directly. Point out that payment is overdue, and ask if there is a problem that you can help with. You can send an e-mail message or a letter instead of making a personal call, but we've found that a one-on-one phone conversation can get action when other methods fail. Be respectful of your client and be polite, but be firm when you ask for payment. The sooner you follow up on a late payment, the sooner you'll get paid.

Call in a Pro

As much as we would prefer to avoid having to bring a collections firm or a lawyer into client relationships, sometimes we have no choice. When a client refuses to pay a late invoice, you have to take action. Unfortunately, if you can't get it done yourself, then you need to call in a pro. The first choice for most late pays is a collections firm that uses its powers of persuasion to try to get your client to pay. For the privilege of helping you out, the firm is paid a significant portion of the money they collect, probably along the lines of 20 percent to 40 percent. Of course, if you get any money out of a client who refuses to pay, then you're doing a lot better than nothing, and the high fee is worth paying. If the invoice is particularly large, or if legal issues are involved (such as whether or not the consulting contract was complied with, or client fraud), then you probably need to call on the services of a lawyer who has experience working with consulting firms.

To find the pro who's right for you, we suggest first asking around for a referral. Ask other consultants or colleagues if they have anyone they recommend. Alternatively, you can do an Internet search, which will provide you with enough names to keep you busy for months. However, absent a recommendation from someone you trust, you just don't know what you're going to get.

Chapter 24

Ten Effective Marketing Strategies for New Business

In This Chapter

▶ Trying different approaches

▶ Getting the word out

Marketing is a wonderful thing. Really. As you can probably guess, part of your job as a consultant is to do great work for your current clients. However, attracting and signing future work with new clients is equally important. Without a steady stream of new work coming in — from new clients — your business is always at risk of failure if and when key current clients decide that you're no longer in their budget. Although you can approach your marketing in a haphazard, fly-by-the-seat-of-your-pants fashion, the best marketing comes from identifying your target clients and then strategizing how best to reach them. What do they read? Where are they? What do they like to do? Before you develop your marketing plan, review the following marketing strategies.

Choose Your Targets

Before you do anything else, your first task when developing your marketing plan is to identify your target clients. As you choose your targets, you should always have two questions in mind:

✔ Who are your best clients?

✔ How can they best be reached?

The answers to these questions help you select the most effective ways to get the message to your targeted audience. If you're a political consultant, then you know that your target clients are people who are running for (or thinking about running for) elected office. You know that sticking an advertisement on the bulletin board at your local supermarket won't generate any new clients.

However, getting interviewed in a local newspaper or a national publication, such as *USA Today,* may lead to lots of business.

And notice that the question is, "Who are your *best* clients?" Some clients are better than others — some pay their bills on time, and others don't. Some appreciate the hard work you do, others not so much. Some make being a consultant a pleasurable challenge, while others make it a living hell. Focus on attracting the best clients for your business, not the worst.

Discover What Works

Good marketing is a state of constant experimentation to discover what works and what doesn't. Your goal is to build on what works, and discard any strategies that don't pan out. When you develop plans for marketing your business, first identify every possible way to get your message out to your targeted audience.

It often helps to ask your current or past clients how they discovered you. A simple survey of these clients might indicate that most found out about you from an advertisement or from a particular referral. You can then build on these successes or augment them with related approaches.

You can try one approach at a time or several at once — it all depends on your budget and how much time you can devote to tracking the results. What is the response from your direct mailing campaign? Good? Then try it again with a somewhat wider distribution. How did the newspaper ad fare? Not well? Then drop it. Keep trying new things and fine-tuning your marketing campaign accordingly.

To determine whether a technique works, you must set up criteria in advance to judge its effectiveness. For example, each newspaper advertisement should generate ten prospects, of which two can be converted to clients. Not only that, but you'll also need to have a way to trace a prospect to your marketing effort. If you run a newspaper advertisement, for example, you may include an incentive if they mention the ad. This is especially important if you are undertaking several different marketing efforts at the same time. If your newspaper advertisement generates only two prospects, then you know that your approach needs work. If, on the other hand, it generates 50 prospects, then you know you've hit the sweet spot.

Use Client Success Stories

Nothing breeds success like success. As you successfully complete jobs for your clients, you automatically create a pool of client success stories that you can draw from to publicize your firm. And the more work you do, the larger the pool grows. The beauty of using success stories for publicity is that potential clients get an idea of the kind of work you do; at the same time, the success stories build a positive impression of your abilities and expertise. Use client success stories whenever you can: in proposals, advertisements, newsletters, Web sites, speeches, seminars, and so forth. Even better, ask your clients whether you can get an endorsement or testimonial from their organization for use in your publicity materials.

Whichever way you decide to use client success stories, be sure to get your clients' permission first if you plan to use their names. And make sure to never, ever disclose any confidential information about your clients in your enthusiasm to tell of their great success.

Encourage Word-of-Mouth Referrals

Some of the best marketing you can get is from your satisfied clients. And it's free! Encourage your clients to tell their friends and business associates about your business. You can encourage this word-of-mouth advertising by meeting or exceeding your commitments, being reliable, doing great work, and asking for referrals. Give your clients extra business cards, brochures, and other promotional materials to pass on to other potential clients. You can thank your clients for referring you to others by sending a thank-you note or by giving them a nominal reward, such as a free subscription to your newsletter or a copy of a report on industry trends.

Peter does no advertising at all, instead relying on referrals from his many happy clients to bring in a steady stream of new business. His Web site, `www.petereconomy.com`, is specifically designed to serve as a high-tech business card, showcasing his many successful projects and relationships with coauthor-clients. For tips on how to build a Web site of your own, see Chapter 22.

Become a Media Animal

If you want to get prospective clients' attention, you have to be relentless in your campaign to do so. Depending on the nature of your consulting business, you have to select the media outlets that are most effective in getting your message to your clients and then bombard them with newsworthy materials. If you're serious about getting publicity, get on the phone, write letters, send e-mail, make personal visits — in short, do whatever it takes to land an interview, place an article, or end up on the 5 o'clock news. Don't take no for an answer. Keep pushing until you get the attention you want. Of course, positive media is the best media. You certainly don't want to find a *60 Minutes* news team in your office waiting to interview you!

Bob turned his book *1001 Ways to Reward Employees* into a huge bestseller (more than 1.5 million copies sold to date) by constantly pushing the media — from print, to broadcast and online — to get and keep his name in the public eye. And the more media attention Bob gets, the further media attention he attracts. Media is like a snowball rolling down a hill — once you reach the tipping point, it gets bigger and moves faster.

Hire a Good Public Relations Person

Good public relations people are definitely worth their weight in gold. If you're a media novice and you try to approach the media on your own, you can waste a lot of time (and don't forget: for consultants, time equals money). Public relations experts already know how the system works, which media outlets are best to tell your story, and the most effective ways to convince the people in power to take time to listen. And the good ones have already developed scads of personal relationships with editors, producers, and the other people who can get your message in front of the widest possible audience. Not only can public relations specialists line up media opportunities, but many are happy to create your press kits, press releases, biographies, brochures, and other marketing materials. Be sure you know what your PR person will provide to you. Get referrals from friends and colleagues whose opinions you trust. To keep things affordable, you can hire the person on an hourly basis and authorize specific tasks as the need arises, or you can specify a retainer arrangement that provides you with a constant level of service for a set fee every month. The choice is up to you and your budget.

Start a Newsletter

Newsletters are great publicity tools for every kind of consulting business. Not only are they an inexpensive (especially when you choose the e-mailed variety over the printed and mailed variety) and effective way to target potential clients, but they're also effective for retaining and developing new business with current clients, who typically want to be on the inside track about what you're doing. Newsletters also add to your credibility.

The heart and soul of most consulting newsletters are stories describing the numerous successful projects that the firm has undertaken. These success stories make terrific publicity — both for your firm and for the firms that you serve. Typical newsletters also contain statements of the owner's vision for the firm and its clients, letters to the editor, tips on how to improve a certain aspect of your business, and general industry news. And although subscriptions to some newsletters are free, others — particularly those produced by popular management consultants — can run in the hundreds of dollars per year. Plus, if you e-mail your newsletters, the money you earn is all profit!

Offer Free Samples

Countless businesses have found offering free samples to be a highly effective way to secure new clients. What better way to show your potential clients the value of your service than to let them try it at no risk and no obligation? Depending on the exact nature of your business, you can offer a free needs analysis, inspection, initial use, product sample, or other such avenue for letting your clients get a taste of what you offer. Some consultants — financial planners, investment counselors, and so on — offer free public information sessions. These sessions commonly include a short program of investment advice and an overview of the services that their firms provide, sometimes accompanied by a free meal. A freelance ad copywriter might send prospective clients samples of his or her work clipped from the local newspaper. What do you have to offer to your clients to get their future business?

Be Responsive to Media

Newspapers, television, radio, magazines — and, increasingly, bloggers — are among the quickest and most effective ways to reach a wide audience of potential clients. Whenever the media wants to talk to you, you should always drop everything and run, don't walk, to the phone or to your computer keyboard. Unless you just gave birth to quintuplets, you usually can't get media attention without spending a lot of time, money, and effort; therefore, when the media is ready for you, you need to be ready for it. Go out of your way to be responsive to the needs, deadlines, and opportunities of media outlets.

Help Clients Even If You Can't Do the Work

From time to time, you'll get requests from clients to do work that is outside of your firm's focus or experience or that exceeds your current capacity to fulfill it. Instead of just telling your clients that they need to go elsewhere, do everything you can to help connect them to someone who can get the work done. Why pass on perfectly good clients to someone else? One, because what goes around comes around and the firms to which you pass your clients just might return the favor someday; and two, because the client may need your services in the future, and he will be grateful that you helped out in his time of need. This is an opportunity to begin to build a long-term relationship with a prospective client. And you establish a network of future partners — both on the delivery side and on the client side.

Keep a list of consultants you trust to do good work in your industry. Not only will such a list be of benefit to your clients when you're unable to fulfill a request, but the list can also benefit you when you need an extra hand completing a project because you're overwhelmed with work.

Chapter 25

Ten Ways to Build Business with a Client

In This Chapter
▶ Delighting your clients
▶ Asking your clients to help you build your business

*H*ere's consulting Rule #1: Your current clients are your best friends. You should love, honor, and cherish them until death do you part. Why the drama? Because your current clients are the source of the revenue that keeps your lights lit, your computer humming, and the finance company from repossessing your car. In addition, if you are successful at building long-term relationships, your clients are your absolute best source of future business — both through additional business and through referrals. Besides, it's widely believed that the cost of getting new clients can be several times more expensive than keeping your current clients happy and coming back for more. You can significantly improve your odds of building business with your current clients by heeding the advice in this chapter.

Always Be On Time and Within Budget

In our experience, dependability is a particularly important quality for consultants to possess. It only takes getting burned once or twice by an undependable consultant for most clients to realize that getting what you're paying for — done right, and on time — is ultimately more important than finding the least expensive consultant for the job.

Being dependable means doing what you promised to do, when you promised to do it, and for the price you agreed to. A lot of people make a lot of promises, but few actually live up to the standards they set for themselves. Being on time and within budget sets you apart from those individuals who promise the moon but then deliver too little too late. If your clients can't depend on you to do what you promise to do, then before long, they'll start looking for someone they *can* depend on. Set realistic time and budget goals when you negotiate your contract, and then do whatever it takes to achieve them. Better yet, deliver more than you promise! As a later section explains, when you deliver more than the client expects and than you promise, you create client delight. And client delight gives you a client for life.

Anticipate Your Clients' Needs (And Suggest Ways to Address Them)

When you're working on a job for a particular client, you often see other things that need fixing, too. This situation is like taking your car to a repair shop to get a tune-up, only to find that the tires and catalytic converter also need to be replaced. So how can you anticipate your clients' needs? One of the best ways is to keep up on emerging industry trends — by reading business magazines, newspapers, and industry journals; visiting appropriate Web sites and blogs; by attending conferences; and by gaining insight from your experience with your other clients. By anticipating your clients' needs, you can bring solutions to your clients before they even know that they need them.

As a consultant, you are in the enviable position of having a clear view of the inner workings of the organization, as well as having the ear of the organization's management. As you work, keep your eyes and ears open to other needs that your client may have. After you identify these needs, talk to your client about them and submit a proposal with your suggested solution. Your client will appreciate your advice, and you will appreciate the additional business that your attention to your client's needs generates. If you do identify a real need that you can't help your client with but you can recommend someone else, your credibility grows in your client's eyes.

But, a note of caution: Don't create work where there really is none. Consultants who find problems where they do not exist — simply to churn up new business with an existing client — risk damaging the trust and credibility they have worked hard to develop. And if your client can't trust you, then why should they hire you?

Be Easy to Work With

Who would you rather hire: an individual who complains every time you give her an assignment or one who is excited by the challenge and eager to please? Your clients will ask themselves the same question when they decide whether to send more business your way.

As a consultant, you're selling more than your products or services — you're selling yourself. You have to offer more than great work; you also have to be easy to work with. Displaying arrogance and throwing temper tantrums are not good ways to turn your clients into long-term partners. Go out of your way to please your clients: Take their phone calls immediately, be responsive to their requests, meet them at their offices whenever possible, and maintain the pleasant and agreeable personality of a person you would want to work with. This way, when your clients have a problem that needs to be solved, your name will be the first one they think of when they start looking for someone to help.

Keep in Touch

What's the old saying — "Out of sight, out of mind"? If you let your clients forget about you, you're going to be an awfully lonely consultant. After you establish working relationships with your clients, keep in touch with them. Make a phone call, send a letter or e-mail message, or drop in on your clients from time to time. How about lunch? Keep them abreast of your latest successes and up-to-date on new services that you add to your repertoire. Offer to help them solve a difficult organizational or technical problem. Send business to your clients. For example, if you worked with a local florist, recommend them to your friends and family and make sure they tell your client that you sent them. Above all, don't let your clients fall off your active list of contacts. Schedule regular contacts with both active and inactive (the ones you want to reactivate) clients into your time-management system. Keeping established communication channels open is much easier than establishing new communication channels with new customers.

Be Honest and Ethical

It almost goes without saying (we say *almost* because we're going to say it anyway): You should always maintain the highest standards of honesty and ethics in all your business practices. Doing so not only makes it easier for you to sleep at night, but also builds a strong foundation of trust between you and your clients upon which to build future business. Ethical lapses and breaches of confidentiality can spell disaster for your client relationships, and, in some cases, they can get you into legal hot water. Make a point of setting the highest standards of conduct — both for yourself and for your employees. You have only one reputation, and it is worth its weight in gold; build and enhance it.

Give More than You Promise

In life, finding people — whether friends, colleagues, or business associates — who do exactly what they say they will do, when they say they will do it, can sometimes be difficult. This is certainly no different when it comes to consultants — many talk a big story about all the great things they're going to do for you, but then fall short when it comes time to deliver the goods. It's simple: When you keep your promises, you have happy clients.

But, what if you want to elevate your clients to a new plateau of excitement — the kind of excitement that generates unsolicited testimonials and referrals? Give a little more. Deliver your report a few days early or include an extra set of data for no extra charge. We can guarantee that if you give more than you promise, your clients will come back for more.

A brother of one of our business associates was in the painting contracting business, focusing on painting the homes of the elderly. He was very patient with his clients in selecting colors and would stop to socialize with them as his crew painted. About three weeks after the end of a job, he would return, unasked, to do any touch-up work that was required. About two months later, he would stop by to do another touch-up, and frequently he would bring a small bouquet of flowers or a bottle of wine or fresh preserves. His clients understandably loved him — and they overwhelmed him with work and with referrals to new clients.

Ask for Testimonials and Referrals

Clients like being bragged about! If you can showcase them as a positive example, such a testimonial can not only leverage additional business with new clients but also strengthen the bond you have with your existing clients. Testimonials are a critical ingredient in your new client proposals: Not only do they lend credibility to your words, but they also give your proposals life. Some consultants have found success by featuring their clients in their advertising. For example, if you are a makeup consultant, before-and-after photographs of your most successful clients are an important way for you to show new clients what results they can expect.

Referrals are one of the most important ways for you to get new business from your current clients. Don't be shy; give your clients extra business cards and brochures to give out to their friends and business associates. And don't forget to thank them — a personal note or spoken word of thanks is usually sufficient — whenever you get a new client as a result.

Offer Incentives or Send a Gift

As you develop a long-term relationship with a client, offering financial incentives to help develop more business can often pay off. For example, you can offer a standing discount of 10 percent to your best customers, or you can give them an occasional free premium.

To thank their clients for their business over the previous year, both Bob and Peter often send clients free autographed copies of their latest books or other tokens of their appreciation. It's not always the cost of the incentive that matters as much as the thought behind it.

Educate Your Clients

Are your clients aware of all the different services that your business offers? Probably not. For example, perhaps you're a consultant who specializes in helping real estate agents improve their sales and you have a Web site devoted to promoting that business. When a client hires you to do work in that area, she may not be aware that you also broker real estate loans at very reasonable rates. And, how would they know unless you tell them?

Your job is to educate your clients about the full range of services that you offer. And after you educate your clients, remind them from time to time about the other kinds of work you can do for them. Your goal is to make them more intelligent consumers of your products and services, to effectively manage their expectations.

Do Great Work

We shouldn't have to tell you that doing great work is what consulting is all about. Your clients hire you because they expect great work, and you went into business for yourself because you were convinced that you could deliver great work. Always do the best job you possibly can, even if you occasionally have to spend more time on a job than you anticipated. Great work creates, maintains, and enhances your reputation as a professional consultant. And delivering great work is one of the best ways to build future business with your current clients.

But, what if you can't do great work on a particular job — what if you're in too deep and can't deliver what you promised? You have a couple of choices: Either bring in someone (perhaps another consultant) to help you, or inform your client that you can't do the work. In either case, you need to act fast. Bringing in someone to help should be your first approach — that way you're able to preserve your client relationship. However, if you're stuck with no way out, then it's better to tell a client that you cannot perform, in advance of your contracted delivery date — and then to help them find other solutions — than to deliver a poor product or service, or to deliver nothing at all.

Index

• C •

Notes

BUSINESS, CAREERS & PERSONAL FINANCE

0-7645-9847-3

0-7645-2431-3

Also available:

- Business Plans Kit For Dummies
  0-7645-9794-9
- Economics For Dummies
  0-7645-5726-2
- Grant Writing For Dummies
  0-7645-8416-2
- Home Buying For Dummies
  0-7645-5331-3
- Managing For Dummies
  0-7645-1771-6
- Marketing For Dummies
  0-7645-5600-2

- Personal Finance For Dummies
  0-7645-2590-5*
- Resumes For Dummies
  0-7645-5471-9
- Selling For Dummies
  0-7645-5363-1
- Six Sigma For Dummies
  0-7645-6798-5
- Small Business Kit For Dummies
  0-7645-5984-2
- Starting an eBay Business For Dummies
  0-7645-6924-4
- Your Dream Career For Dummies
  0-7645-9795-7

HOME & BUSINESS COMPUTER BASICS

0-470-05432-8

0-471-75421-8

Also available:

- Cleaning Windows Vista For Dummies
  0-471-78293-9
- Excel 2007 For Dummies
  0-470-03737-7
- Mac OS X Tiger For Dummies
  0-7645-7675-5
- MacBook For Dummies
  0-470-04859-X
- Macs For Dummies
  0-470-04849-2
- Office 2007 For Dummies
  0-470-00923-3

- Outlook 2007 For Dummies
  0-470-03830-6
- PCs For Dummies
  0-7645-8958-X
- Salesforce.com For Dummies
  0-470-04893-X
- Upgrading & Fixing Laptops For Dummies
  0-7645-8959-8
- Word 2007 For Dummies
  0-470-03658-3
- Quicken 2007 For Dummies
  0-470-04600-7

FOOD, HOME, GARDEN, HOBBIES, MUSIC & PETS

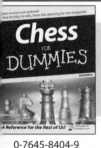

0-7645-8404-9

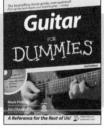

0-7645-9904-6

Also available:

- Candy Making For Dummies
  0-7645-9734-5
- Card Games For Dummies
  0-7645-9910-0
- Crocheting For Dummies
  0-7645-4151-X
- Dog Training For Dummies
  0-7645-8418-9
- Healthy Carb Cookbook For Dummies
  0-7645-8476-6
- Home Maintenance For Dummies
  0-7645-5215-5

- Horses For Dummies
  0-7645-9797-3
- Jewelry Making & Beading For Dummies
  0-7645-2571-9
- Orchids For Dummies
  0-7645-6759-4
- Puppies For Dummies
  0-7645-5255-4
- Rock Guitar For Dummies
  0-7645-5356-9
- Sewing For Dummies
  0-7645-6847-7
- Singing For Dummies
  0-7645-2475-5

INTERNET & DIGITAL MEDIA

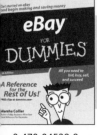

0-470-04529-9

0-470-04894-8

Also available:

- Blogging For Dummies
  0-471-77084-1
- Digital Photography For Dummies
  0-7645-9802-3
- Digital Photography All-in-One Desk Reference For Dummies
  0-470-03743-1
- Digital SLR Cameras and Photography For Dummies
  0-7645-9803-1
- eBay Business All-in-One Desk Reference For Dummies
  0-7645-8438-3
- HDTV For Dummies
  0-470-09673-X

- Home Entertainment PCs For Dummies
  0-470-05523-5
- MySpace For Dummies
  0-470-09529-6
- Search Engine Optimization For Dummies
  0-471-97998-8
- Skype For Dummies
  0-470-04891-3
- The Internet For Dummies
  0-7645-8996-2
- Wiring Your Digital Home For Dummies
  0-471-91830-X

* Separate Canadian edition also available
† Separate U.K. edition also available

SPORTS, FITNESS, PARENTING, RELIGION & SPIRITUALITY

0-471-76871-5

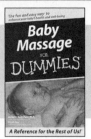

0-7645-7841-3

Also available:
- Catholicism For Dummies
  0-7645-5391-7
- Exercise Balls For Dummies
  0-7645-5623-1
- Fitness For Dummies
  0-7645-7851-0
- Football For Dummies
  0-7645-3936-1
- Judaism For Dummies
  0-7645-5299-6
- Potty Training For Dummies
  0-7645-5417-4
- Buddhism For Dummies
  0-7645-5359-3

- Pregnancy For Dummies
  0-7645-4483-7 †
- Ten Minute Tone-Ups For Dummies
  0-7645-7207-5
- NASCAR For Dummies
  0-7645-7681-X
- Religion For Dummies
  0-7645-5264-3
- Soccer For Dummies
  0-7645-5229-5
- Women in the Bible For Dummies
  0-7645-8475-8

TRAVEL

0-7645-7749-2

0-7645-6945-7

Also available:
- Alaska For Dummies
  0-7645-7746-8
- Cruise Vacations For Dummies
  0-7645-6941-4
- England For Dummies
  0-7645-4276-1
- Europe For Dummies
  0-7645-7529-5
- Germany For Dummies
  0-7645-7823-5
- Hawaii For Dummies
  0-7645-7402-7

- Italy For Dummies
  0-7645-7386-1
- Las Vegas For Dummies
  0-7645-7382-9
- London For Dummies
  0-7645-4277-X
- Paris For Dummies
  0-7645-7630-5
- RV Vacations For Dummies
  0-7645-4442-X
- Walt Disney World & Orlando
  For Dummies
  0-7645-9660-8

GRAPHICS, DESIGN & WEB DEVELOPMENT

0-7645-8815-X

0-7645-9571-7

Also available:
- 3D Game Animation For Dummies
  0-7645-8789-7
- AutoCAD 2006 For Dummies
  0-7645-8925-3
- Building a Web Site For Dummies
  0-7645-7144-3
- Creating Web Pages For Dummies
  0-470-08030-2
- Creating Web Pages All-in-One Desk
  Reference For Dummies
  0-7645-4345-8
- Dreamweaver 8 For Dummies
  0-7645-9649-7

- InDesign CS2 For Dummies
  0-7645-9572-5
- Macromedia Flash 8 For Dummies
  0-7645-9691-8
- Photoshop CS2 and Digital
  Photography For Dummies
  0-7645-9580-6
- Photoshop Elements 4 For Dummies
  0-471-77483-9
- Syndicating Web Sites with RSS Feed
  For Dummies
  0-7645-8848-6
- Yahoo! SiteBuilder For Dummies
  0-7645-9800-7

NETWORKING, SECURITY, PROGRAMMING & DATABASES

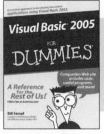

0-7645-7728-X

0-471-74940-0

Also available:
- Access 2007 For Dummies
  0-470-04612-0
- ASP.NET 2 For Dummies
  0-7645-7907-X
- C# 2005 For Dummies
  0-7645-9704-3
- Hacking For Dummies
  0-470-05235-X
- Hacking Wireless Networks
  For Dummies
  0-7645-9730-2
- Java For Dummies
  0-470-08716-1

- Microsoft SQL Server 2005 For Dummi
  0-7645-7755-7
- Networking All-in-One Desk Referen
  For Dummies
  0-7645-9939-9
- Preventing Identity Theft For Dummie
  0-7645-7336-5
- Telecom For Dummies
  0-471-77085-X
- Visual Studio 2005 All-in-One Desk
  Reference For Dummies
  0-7645-9775-2
- XML For Dummies
  0-7645-8845-1

EALTH & SELF-HELP

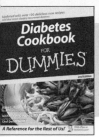

0-7645-8450-2

0-7645-4149-8

Also available:

✔Bipolar Disorder For Dummies
0-7645-8451-0

✔Chemotherapy and Radiation
For Dummies
0-7645-7832-4

✔Controlling Cholesterol For Dummies
0-7645-5440-9

✔Diabetes For Dummies
0-7645-6820-5* †

✔Divorce For Dummies
0-7645-8417-0 †

✔Fibromyalgia For Dummies
0-7645-5441-7

✔Low-Calorie Dieting For Dummies
0-7645-9905-4

✔Meditation For Dummies
0-471-77774-9

✔Osteoporosis For Dummies
0-7645-7621-6

✔Overcoming Anxiety For Dummies
0-7645-5447-6

✔Reiki For Dummies
0-7645-9907-0

✔Stress Management For Dummies
0-7645-5144-2

DUCATION, HISTORY, REFERENCE & TEST PREPARATION

0-7645-8381-6

0-7645-9554-7

Also available:

✔The ACT For Dummies
0-7645-9652-7

✔Algebra For Dummies
0-7645-5325-9

✔Algebra Workbook For Dummies
0-7645-8467-7

✔Astronomy For Dummies
0-7645-8465-0

✔Calculus For Dummies
0-7645-2498-4

✔Chemistry For Dummies
0-7645-5430-1

✔Forensics For Dummies
0-7645-5580-4

✔Freemasons For Dummies
0-7645-9796-5

✔French For Dummies
0-7645-5193-0

✔Geometry For Dummies
0-7645-5324-0

✔Organic Chemistry I For Dummies
0-7645-6902-3

✔The SAT I For Dummies
0-7645-7193-1

✔Spanish For Dummies
0-7645-5194-9

✔Statistics For Dummies
0-7645-5423-9

Get smart @ dummies.com®

- **Find a full list of Dummies titles**
- **Look into loads of FREE on-site articles**
- **Sign up for FREE eTips e-mailed to you weekly**
- **See what other products carry the Dummies name**
- **Shop directly from the Dummies bookstore**
- **Enter to win new prizes every month!**